Feminism, Prostitution and the State

This edited volume focuses on charting the rise of neo-abolitionism and offering a critique of the idea, its logics and consequences. A model of state policy which aims to abolish prostitution through legislation, neo-abolitionism criminalises the buyer of sex but not the seller. It is currently law in Sweden and other Nordic states and dominates the framing of policy debates in many other Western liberal contexts. Pressure for the adoption of this policy has come from radical feminists who understand prostitution and sex trafficking as a form of violence against women.

This volume argues that this convergence between radical feminism and states' interests arises from the emergence of, on the one hand, 'governance feminism' which seeks to have its ideals implemented through 'top-down sovereigntist means', and on the other hand, states' interests in legitimising stricter border controls and law enforcement responses in relation to transnational organised criminality, 'illegal' migration and insecurity.

Based around a series of country case studies each chapter will explore the politics surrounding the emergence of neo-abolitionism and its trajectory through those polities, whether the paradigm has been adopted, rejected or is still under debate. The volume will be of great interest to students and scholars of Social and Public Policy, Gender and Women's Studies, Politics and International Relations and Critical Legal Studies/Criminology.

Eilís Ward is Lecturer in the School of Political Science and Sociology National University of Ireland, Galway, Ireland.

Gillian Wylie is Assistant Professor of International Peace Studies, Trinity College Dublin, Ireland.

Routledge Studies in Gender and Global Politics

Series Editor: Laura J. Shepherd, UNSW Australia

This series aims to publish books that work with, and through, feminist insights on global politics, and illuminate the ways in which gender functions not just as a marker of identity but also as a constitutive logic in global political practices. The series welcomes scholarship on any aspect of global political practices, broadly conceived, that pays attention to the ways in which gender is central to, (re)produced in, and is productive of, such practices.

There is growing recognition both within the academy and in global political institutions that gender matters in and to the practices of global politics. From the governance of peace and security, to the provision of funds for development initiatives, via transnational advocacy networks linked through strategic engagement with new forms of media, these processes have a gendered dimension that is made visible through empirically grounded and theoretically sophisticated feminist work.

Masculinity and New War
The Gendered Dynamics of Contemporary Armed Conflict
David Duriesmith

Why Women Rebel
Understanding Women's Participation in Armed Rebel Groups
Alexis Leanna Henshaw

Feminism, Prostitution and the State
The Politics of Neo-Abolitionism
Edited by Eilís Ward & Gillian Wylie

Feminism, Prostitution and the State

The Politics of Neo-abolitionism

Edited by
Eilís Ward and Gillian Wylie

Routledge
Taylor & Francis Group
LONDON AND NEW YORK

First published 2017
by Routledge
2 Park Square, Milton Park, Abingdon, Oxon OX14 4RN

and by Routledge
711 Third Avenue, New York, NY 10017

Routledge is an imprint of the Taylor & Francis Group, an informa business

British Library Cataloguing in Publication Data
A catalogue record for this book is available from the British Library

Library of Congress Cataloging in Publication Data
Names: Ward, Eilis, editor. | Wylie, Gillian, 1969- editor.
Title: Feminism, prostitution and the state : the politics of neo-abolitionism / [edited by] Eilâis Ward and Gillian Wylie.
Description: Abingdon, Oxon ; NewYork, NY : Routledge, 2017. |
Series: Routledge studies in gender and global politics | Includes bibliographical references and index.
Identifiers: LCCN 2016046379| ISBN 9781138945401 (hardback) | ISBN 9781315671437 (ebook)
Subjects: LCSH: Prostitution–Political aspects. | Human trafficking. | Antislavery movements. | Feminism.
Classification: LCC HQ118 .F46 2017 | DDC 306.74–dc23
LC record available at https://lccn.loc.gov/2016046379

ISBN: 978-1-138-94540-1 (hbk)
ISBN: 978-1-31567-143-7 (ebk)

Typeset in Times New Roman
by Taylor & Francis Books

Contents

Contributors

Gillian Abel is Associate Professor and Head of Department in the Department of Population Health at the University of Otago in Christchurch, New Zealand. Her most extensive research work has been in the field of sex work; her exploration of how decriminalisation has impacted on the health, safety and human rights of sex workers has been influential in informing policy in New Zealand.

Barbara G. Brents is a professor in the Sociology Department at the University of Nevada, Las Vegas. She is co-editor of a special cluster in the journal *Sociological Perspectives* on Sex Work and Human Trafficking and is co-author of *The State of Sex: Tourism, Sex and Sin in the New American Heartland* (Routledge, 2010).

Anna Carline is a senior lecturer in Law at the University of Leicester. Her main areas of expertise are criminal law and justice, in particular violence against women and sexual offences, and feminist/gender theory. She has published extensively on rape and sexual assault, domestic homicide, prostitution and trafficking.

Sara Vida Coumans holds a Master's degree in International Development Studies from the International Institute of Social Studies of Erasmus University Rotterdam, in the Hague, the Netherlands. Sara has many years of experience in working on young people's sexual and reproductive rights and currently works at Amnesty International as International Youth Coordinator with responsibility for designing and managing the global program of youth engagement. Sara has contributed to this book in her personal capacity and the work does not necessarily reflect the views of Amnesty International.

Silke Heumann is a sociologist and assistant professor in Women's and Gender Studies at the International Institute of Social Studies of Erasmus University Rotterdam, in The Hague, the Netherlands. Her research interests include gender, sexual politics and (their relation to) social justice; social movements and discourse analysis. She has written on the adverse impact of anti-trafficking policies on undocumented migrant sex workers and the need for a labour approach to address labour precarity in the sex industry.

Crystal A. Jackson is an assistant professor of Sociology, and affiliated Gender Studies faculty, at the John Jay College-City University of New York. She specialises in studying gender and sexuality, including sex work, social justice, inequalities and feminism. Crystal is co-author of *The State of Sex: Tourism, Sex, and Sin in the New American Heartland* (Routledge, 2010).

Erin O'Brien is a senior lecturer in the School of Justice, Faculty of Law, at the Queensland University of Technology. Her research examines the interplay between political activists and the state in the construction of knowledge and formation of policy on issues of sex, gender and justice. She is co-author of *The Politics of Sex Trafficking: A Moral Geography* (Palgrave Macmillan, 2013).

Jennifer J. Reed is a PhD candidate in Sociology at the University of Nevada, Las Vegas. Her scholarly research interests centre around inequalities and social justice from an intersectional perspective. She has an invited piece published in *Sociologists in Action on Inequalities: Race, Class, Gender and Sexuality* based on her work for evidence-based sex trafficking policy during the 2013 Nevada legislative session.

Jane Scoular is a professor in Law, based at the University of Strathclyde, Scotland, UK. She is a socio-legal scholar working across issues relating to law and gender and sexuality and her scholarship is a primary reference in the field of the legal regulation of commercial sex.

Tamar Shiboleth is a criminologist schooled in Global Criminology at the Willem Pompe Institute in Utrecht, the Netherlands. Her research interests lie in global crimes, cultural criminology, technology and crime, and prostitution. Shiboleth wrote the book *Being a John* which describes her research on why men in the Netherlands buy sexual services, and how they incorporate 'being a client' in their everyday lives. She lectures in Social Sciences at the University of Applied Sciences Avans Den Bosch.

Yvonne Svanström is a senior lecturer and Associate Professor at the Department of Economic History at Stockholm University. Her research focuses on gender issues during the 1800–1900s. Her PhD (2000) *Policing Public Women: The Regulation of Prostitution in Stockholm*, on prostitution in the nineteenth century was published in an expanded and popularised version *Offentliga kvinnor. Prostitution I Sverige 1812–1918* and she has published widely on prostitution policies in Sweden.

Eilís Ward is lecturer in the School of Political Science and Sociology, NUI Galway, Ireland. Her background is in international relations and gender politics and she has published on Irish prostitution regimes, trafficking, prostitution in Northern Ireland (Huschke, Ward *et al.* 2014) and the politics of researching the sex trade including with Gillian Wylie.

Marieke Ridder-Wiskerke holds a Master's degree in Organisational Science – Strategic Management. Alongside her work as a Chief of Party at the Aids Fonds' Stop Aids Now!, she is currently a PhD student with a special focus on the development of community-led initiatives for sex workers based on comparative research in three countries. She has worked as an expert in the sex industry for the last 15 years, with and for sex workers, in over 20 countries. She is also responsible for the national STI/HIV sex work program in the Netherlands.

Gillian Wylie is Assistant Professor in International Peace Studies at Trinity College Dublin. She has researched and co-authored work on political discourses surrounding sex trafficking in Ireland with Eilís Ward and is author of *The International Politics of Human Trafficking* (Palgrave, 2016).

Acknowledgements

Our thanks go firstly to the contributors to this book who have been exemplary colleagues. They were all enthusiastic about the project from the outset and have been a joy to work with in terms of their timeliness, responsiveness and general good nature.

Our thinking on this topic has developed over a number of years and we've learned a lot from working together but we are also surrounded by wider networks of researchers who have given us invaluable insights and supports. We would like to thank colleagues in the Commercial Sex Researchers Network of Ireland (CSNRI), the NUI Galway-UL Gender Arc and those involved in the QUB research into prostitution in Northern Ireland. Eilís would particularly like to thank her colleagues in the EU COST Prospol network and especially those who participated in the workshop on neo-abolitionism and neo-liberalism in Ljubljana in early 2016. We both benefitted very much from the invitation to present the themes of this book there.

Our thanks also to the team at Routledge and the series editor for accepting our proposal and helping it come to fruition.

And finally many thanks are due to our departmental colleagues, friends and families without whose support nothing would get done.

Introduction

Eilís Ward and Gillian Wylie

Introducing neo-abolitionism: definition, drivers and debates

When the Swedish government adopted its Sex Purchase Act in 1999, it was hardly imaginable that the measure would gild the state as a global 'supermodel' for prostitution policies in the following decades.

While prostitution policies have traditionally not received much political attention – with some notable exceptions such as New Zealand and the Netherlands – states in the Western world have recently begun to debate commercial sex as a pressing priority and a compelling realm of action. Within these debates one view is always vociferous and indeed dominates in several international organisations and nation-states: that criminalising those who purchase sex is working in Sweden and, perforce, will do so elsewhere to both reduce the sex trade and, most potently, reduce trafficking for the purpose of sexual exploitation.

For scholars there is much richness to unpick in this phenomenon and much complexity that needs untangling. One central issue requiring analysis is the oft-posed question – how has this neo-abolitionist model come to dominate the way that many governments and civil society organisations think about prostitution and the sex trade? This question is at the heart of this book.

This book attempts to offer some explanations for the spreading influence of neo-abolitionism, informed by case studies of policy activism and state practices in a select number of jurisdictions. Our interest is in a critical evaluation of the rise and rise of neo-abolitionism and its grounding in a set of beliefs about its success in the exemplar, Sweden. Sweden's policy has been legitimised in turn by a strong international discourse that has successfully framed how political and civil actors think about prostitution and the sex trade in the early twenty-first century.

Herein lies the challenge to both policy makers and to scholars. While proponents of neo-abolitionism, be they radical feminist activists, faith-based lobbyists or politicians, argue that this is the *only* response to the changed circumstances of the sex trade today, other voices trouble both the assumptions contained in the model and its suitability as a 'one size fits all' response. So the debate has become polarised and the complex reality of acknowledging multiple positions, multiple situations and the relevance of context when creating policies around the sex trade has become somewhat lost. Indeed, the exemplary power of Sweden-as-model is reflected in the central focus of this book itself – how to explain the manner in which this approach has come to set the norm against which all others are measured.

Before entering the discussions to follow, it is necessary to clarify what is meant by neo-abolitionism. Neo-abolitionism can be conceived as a new version of an established approach to prostitution, abolitionism, that seeks to shut down the spaces and places wherein commercial sex is transacted. This works by criminalising activities attendant to sex work such as pimping, profiteering, living off the earnings of prostitution, organising and so on. We can think about this as a regime that attempts to squeeze 'supply' by criminalising its technologies, human or otherwise, but on paper at least, does not punish the seller.

Neo-abolitionism continues to argue that states ought to attempt to abolish prostitution but shifts attention towards demand as the pivot to this end goal. If demand for commercial sex is made a crime, then supply will wither on the vine. This shift was first adopted in the Western world in Sweden as part of its radical feminist statecraft agenda and posited commercial sex, in which women were sellers and men buyers, as an unacceptable and violent expression of patriarchy, requiring ameliorative state intervention. It was thus conceived as a policy designed to abolish prostitution *per se*. Through a process described elsewhere (see Swanström in this volume) it swiftly became reworked again to address trafficking in women for the purposes of sexual exploitation, in response to the presence of migrant women in the Swedish sex trade, and shadowing international anti-trafficking frameworks then emerging in the UN, the EU and elsewhere.

This brief social history of the idea isolates the two defining themes of neo-abolitionism. Firstly that it understands prostitution *per se* as a form of violence against women, in keeping with radical feminist accounts of gender relations and gendered power. Secondly, that it conceives prostitution and sex-trafficking as inseparable both conceptually (how we *think* about them) and in terms of policy fields (how states *respond* to them). Hence neo-abolitionism disaggregates 'sex trafficking' from other forms of trafficking (such as labour or organ trafficking) and, in policy terms, delinks prostitution from social policy frameworks such as harm reduction and anti-poverty measures and focuses instead on criminal justice and law enforcement responses.

Since Sweden's Act came into effect in 1999, Finland, Norway, Northern Ireland, France and the Republic of Ireland have all adopted, or are on verge of adopting, neo-abolitionism, though not always faithfully. In Northern Ireland for instance, those selling sex in groups of more than one person can be prosecuted for brothel keeping thus producing a strange variant of neo-abolitionism that conceives of the person selling sex as simultaneously a victim and a perpetrator of a crime, a profound contradiction surely.

While advocacy of neo-abolitionism owes much to radical feminism, it is notable that other, very different, lobbyists also support the idea. Most obviously in the US context, but also in other places such as Northern Ireland, conservative and fundamentalist religious forces are at play (Bernstein 2012; Weitzer 2007; Zimmerman 2013). The unlikely collaboration of feminism and fundamentalism manifests in a form of feminist governance (Halley 2006) or 'carceral feminism' (Bernstein 2012) and has become a key component of US foreign policy with direct implications for international relations. The anti-prostitution pledge required of US aid recipients during the Bush administration being one key example of this impact.

Here, we find an additional and initially perhaps puzzling aspect of neo-abolitionism's popularity; its dalliance with neo-liberalism as both a form of governance and/or a set of ideas or an ideal. Evidence of this convergence is found for example in Bumiller's (2008) critique of radical feminism's alliance with the neo-liberal state in relation to sexual violence and in relation to the law and sexual politics more generally (Halley 2006). On this view, the formulation of prostitution as a form of violence against women fits with certain neo-liberal values, or at least, does not cause problems for neo-liberal states. For example, neo-abolitionism's influence on prostitution diversion programmes in the US fits well with a neo-liberal paradigm of deflecting responsibility for social welfare from the state and onto hyper-responsibilising individuals (Leon Crysanthi, Shdaimah and Corey 2012: 269); a theme also identified in relation to the UK (Scoular and O'Neill 2007; Carline and Scoular this volume). Examples such as these lend weight to a compelling argument that radical feminist ideas, particularly on gender-based violence (to include prostitution *per se*), have found a comfortable home in the punitative neo-liberal state (Halley 2006, Bumiller 2008: 160).

However, although neo-abolitionism appears to flourish in neo-liberal contexts, a superficial survey reveals no clear pattern between type of state and type of prostitution regime. In fact the neo-liberal thesis appears to be confounded by the case of both Sweden and, at the other end of the spectrum, by New Zealand. Sweden is a 'state feminist' welfare state and the sex purchase ban is integral to its interventionist equality agenda. It understands that the state can intervene into sexual acts between adults in order to redress and rebalance gender inequalities and is deeply culturally embedded in Sweden's long history of state welfarism (Carson and Edwards 2011). In contrast, New Zealand has a completely different policy which does not criminalise the act of buying or selling sex and seeks instead to regulate the activity through other laws such as those relating to taxation, health and safety, sexual violence and harassment and so on. New Zealand in effect rejected the idea of a sex purchase ban but Harrington argues that, *contra* the authors cited above, its regime fits snugly into ideas of the marketisation of the economy and society inherent in the neo-liberalism of the state (Harrington 2012). Indeed, the argument is often made that neo-liberalism is good for sex workers because its privileging of individualism and market forces can rationalise the kind of social norms within which women who wish to engage in sex commerce can do so without, necessarily, attendant stigmatisation. In this approach, selling sex become, hence, an act like selling any other 'product'.

The fact that there is no straightforward relationship between neo-liberal regimes and neo-abolitionism may be a function of the contradictions that inhere within the idea of neo-liberalism itself. Wendy Brown (2015) argues that neo-liberalism is a challenged concept, characterised by ambiguity. It is a global phenomenon, yet it is inconsistent and unsystematic in its manifestation. The manner in which diametrically different sex work regimes can 'fit' into neo-liberal frameworks, makes sense, however, when we conceive of neo-liberalism not as a singular, coherent and *politically* liberal ideology, or set of state practices, but as containing contradictions and complex dynamics (Larner 2000) including tendencies towards both conservative and liberal political ideologies.

Setting grand theory aside however, this book suggests that the best approach to considering why neo-abolitionism has become so influential in the contemporary Western world is, in effect, to build theory from the ground up, based on discrete case studies. While neo-abolitionism tends to offer the same policy prescriptions wherever it finds voice, in varying contexts it must adapt to local conditions, histories and subjectivities. It has however not necessarily always being successful precisely because of those local conditions, as some of our cases illustrate. So, the history of sex worker organisation in New Zealand surely is a principle barrier to neo-abolitionism there, while Australian government structures and related division of legislative powers (O'Brien this volume) make it extremely difficult for neo-abolitionist activism to take a foothold there despite a groundswell of support for its agenda.

We here suggest, from the case studies in this book, a set of drivers – factors, actors, forces and institutions – of neo-abolitionism. However they may not be universally found, or they may indeed work contrarily depending on the particularities of each context. Readers will note that these drivers are reflected in one way or another throughout the chapters to follow.

The drivers of neo-abolitionism

1 Sweden as the supermodel

This may seem an obvious point given the ubiquity of references to the 'Swedish model' by advocates but it is a point insufficiently acknowledged and there are reasons why the 'Swedishness' of the model is particularly influential. One of those is the widespread international perception of Sweden as a morally upright and highly successful gender equitable state. Thanks to Sweden's status as a 'good international citizen', neo-abolitionism gains legitimacy by association. A second reason why the model is so successfully promoted lies in the impact of conscientious Swedish statecraft. The state puts funds and political effort into promoting the model abroad (in the EU, for example) and into hosting parliamentary delegations at home as attested to by some of our chapters here. Sweden's role in actively promoting its approach, as a part of its own identity-shaping in the international realm, cannot be underestimated in explaining the power of the idea to find homes elsewhere.

2 Transnational networks in international politics

While most of this book takes the approach of learning about the politics of neo-abolitionism within each country 'from the ground up', there is no doubt that transnational advocacy networks have been influential players in the spread of the idea. Using the spaces created for lobbying around global and regional organisations, networks of neo-abolitionist advocates have influenced international frameworks on sex trafficking, while tying the issue closely to prostitution policies and tackling 'the demand side'. Many of these transnational advocacy groups are associated with the global movement opposing violence against women, which has grown ever more prominent since the Beijing Conference of 1995 and is now embedded in transnational lobby groups such as the European Women's Lobby (EWL) whose key role in promoting neo-abolitionism in Europe is significant. Local civil society activists, aiming to domesticate neo-abolitionist ideals in their own contexts, look to allies in global civil society like the EWL and the Coalition Against Trafficking in Women, to bolster their case.

3 Violence against women movements in domestic politics

While feminism has had a long and continuing debate about its positions on sex work, neo-abolitionism's positing of sex work as inherently a form of violence, carved out a neat fit with gains made by the violence against women movements in various domestic polities. While linked indeed to transnational organisations such as the EWL (its Observatory on Violence Against women, for instance), as referred to above, many small and local woman's organisations have embedded the idea of state intervention and secured state funding to work against domestic and other forms of violence against women. These groups cut their teeth through many years of lobbying at local and national levels for shelters, public education programs and numerous other initiatives. Neo-abolitionism easily drew from and was co-created by these efforts and the lobbyists' expertise to legitimise and popularise the agenda .

4 Old fashioned morality politics

A strong element of the appeal of neo-abolitionist rhetoric lies in its recourse to simplistic values of good versus evil rather than offering rational policy analysis based on rigorous data. Empirical knowledge about the nature and extent of commercial sex often lacks rigour, or acknowledgement of complexity, in many country contexts. Instead debates about prostitution and sex work are often highly emotionally charged, resistant to facts, ruled by a very explicit ideology, peopled by informants with limited knowledge, preeminently concerned with symbolism, and, finally subject to abrupt changes (Wagenaar and Altink 2012). On this view, therefore, the success of neo-abolitionism can be explained as a function of the particular dynamics of prostitution policy formation, perhaps distinct from other policy areas (such as the environment or transport) in that moral concerns often trump evidence. This argument suggests therefore that it is the discursive power of neo-abolitionism, its moral force, that has given it ballast, alongside, as some chapters illustrate, the convergence of 'old fashioned' conservative sexual morality with its close cousin when it comes to the sex trade, the more fashionable cachet of radical feminism.

5 The trafficking imaginary

Neo-abolitionist thinking relies heavily on creating an irreducible equivalence between prostitution and sex trafficking and the power of the idea of sex trafficking as a huge, overwhelming phenomenon. This is not to say that exploitation of people moving globally or locally in the sex trade does not take place (it would be foolish to deny this) but to say that as an idea 'sex trafficking' has been utilised to great political effect in the same way that the white slave trade functioned in the early part of the twentieth century (Doezema 2010, Soderlund 2013). The contemporary imaginary draws an equivalence between prostitution and what's called sex trafficking because both are understood to be founded on violence and the impossibility of consent. Being able to rely on the imaginary of the trafficking victim – innocent, female, exploited – trumps all other approaches, including those that seek to include debates about freedom in relation to the sexual body or bodily autonomy. Contested statistics and the complexity of 'trafficking' notwithstanding (see for instance Sharma 2003), the power of this imaginary points to difficulties encountered in bringing empirical evidence to bear on the debate. Trafficking victims are, by definition, invisible and as such ever present and irrefutable. By virtue of their assumed innocence and victimhood, they will always trump the case made by a sex worker whose status is traditionally, though with some exceptions, considered politically, socially and morally problematic including within feminist theory (Beloso 2012). The trafficking imaginary has been particularly powerful in the USA allowing the state to take on the role of benevolent protector to dovetail with its own territorial interests (Soderlund 2005). Strikingly, Portugal stands alone amongst the older EU member states as absent of neo-abolitionist thought notwithstanding the presence of both a strong feminist movement and a sex trade, a phenomenon possibly explained by the fact that 'trafficking' is not an issue for the state.[1]

6 Religious evangelism

Feminist neo-abolitionists have found themselves as strange bedfellows with evangelical Christians in the anti-prostitution, anti-sex trafficking cause. In the American context right wing Christian evangelicals hold neo-abolitionist ideals despite starting from diametrically different viewpoints from radical feminists. Evangelicals are concerned to shore up nuclear heterosexual family life and oppose 'slavery' because it denies people the freedom to follow Christ (Zimmerman 2013). Arguably this powerful alliance between radical feminism and the religious right ensured neo-abolitionism's valence in the US. Additionally, other traditions within Christianity can also lead to endorsement of neo-abolitionism, such as in France where current neo-abolitionism involves a convergence of feminism and the historically progressive Catholic rescue and social justice movements (Mathieu 2016).

7 The dominant national political culture

As mentioned above neo-liberal thinking is an ideal and set of practices found amongst the advanced democracies discussed in this book. Yet, as also conceded in the previous discussion, the neo-liberal context can work both ways in relation to the sex trade. Free market thinking can legitimise commercial sex, just as the attendant transfer of responsibility for welfare from the state to individuals can promote a confluence between neo-abolitionism and criminal justice approaches to prostitution. Moreover, the internal contradictions of neo-liberalism are also evident in liberal states' desire to allow the free market in goods while determinedly preventing cross-border movements of people. The common tendency for advanced capitalist states to seek control of migration in the name of security can create common cause with those who seek to criminalise sex traffickers and sex buyers. Within these global political currents therefore, the salience of neo-abolitionism in particular places still depends much on the intersection between the ideal and local political cultures. So resistance to neo-abolitionism can stem from the historical individualism of New Zealand, whereas empathy with the idea can be found in the state feminism of Sweden, in the history of moral regulationism in Ireland or in the shift to responsibilisation in England and Wales. National differences, including political institutions and cultures, therefore will play a role in how neo-abolitionism is driven and who drives it.

8 Consensual cross-party politics

A striking theme of neo-abolitionism's success is the degree of cross party consensus achieved within different contexts and different political systems. In Sweden, England and Wales, Ireland and in the Netherlands, parties from across the spectrum, usually divided on other issues of private morality (on issues of abortion rights for instance, or more traditionally, on homosexuality) have found enough common cause to transcend what political scientists customarily term political cleavages. Where this has occurred it is indeed difficult for contrary views to be aired and/or legitimised within that polity.

9 The relative strength or weakness of sex worker organisations

Finally, any discussion of the drivers of neo-abolitionism needs to refer to the presence or absence of sex worker organisations and their strategic or political clout within any polity. It is a tempting symmetry to argue that where there are strong and politically astute sex worker organisations, neo-abolitionism at least will get a good run for its money. In this sense, we could argue, to state a perhaps obvious point, that their absence becomes a driver of neo-abolitionism. In countries where such movements are strong, New Zealand, Australia and the Netherlands, neo-abolitionist politics have not achieved a dominant position.

However, as is treated in the chapter from the Netherlands to follow, this is a symmetry that cannot be assumed. Equally, in the US (the home, after all of one of the original sex worker organisations COYOTE) other factors, such as those identified above, have eclipsed the power and legitimacy of sex worker organisations. In this sense, we can more correctly identify sex worker organisations perhaps as one important variable in the mix rather than a driver. Our case studies here again seem to indicate that the blend of local particularities, including the relative power and status of sex worker organisations, will prove significant in determining the outcome of any law or policy reform process.

Structure of the book

Woven into the listing of the drivers of abolitionism are references to several of the countries that provide the case studies contained in each chapter in this book. Each chapter explores the dynamics surrounding neo-abolitionism in a defined context, examining whether and to what extent the various drivers of neo-abolitionism feature in shaping the particularities of local policies.

Before looking into each of these cases in greater depth, the book opens with a reminder of the global currents within which these particular country cases sit. Chapter 1 therefore sets the scene at a global level and author Gillian Wylie identifies the multiple layers and trajectories of neo-abolitionism at the international level. The transnational politics of neo-abolitionism and its intersection with the concerns expressed by states in the face of neo-liberal globalisation and its contradictions, set the wider scene for making sense of why neo-abolitionism has become an influential force in feminist and state politics.

The chapter on Sweden, Chapter 2, opens our case study approach and is given pride of place, of course, arising from Sweden's role as neo-abolitionist 'supermodel'. In this chapter Yvonne Swanström charts how absolute political consensus was forged across the party spectrum behind the initially controversial sex purchase ban of 1999. She reminds us that the sex purchase ban was possible in the first instance because of the 'state feminism' of Swedish welfarism but it became unchallengeable by 2010 once it was linked in political minds to sex trafficking and thus became a policy vehicle enlarged beyond the scope of gender politics.

In the European context, the Netherlands is often presented as Sweden's mirror image. Neo-abolitionism is cast as being at odds with that state's legalisation approach, in turn, cast as the classical 'liberal' approach to sex work. Yet, as Silke Heumann and co-authors reveal, in Chapter 3, the apparently liberal consensus in the Netherlands was partially motivated by political intent to separate, and so control, legal from illegal sex work, and migration. Nor is the liberal consensus necessarily secure at either national or local authority level, where for example, the lure of neo-abolitionism attracts politicians protecting gentrified neighbourhoods.

Neo-abolitionism's influence in the domestic politics of the United States is very marked as was its international influence in the Bush administration years, through the anti-sex trafficking and anti-prostitution emphases of the Office to Monitor and Combat Trafficking in Persons. Chapter 4 then, by Crystal Jackson, Jennifer Reed and Barbara Brents, provides us with insight into the strange confluence of radical feminist and evangelical Christian activism which became the essential driver of neo-abolitionism in domestic and foreign policy and continues to be influential, though not unchallenged, today.

As a state that, at the time of writing, seemed destined to adopt a Swedish-style approach, the case study of Ireland tells us a lot about the dynamics of prostitution law reform and neo-abolitionism. In Chapter 5, Eilís Ward identifies how a political consensus was shaped around radical feminist understandings of prostitution and came to dominate in parliamentary proceedings in a state with a strong tradition of morality politics.

In England and Wales, around the same time, the traditional harm reduction approach to the sex trade has come under pressure as here too political consensus has built up around the desirability of neo-abolitionism. The authors, Jane Scoular and Anna Carline, pay particular attention to the way British neo-liberalism has created a peculiar adaptation by authorities of the 'Swedish model' to fit with punitive and responsibilisation approaches to public nuisance and commercial sex offences which construct the sex worker, contradictorily, as both victim and offender.

Two countries that have proven resistant to neo-abolitionism, though for different reasons, form the final cases. Several of Australia's state level governments have legalised sex work, much to the chagrin of neo-abolitionist campaigners. As Erin O'Brien explains in Chapter 7, these advocates used federal level trafficking hearings to push their agenda. However the political structures that prevent federal interference in state governance militate against success for neo-abolitionist ideas, although there is an increasing readiness to listen to that view from a federal government that finds a potential ally in governance feminism as it seeks to repel migration.

Finally New Zealand's approach to sex work is discussed by Gillian Abel in Chapter 8, bookending our discussion of neo-abolitionism by highlighting a contrary regime. The reasons for the failure of neo-abolitionism to gain traction in this context are the strength of the sex worker's movement, a consensus on a harm reduction framework for managing the sex trade and, more broadly, the deeply held cultural value of fairness with which New Zealand is steeped and which finds sympathy in the state's adoption of neo-liberalism.

Taken together in their comparability and diversity, each of these case studies reveals the importance of our range of drivers in promoting the politics of neo-abolitionism, as radical feminism intersects in curious ways with state interests and neo-liberal agendas.

Note

1 The authors would like to thank Alexandra Oliveira for this helpful insight.

References

Beloso, B. M. (2012) 'Sex, Work and the Feminist Erasure of Class', *Signs*, 38(1): 47–70.

Bernstein, E. (2012) 'Carceral Politics as Gender justice? The "Traffic in Women" and Neo-Liberal Circuits of Crime, Sex and Rights', *Theory and Society*, 41(3): 233–259.

Brown, W. (2015) *Undoing the Demos: Neoliberalism's Stealth Revolution*. Boston, MA: MIT Press.

Bumiller, K. (2008) *In an Abusive State: How Neo-liberalism Appropriated the Feminist Movement against Sexual Violence*. Durham, NC and London: Duke University Press.

Carson, L. and Edwards, K. (2011) 'Prostitution and Sex Trafficking: What are the Problems Represented to Be? A Discursive Analysis of Law and Policy in Sweden and Victoria, Australia', *Australian Feminist Law Journal*, 34(1): 63–87.

Doezema, J. (2010) *Sex Slaves and Discourse Masters: The Construction of Trafficking*. London: Zed Books.

Halley, J. (2006) *Split Decisions: How and Why to Take a Break from Feminism*. Princeton, NJ: Princeton University Press.

Harrington, C. (2012) 'Prostitution Policy Models and Feminist Knowledge Politics in New Zealand and Sweden', *Sexuality Research and Social Policy*, 9: 337–394.

Larner, W. (2000) 'Neo-liberalism: Policy, Ideology, Governmentality', *Studies in Political Economy*, 63: 5–21.

Leon Chrysanthi, S., Shdaimah, S. and Corey, S. (2012) 'JUSTifying Scrutiny: State Power in Prostitution Diversion Programs', *Journal of Poverty*, 16(3): 250–273.

Mathieu, L. (2016) unpublished paper presented at Workshop on Neo-Liberalism and Neo-abolitionism, EU COST Pros Pol conference, Ljubljana, 22 March 2016.

Scoular, J. and O'Neill, M. (2007) 'Regulating Prostitution', *British Journal of Criminology*, 47(5): 764–778.

Sharma, N. (2003) 'Travel-Agency: A Critique of Anti-Trafficking Campaigns', *Refuge: Canada's Journal of Refugees* 21(3): 53–65.

Soderlund, G. (2005) 'Running from the Rescuers: New US Crusades Against Sex Traffic and the Rhetoric of Abolition', *Feminist Formations*, 17(3): 68–87.

Soderlund, G. (2013) *Sex Trafficking, Scandal and the Transformation of Journalism: 1885–1917*. Chicago, IL: University of Chicago Press.

Wagenaar, H. and Altink, S. (2012) Prostitution as Morality Politics or Why It Is Exceedingly Difficult To Design and Sustain Effective Prostitution Policy', *Sexuality Research and Social Policy*, 9(3): 279–292.

Weitzer, R. (2007) 'The Social Construction of Sex Trafficking: Ideology and Institutionalisation of a Moral Crusade', *Politics and Society* 35(3): 447–475.

ZimmermanY. (2013) *Other Dreams of Freedom: Religion, Sex, and Human Trafficking*. Oxford: Oxford University Press.

1 Neo-abolitionism and transnational advocacy networks

Globalising an idea

Gillian Wylie

Introduction

As each of the case study chapters of this book will illustrate, the resonance or not of neo-abolitionism in different polities is very much affected by the 'moral geography' of each state and society. 'Moral geography' is a term that captures the ways in which ideas of morality are bounded by the particularities of place and space (O'Brien *et al.* 2013). That said, 'place and space' today are, more than ever, enmeshed in the context of globalisation and neither physical nor moral boundaries can be hermetically sealed in the contemporary world. That neo-abolitionism is simultaneously on the agenda in so many advanced capitalist states speaks to its presence as a globalising ideal and although ideas do not just 'jump' between states (Carline and Scoular this volume), determined transnational lobbying is part of the dynamic by which this idea, like many others, spreads.

Transnational 'moral entrepreneurs', in the term coined by Martha Finnemore and Kathryn Sikkink (1998), work actively at the international level to frame concepts, lobby policy makers and socialise them to new ideas, ultimately aiming to get international bodies and their constituent states to adopt new normative frameworks. As this chapter will show, neo-abolitionism – like historical prostitution abolitionism before it – has taken such transnational form through the activities of radical feminist international advocacy networks. They have found allies in particular states too, with Swedish and American administrations providing crucial support as exemplars and advocates. The influence of such 'moral entrepreneurs' can be seen behind the formation of international law and in interactions within domestic civil and political societies as nation-states engage in policy debates about neo-abolitionism.

This chapter will use two examples to illustrate these dynamics. The first draws on the negotiation of the anti-trafficking Palermo Protocol at the United Nations in 1999–2000. International women's groups shadowed these talks putting forward vociferous but often contending views. While the final Protocol undoubtedly reflects multiple influences, the chapter will focus on the discernible impact that neo-abolitionist activism had on the outcome of the negotiations and the Palermo text. The second example focuses on the regional level of international politics, analysing the role of transnational civil society lobbying in and around the European institutions, particularly the European Parliament (EP). As this case shows, in recent years the parliament adopted an increasingly neo-abolitionist stance and the role of radical feminist activism, particularly centred in the European Women's Lobby, has been instrumental in this.

From these examples, it is possible to see and comprehend the successes of internationally networked radical feminism in promoting the spread of neo-abolitionism. Yet, as will be proposed at the end of this chapter, there are costly consequences in this transnationalisation of neo-abolitionism. Arguably, governments are not only drawn to neo-abolitionism and anti-trafficking action by consideration of moral harm in prostitution or particular conceptualisations of gender equality. Rather the more 'carceral' approach (Bernstein 2010) to prostitution and trafficking embedded in neo-abolitionism chimes well with the interests of advanced liberal-democratic states in controlling their physical borders in the globalising world of neo-liberal economy and insecurity. The punitive approach towards the organisers and buyers of prostitution which neo-abolitionism legitimates has the consequence of enabling ever-increasing state control over female migrants' lives. This is surely a problematic outcome for a purportedly feminist politics and goal.

In order to set the context for the discussion of these examples of transnational neo-abolitionist lobbying, the chapter begins by setting out a theoretical framework drawn from International Relations theory, to provide a way of conceptualising how ideals spread and have influence in international politics. The idea of the 'norm lifecycle' captures how ideals are firstly promoted by 'moral entrepreneurs', then gain influential allies, and so cascade from the global to the regional and the local. This theory will provide a necessary framework to make sense of the detailed discussion of the activism and influence of neo-abolitionist entrepreneurs at the UN and the EP, ultimately revealing how transnational neo-abolitionism comes to intersect in ways that are both influential upon and constrained by the moral geography of particular places and spaces.

Moral entrepreneurs and the lifecycle of international norms

Norms are ideas about what constitutes appropriate behaviour. They can be 'regulative' in terms of defining what an actor ought to do and/or 'constitutive' in terms of determining what kind of behaviour is required for an actor to be considered legitimate in their context (Risse 2000). So, in the world of international politics, protection of human rights or environmental standards could be examples of norms that define what nation-states ought to do, whereas respecting the ideal of sovereign equality is a norm that constitutes what it is to be a state. Having said this, within the academic discipline of International Relations there are different perspectives on whether normative ideals matter at all in explaining the way the world works. Realist theorists argue that power balance and national interests matter far more than ideas about how actors ought to behave. However, since the unexpected end of the Cold War – which was provoked in large part by unconventional ideas and actors – caused a turn towards more sociological readings of international politics, the idea that norms matter in shaping how states understand themselves and act has become more widely accepted (Katzenstein 1996).

In their seminal attempt to answer the question of how international norms form and take effect, Finnemore and Sikkink (1998) suggest that it's possible to trace 'norm lifecycles', spanning the social life of ideas from their inception to adoption. According to this lifecycle model, normative change starts with the efforts of 'norm entrepreneurs' or 'moral proselytisers' who seek to shape and frame international understanding of their chosen cause. Furthering the cause involves moral entrepreneurs in building transnational networks and alliances, lobbying at global forums and working to influence the negotiation of international laws or conventions. Once a new normative framework emerges in these venues, states begin to sign and then ratify international agreements (by transposing new international commitments into domestic laws). Finnemore and Sikkink suggest this process reaches a 'tipping' point once a critical mass of member states sign up (they suggest about 40), leading the norm to 'cascade' into the international system. During a cascade there is increasingly rapid endorsement of the new norm, as governments become aware that its adoption has become an expected aspect of legitimate international behaviour. By its lifecycle's end, the norm is embedded in global and regional international frameworks and domestic politics, coming to seem 'common-sensical' to governments and peoples alike (see Finnemore and Sikkink 1998 for a detailed description of the norm lifecycle). All the while, 'transnational moral entrepreneurs' remain part of these processes, lobbying regional institutions and governments and lending support to local civil society activists to spread the norm.

In the reality of international politics, the story of international norm change is much more convoluted than the neatness the lifecycle model implies (Wylie 2016). Norm evolution is made fraught by pre-existing normative commitments, issues of power politics, the material interests of states and 'norm battles' (van Kersbergen and Verbeek 2007) between entrepreneurs who are oftentimes at loggerheads over the value, meaning or interpretation of ideals. Moreover, new international norms do not automatically transfer to domestic political scenarios but are accepted, reshaped or contested, depending on the mores of national contexts (Acharya 2004), that is the 'moral geography' of places and spaces.

Yet, bearing plenty of such caveats in mind, it is helpful to use the lifecycle model to trace the trajectory of neo-abolitionism as a globalising norm. There are transnational radical feminist networks that have elaborated linkages between contemporary prostitution and international sex trafficking to support their calls for neo-abolitionist policies; they have utilised the spaces of international conferencing and regional governance to push this agenda; and they have built alliances with local civil and political actors in advanced democracies to encourage the socialisation of states to neo-abolitionist norms. In the next sections of this chapter, the moral entrepreneurship driving the lifecycle of anti-trafficking activism, particularly in its neo-abolitionist guise, through the global institution of the United Nations and the regional architecture of the European Union will be described to illustrate these dynamics.

Transnational neo-abolitionism in the late-twentieth century

The focus of this chapter is on contemporary manifestations of transnational feminist abolitionism. However, it is worth remembering that international abolitionist networking linking the exploitation of women and children in prostitution with sex trafficking has a long history, which still permeates into today's framing of the issue.

Global civil networking, in general, is a practice with a longer history than is often credited in conventional state-centric accounts of International Relations. As outlined in Robert Holton's work on globalisation, global civil society interaction, whether constituted by formal links between organisations or less formal expressions of social interaction, has a history going back many centuries (Holton 2005: Chapter 6). Yet colonial linkages, new forms of communication, social change and emergent social movements certainly enabled an intensification of global civil life by the nineteenth century. Transnational social movements for the abolition of slavery, for example, emerged in the eighteenth-nineteeth centuries (Hochschild 2005). Likewise, the first wave of feminism dates to this timeframe, and transnational linkages were vital to the evolving movement (Keck and Sikkink 1998).

Within early international feminism, energetic transnational norm entrepreneurship explicitly linking prostitution with sex trafficking was very evident in the late-nineteenth century. For example, Josephine Butler of the International Abolitionist Federation was involved in relentless international efforts to promote the cause of abolishing state regulation of prostitution and the double standards that brought moral opprobrium on the sellers but not the buyers of sex (Jordan 2007). Moreover, concerns about the imagined 'white slavery' of European women in the colonised world, boosted abolitionist efforts (Doezema 2010; Soderlund 2013; Limoncelli 2010). Moving into the twentieth century, international abolitionists became influential lobbyists at the League of Nations, with marked effect on the League's anti-trafficking work and the subsequent 1949 UN Convention for the Suppression of the Traffic in Persons and of the Exploitation of the Prostitution of Others, which equated 'the evil' of trafficking with prostitution and defined all prostitution as 'incompatible with the dignity and worth of the human person' (UN 1949). Although the 1949 text was not widely ratified, the abolitionist tone which evolved through the League of Nations and into the early UN framework set a historical normative precedent which lends international weight to more recent abolitionist entrepreneurs, who look back on the 1949 Convention as an 'abolitionist victory' (Marcovich 2002: 9).

After 1949, the Cold War years saw a diminution of international political concern with sex trafficking and prostitution issues, but that period of quiet ended in the latter part of the twentieth century. Anti-trafficking activism was provoked into new life for states and civil society actors by a confluence of the uncertainties of the post-Cold War world, new migration patterns, and a revamped international women's movement inspired by (amongst other things) the series of UN women's conferences that culminated in Beijing.

At Beijing there were 'norm battles' between women's NGOs taking radically opposing views on whether prostitution *per se* is a form of violence against women. Radical feminist groups stressed the harms, inequalities and human rights violations they perceived in all prostitution and sex trafficking, while others argued for recognising differentiations in the experiences of those involved in prostitution and refusing the collapse of all prostitution under the concept of sex trafficking (Raymond 1998). The impact of both camps can be traced in the final Beijing Platform for Action because while trafficking in women 'for sexual exploitation, pornography and prostitution' is considered violence against women, most references to prostitution throughout the Platform for Action qualify the problem as specifically relating to 'forced prostitution' (UNWomen 1995). Other feminist international civil society gatherings in the 1980s and 1990s were equally marked by contestation between neo-abolitionists, equating prostitution and trafficking and arguing for a shift to focus on criminalising demand, and those coming from a sex workers' rights perspective (Milivojevic and Pickering 2013). Out of these meetings came the most influential of contemporary neo-abolitionist international networks, the Coalition Against Trafficking in Women (CATW) (Milivojevic and Pickering 2013: 590).

CATW is based in the United States but it is a transnational coalition, counting amongst its membership organizations in Mali, the Philippines, Mexico, Venezuela, Georgia, Japan and India (CATW 2016). CATW consciously links itself back to historical precursors in earlier abolitionism, celebrating the work of women such as Josephine Butler and holding to the tenets of the 1949 UN Convention (Marcovich 2002). A more contemporary theoretical touchstone for its stance is found primarily in the writings of Kathleen Barry. According to Barry's feminist structuralist analysis, the prostitution of women's sexuality is the outcome of the exploitative exercise by men of patriarchal power over women (Barry 1979 and 1995). This bald analysis of patriarchy as the overarching social reality, makes Barry the archetypal 'power feminist' in Janet Halley's term, i.e. the feminist who thinks 'everything about the relationship of males to females manifests domination and subordination' and 'characterize male sexuality as a vast social problem' (Halley 2006: 33–57 and 27). CATW therefore advocates for the neo-abolitionist aim of criminalising male demand for commercial sex.

The chapter on the USA in this book provides further insights into the formation and thinking of CATW and the influential roles of women such as Laura Lederer, Janice Raymond and Donna Hughes in developing the thinking and activism of the network (Jackson, Reed and Brents this volume). As Jackson *et al.* make clear, CATW's influence was profoundly felt in US domestic politics, particularly during the Bush Administration in the framing of the Trafficking in Persons Victims Protection Act (2000, then reauthorised in 2003, 2005, 2008) and the work of the Office to Monitor and Combat Trafficking in Persons. For the purposes of this chapter though, emphasis is on transnational neo-abolitionism and the global and regional spaces where its advocates have worked to influence outcomes. I therefore turn to examine the role of CATW and its allies in influencing the negotiations at the UN which culminated in the UN Protocol to Prevent, Suppress and Punish Trafficking in Persons, especially Women and Children – the Palermo Protocol of 2000.

The Palermo Protocol: a first example of neo-abolitionist lobbying in action

In the late 1990s, concerns about global organised crime led the UN to task its Committee on Crime Prevention and Control with drafting a new convention on the general issue of organised crime and a number of related protocols, including one on human trafficking. As has become normal practice at such UN forums, accredited civil society organisations were allowed to shadow and lobby these meetings (Reimann 2006). Amongst the many lobbyists on the human trafficking issue was a radical feminist coalition termed the International Human Rights Network (most prominently featuring CATW but including the European Women's Lobby, the Movement for the Abolition of Pornography and Prostitution (MAPP) and Equality Now among others) and an alternative pro-sex workers' rights feminist coalition under the moniker of the Human Rights Caucus (that included the Global Alliance Against Traffic in Women (GAATW), La Strada International and the International Human Rights Law Group). As Gallagher points out, such intense NGO excitement around the UN Crime Committee's meetings was an unusual occurrence (2001: 1001). First hand accounts from those who lobbied at the negotiations testify to difficult and emotional negotiations (Raymond 2002; CATW 2001; Ditmore and Wijers 2003; Doezema 2005), with enormous efforts expended by opposing lobbyists in trying to influence state negotiators through verbal lobbying, submitting position papers, seeking allies in the UN system and bringing in ever 'larger numbers of representatives to have greater impact' (Ditmore and Wijers 2003).

If one follows the paper trail left by the eleven ad hoc committee meetings producing the Palermo Protocol between January 1999 and July 2000, it's clear that the issues particularly exercising state parties and lobbyists included the question of whether trafficking should be widely defined to include ends beyond sexual exploitation, whether consent to prostitution was possible, and whether tackling 'demand' for prostitution should be named as integral to sex trafficking prevention efforts (Wylie 2016).

As mentioned above, the UN's previous 1949 Convention exclusively associated trafficking with prostitution involving women and children. In the

Palermo negotiations, this was a position reaffirmed both by some very active states (with Argentina in the lead) and by the coalition of NGOs in the International Human Rights Network (IHRN). However, the US administration of the time (the Clinton Administration) and the Human Rights Caucus (HRC) pushed for a broadening of the trafficking definition to include other exploitative ends, such as labour, servitude and organ trafficking. The controversies about this wound their way through the negotiations to end in UN fudge, with all exploitative ends named in clause 3a of the Palermo definition but a tacit understanding that the problem really affected 'especially women and children' being preserved in the Protocol's title (i.e. The Protocol to Prevent, Suppress and Punish Trafficking in Persons, Especially Women and Children).

Issues of prostitution and consent were equally contentious through the work of the ad hoc committee. Following on from the 1949 Convention, Argentina proposed that trafficking involved 'transporting a woman or facilitating her entry into another state' for 'illicit purpose' including prostitution, 'even with the consent of that person' (UN Office on Drugs and Crime (UNODC) second session 1999). Other delegations, however, did not accept that prostitution is by definition coercive. At the ninth committee session 'several delegations expressed that it was essential to distinguish victims of prostitution from those who chose to engage' (UNODC ninth session 2000). Once again these two positions were volubly supported by the IHRN and the HRC respectively. The outcome was, once again, a compromise. The well-known, convoluted Palermo definition of trafficking lays out the act, means and purposes of trafficking (article 3a), followed by article 3b, which states that 'the consent of a victim of trafficking in persons to the intended exploitation … shall be irrelevant where any of the means set forth in [3a] have been used' (UNODC 2000). The list of 'means' in 3a includes coercion, deception, force, fraud, abuse of power, or abuse of a position of vulnerability (UNODC 2000). The neo-abolitionist IHRN interpreted article 3b as a victory because according to their 'power feminist' interpretation of gender relations, in which all men dominate all women, prostitution is by definition an abuse of power or vulnerability and so can never be consented to (CATW 2001: 8). Yet the HRC read this clause differently. Because those from a sex workers' rights perspective do not agree that prostitution is always coercive, they took heart from the fact that article 3b specifically states that consent is only negated if any of the means have been used and therefore not in every situation in which sex is transacted.

It is often stated that the anti-trafficking approach of the UN can be summarised as involving '3Ps' – prosecution, prevention and protection (Cho 2015). A common criticism of the Palermo text is that the protection of victims is negligible and weak when compared to the sections designed to criminalise and prevent trafficking. Indeed as the Protocol's drafts evolved through the ad hoc committee meetings, the crime control element of the Protocol came to the fore with the incorporation of an ever-lengthening list of state border control and policing cooperation measures intended to prosecute and prevent trafficking. These elements of the Protocol testify to the fact that Palermo was always more about transnational crime control than human rights protections (Jordan 2002: 2). However, neo-abolitionist entrepreneurs were satisfied that among the prevention measures was article 9.5, which states that:

> parties shall adopt or strengthen legislative or other measures, such as educational, social or cultural measures, including through bilateral and multilateral cooperation, to discourage the demand that fosters all forms of exploitation of persons, especially women and children, that leads to trafficking.
>
> (UNODC 2000)

From an IRHN perspective this article preserved the abolitionist tenor of the 1949 Convention and could be read as a clause that commits signatories to tackle demand for sexual exploitation. As such IHRN welcomed Palermo as 'the first international instrument that mentions the demand that creates all forms of exploitation that leads to trafficking' (Ekberg 2004: 1202). Again, however, it is the case that because the article does not specifically mention sexual exploitation, others could interpret it more broadly. Thus those associated with the HRN were able to read the article as calling on state parties to protect all workers made vulnerable by demand for their labour in the dirty, dangerous and demeaning '3D' industries and their often irregular migration status (Jordan 2002: 30).

The Palermo negotiations can be analysed to reveal that both feminist transnational advocacy on neo-abolitionism, and its opponents, had an impact. Although the actual Palermo text is interpretable in many directions and the discussion above has shown that both feminist networks could claim credit for influencing wording, the IHRN were able to claim their lobbying resulted in a text that could be interpreted as a validation of their views in relation to demand, consent and the overall emphasis on the sex trafficking of women and children. Palermo has therefore provided a global normative framework which neo-abolitionists employ as they work to further the cascade of the norm through the international system and the adoption of particular anti-trafficking frameworks in regional and domestic political contexts. It is to this cascade to the regional level of international politics that this chapter now turns with an examination of neo-abolitionist advocacy and its impact on the European institutions, most specifically the European Parliament.

The European Parliament: a second example of neo-abolitionist lobbying in practice

When mapping out the trajectory of the social life of ideas, Finnemore and Sikkink (1998) suggest that after the global emergence of a norm in international spaces and frameworks, the norm will inexorably cascade from the global to the regional and the local if it reaches a critical mass or tipping point (of about 40 state signatories). It certainly is the case that Palermo gained plentiful signatories after it opened for signing in 2000 and consequently a plethora of new regional frameworks and domestic legal, political and social responses to human trafficking have blossomed since 2000.

Although the idea of a tipping point seems to imply a natural spread of ideas, the political momentum by which a new norm travels from the global to the regional and local is more complex than this implies. Factors causing the cascade include the accrual of new obligations that states acquire as a consequence of signing international conventions and elite socialisation processes, as government representatives learn what is expected of states through their work at international level. Socialisation happens therefore when states perceive an interest or an appropriateness in 'copying the behaviour of others' (Greenhill 2010: 129). However, norm socialisation can also receive an almighty push when backed by powerful international actors. That was certainly the case with the spread of the anti-trafficking norm after it was enthusiastically endorsed by the G.W. Bush Administration. As Jackson *et al.* explain (this volume) the Bush Administration came willingly under the sway of a neo-abolitionist coalition of Christian evangelical and radical feminist lobbyists. Activists from these contrasting backgrounds were prominent witnesses at Congressional Hearings leading to the passing of the Trafficking Victims Protection Act (TVPA) of 2000 and its 'reauthorisations' in subsequent years (O'Brien *et al.* 2013). Following the TVPA and Palermo, the US has been described as acting as a 'global sheriff' (Chuang 2006), enforcing anti-prostitution and anti-sex trafficking measures around the world. One way this occurred (and continues to occur under different administrations), for example, is through the annual compilation of the State Department's Trafficking in Persons (TiP) report, which produces trafficking statistics for every country and assesses whether states are in compliance with American defined anti-trafficking and anti-prostitution standards. The TiP report places all states into tiers, and a poor ranking can lead to humanitarian sanctions against those deemed to be not performing (Wooditch 2011).

That these intersecting dynamics of elite socialisation processes, power politics and skillful lobbying were played out as the new trafficking norm moved from the global to the regional level in international relations, will be exemplified here in relation to the European context. Over the last decade European institutions have successively taken up the anti-trafficking issue, responding in part to the impetus coming from the Palermo Protocol and to the disciplining power of the State Department's TiP reports. So, for example, the Council of Europe developed a Convention on Action against Trafficking in Human Beings (2005) and the Organisation for Security and Cooperation in Europe (OSCE) also established an anti-trafficking secretariat. And countries that became aware they were hovering on the verge of poor TiP rankings, moved to introduce new anti-trafficking policies (such as Portugal and

Ireland). However, in this regional context it is the institutions of the European Union that play the most prominent role in socialising member states into new normative expectations (Krasnodębska 2014). And what is clear here is that pan-European neo-abolitionist lobbying has exercised an increasing impact on the tenor of EU interventions over the last decade.

The EU passed a number of anti-trafficking Directives and Framework Decisions[1] throughout the 2000s. One notable facet of these initiatives to date is that, while mentioning human rights, they tend to focus on trafficking as an issue of crime and border control (Krieg 2009). So, for example, the 2004 European Council Directive on protections for victims of trafficking offered temporary residence to people identified as victims of trafficking, but on the pre-condition that they collaborate with the police authorities to assist in the prosecution of traffickers. Equally notable is that, in more recent years, neo-abolitionist perspectives are increasingly obvious in the overarching EU anti-trafficking framework. For example, the 2011 European Directive picks up the issue of 'demand' for sexual services, by stating that member states should, seek to 'discourage and reduce the demand that fosters all forms of exploitation related to trafficking in human beings' (Article 18).

In addition, neo-abolitionist tendencies have become most powerfully present in the research and deliberations of the European Parliament's Women's Rights and Gender Equality Committee. This can be seen clearly in its report on 'Sexual Exploitation and Prostitution and its Impact on Gender Equality' (aka the Honeyball[2] Report (2014)), which led to a resolution of the same title being put before the European Parliament. This report and its subsequent resolution took an avowedly neo-abolitionist line. It defined prostitution as a gendered phenomenon, as both a form of slavery and of violence against women, as incompatible with dignity and rights, linked to human trafficking and maintained through demand. The resolution then advocated 'the Nordic model' (European Parliament Motion 2013/2103/INI, points 31 and 32) arguing that such legislation should be introduced to combat trafficking and to establish 'what acceptable norms are in society' (point 36). The European Parliament adopted the non-binding Honeyball Resolution in February 2014 by 343 votes to 139, with 105 abstentions (European Parliament News 2014). While Resolutions of the European Parliament do not bind member states they do signal 'a political desire to act in a certain area' (Europaedia 2011), therefore the success of the Honeyball Resolution reveals cascading support for this interpretation of prostitution and trafficking in the European institutional context.

The move towards support for neo-abolitionism in the European Parliament came from the members of the Women's Rights Committee but also as a result of enthusiastic self-promotion of the Swedish policy in the European context by that country (see Swanström and Heumann *et al.* in this volume) and as a consequence of highly efficient and collaborative advocacy between the Women's Committee and the European Women's Lobby (EWL).

Most European institutions are shadowed by umbrella groups composed of the NGOs associated with the sector they relate to (Greenwood 2010: 202–207) and the EWL, as the umbrella body for 2,000 NGOs, performs this function in relation to the institutions of the EU for issues of feminist concern and women's interest. The stance of EWL on many issues, including prostitution and sex trafficking, is derived from radical feminist thinking. Since 1997 the EWL has maintained its 'Observatory on Violence against Women (VaW)', which is a group of 33 experts whose role is to define and research VaW and offer related policy advice to EWL. The Observatory succinctly defines prostitution and trafficking as violence (EWL Factsheet 2016) with prostitution classified as a form of violence against women and a consequence of patriarchy, 'the ultimate way in which men control women's bodies and sexuality, through an exchange of money' (European Women's Lobby 2010: 2 and 8).

Lobbying for neo-abolitionist goals has been a key aim of EWL in recent years. For example, in 2012 it launched its 'Brussels' Call – 'Together for a Europe Free of Prostitution' declaring that 'abolition of prostitution is a shared value across Europe' and claiming that 'the system of prostitution fuels and perpetuates trafficking in human beings for sexual exploitation' (European Women's Lobby 2012). The EWL website showcases the 200 organisations who have joined the cause. Moreover, members of the European Parliament were lobbied on this call and at least 50 signed up, with their public support recorded on the EWL website. Signatories included Mary Honeyball and other members of the Women's Rights Committee.

It is clear from following Mary Honeyball's blog posts in the period 2012–2014 that she welcomed being lobbied by EWL and readily offered her support to their policy position on prostitution. So, her blog of 7 December 2012 notes that 'the European Women's Lobby visited the European Parliament earlier this week to put forward their proposals for a 'Europe free from prostitution'. And her response to this lobby was that, 'Following the EWL's calls I said, 'I fully supported the adoption of a model similar to the one in place in Sweden' (The Honeyball Buzz 2012). Later, in anticipation of the vote on the Honeyball Report in the Women's Rights Committee, the EWL hosted a day seminar for European parliamentarians on 'the reality of prostitution' with speakers from the Swedish and German police as well as neo-abolitionist advocates (1 October 2013). Since the resolution passed in the EP in 2014, the EWL has kept up the pressure for its political uptake by celebrating its anniversaries and continuing the lobby. What these interactions between EWL, MEPs and the Committee illustrate is the intense activism of neo-abolitionist lobbyists within the European regional framework, working to spread and cascade their normative take on trafficking and prostitution in the EU (and so its member states) in the wake of the new international framework kick-started with Palermo.

As Carline and Scoular (this volume) remind us, ideas do not just jump from one context to the other. Norms do not automatically cascade from the global to the regional to the local. The social mores (or moral geography) in different contexts might result in norms being accepted, adapted or rejected as they spread (Acharya 2004). Therefore, although neo-abolitionism has gained traction in the European Parliament and in the EWL as the transnational lobby that pulls together multiple women's groups, not all member states or civil society organisations are convinced. States like Germany and the Netherlands maintain different forms of prostitution governance, although as Heumann *et al.* reveal (this volume), the EWL's influence is part of the reason for growing neo-abolitionist tendencies in the Netherlands. Moreover, concerted opposition to the Honeyball Resolution was mustered under the umbrella of the International Committee on the Rights of Sex Workers in Europe, which lodged a petition of 560 NGOs and 94 academics calling for the rejection of the Resolution (ICRSE 2014). But in other European member states, the synergy between the European lobby and local civil society actors is part of the production of powerful advocacy for the adoption of neo-abolitionism. Examples of this would include France and Northern Ireland. Very clearly the highly efficient Turn Off the Red Light coalition in the Republic of Ireland (Ward this volume) was boosted by its association with EWL (and vice versa), as ToRL provided a host of Irish signatories for the Brussels Call. Equally, being able to make frequent reference to a positive interpretation of the Swedish model and encouraging visits by political leaders to Sweden was another facet of the localisation of a sex purchase ban in Ireland through connection to regional framings of the issue.

The harmful consequences of transnationalising neo-abolitionism

The two examples discussed in this chapter draw attention to the work of transnational neo-abolitionist coalitions as norm entrepreneurs; framing, influencing and pushing the cascade and socialisation of their understandings of prostitution and sex trafficking in global and regional political forums. As we saw in the case of the institutions of the EU and the UN, transnationally connected radical feminists acted as 'moral proselytisers' in the promotion of the renewed lifecycle of the anti-trafficking norm. Their lobbying was integral to the cascading and internalising of the neo-abolitionist aspects of Palermo and the analysis found in the Honeyball Report and Resolution. Although meeting continual resistance from civil society lobbyists and political elites who disagree with them, and while not enjoying the same influence everywhere, there is no doubt that these transnational networks have helped to legitimise and spread neo-abolitionism. Vociferous lobbying in the spaces provided by the UN and the EU has ensured that the stamp of their worldview can be detected in the wording of the Palermo Protocol and in the recent stance of the European Parliament. The support lent to activists within nation-states by their transnational allies has furthered or consolidated the sway of neo-abolitionism in places like Ireland, Northern Ireland and even surprisingly, the Netherlands. These dynamics can also be seen beyond Europe, as shown in Erin O'Brien's chapter on Australia, which references the persistence of the Australian CATW (part of the global CATW coalition) in trying to press the neo-abolitionist case in a resistant context.

Neo-abolitionists celebrate their inroads in some states and outright successes in others. Their analytical linkage of prostitution with sex trafficking and both with patriarchal violence against women make them secure in their sense of the rightness of advocating for sex purchase bans and buyer criminalisation. But there is a dark side to these measures, allying feminism with many governments' law and order approaches to social problems and so forging a 'carceral' form of feminism (Bernstein 2010) which relegates women to the role of perpetual victim and men to assumed criminality. Likewise, as the section of this chapter on the Palermo Protocol already hinted, anti-trafficking measures all too often further statist agendas related to border and migration control. In the context of the neo-liberal world economy, which rests on a great contradiction of espousing freedoms of movement for everything except people (Munck 2008), the world's prosperous states are trying to shore up their borders against freedom of migration. Ironically, anti-trafficking rhetoric and measures have become part of the mechanisms of border control (see also O'Brien in this volume). The exponential increase of border control clauses in the drafting process of the Palermo Protocol, as mentioned, exemplifies this aspect of anti-trafficking law making. This consequence of anti-trafficking activism has become ever more obvious in the use of anti-trafficking rhetoric to justify European governments' erection of physical barriers against refugees entering Europe in 2015 and 16 (see, for example, Hungarian Prime Minister Victor Orban's speeches naming the Hungarian border fence an 'anti-trafficking' device (Wylie 2016: 172)). In this context, radical feminist thinking that casts women as victims of prostitution and international sex trafficking, bolsters Western governments' leveraging of 'the idiom of the vulnerable female, trafficked migrant to extend ... border and immigration control capacity' (Fitzgerald 2012: 228). Ironically, this strand of feminist thought and action ends up enabling states to discipline and regulate the international movement of women.

Conclusion

This book is formed largely from a set of individual case studies of the politics of neo-abolitionism inside particular nation-states. As you will read each case does display different dynamics, arising from the peculiar ways in which political frameworks, feminist tendencies and social mores play out in each place. Having said this none of the cases are hermetically sealed from the impact of global or regional political frameworks, transnational activism or the contemporary global politics of neo-liberal economy, border control and migration securitisation discourses. Although ideas do not simply jump over borders or cascade from the global to the local, this broader context and the impact of these factors need to be taken into account to understand the increasingly global spread of neo-abolitionism and its impact on states and societies.[3]

Notes

1 An EU Directive is a legislative act that sets out a goal that all EU countries must achieve. However, it is up to the individual countries to devise their own laws on how to reach these goals. A Framework Decision is a kind of legislative act of the European Union used exclusively within the EU's competences in police and judicial co-operation in criminal justice matters. See https://europa.eu/european-union/law/legal-acts_en.

2 Mary Honeyball is a Member of the European Parliament, representing London for the UK Labour Party. She is a member of the EP Committee on Women's Rights and Gender Equality.

3 Some material in this chapter has already appeared in Wylie, G. (2016) *The International Politics of Human Trafficking*, London: Palgrave Macmillan, reproduced with permission of Palgrave Macmillan.

References

Acharya, A. (2004) 'How Ideas Spread: Whose Norms Matter? Norm Localization and Institutional Change in Asian Regionalism', *International Organization*, 58(2): 239–275.

Barry, K. (1979) *Female Sexual Slavery*. New York: University Press.

Barry, K. (1995) *The Prostitution of Sexuality: The Global Exploitation of Women*. New York: University Press.

Bernstein, E. (2010) 'Militarized Humanitarianism Meets Carceral Feminism: The Politics of Sex, Rights, and Freedom in Contemporary Antitrafficking Campaigns', *Signs: Journal of Women in Culture and Society*, 36(1): 45–71.

CATW (2016) *Coalition Against Trafficking in Women: Who we are: Mission*. Available from www.catwinternational.org/WhoWeAre/Mission.

CATW (2001) *Coalition Report: Coalition Against Trafficking in Women Annual Report 2001*. Available from, www.catwinternational.org/Content/Documents/Reports/ReportOct2001.pdf.

Cho, S-Y. (2015) 'Evaluating Policies Against Human Trafficking Worldwide: An Overview and Review of the 3P Index', *Journal of Human Trafficking*, 1(1): 86–99.

Chuang, J. (2006) 'The United States as Global Sheriff: Using Unilateral Sanctions to Combat Human Trafficking', *Michigan Journal of International Law*, 27: 437–494.

Ditmore, M. and Wijers, M. (2003) 'The Negotiations on the UN Protocol on Trafficking in Persons: Moving the Focus from Morality to Actual Conditions', *Nemesis*, 4: 79–88.

Doezema, J. (2005) 'Now You See Her, Now You Don't: Sex Workers at the UN Trafficking Protocol Negotiation', *Social and Legal Studies*, 14(1): 61–89.

Doezema, J. (2010) *Sex Slaves and Discourse Masters: The Construction of Trafficking*. London: Zed Books.

Ekberg, G. (2004) 'The Swedish Law that Prohibits the Purchase of Sexual Services Best Practices for Prevention of Prostitution and Trafficking in Human Beings', *Violence Against Women*, 10(10): 1187–1218.

Europaedia (2011) *Europaedia – The Legal System of the European Union*, from www.europedia.moussis.eu/books/Book_2/.

European Parliament (2013) *Motion for a European Parliament Resolution on Sexual Exploitation and Prostitution and its Impact on Gender Equality*, www.europarl.europa.eu/sides/getDoc.do?pubRef=-//EP//TEXT+REPORT+A7-2014-0071+0+DOC+XML+V0//EN#title1, Brussels.

European Parliament News (2014) *Punish the Client, not the Prostitute.* Available from www.europarl.europa.eu/news/en/news-room/content/20140221IPR36644/html/Punish-the-client-not-the-prostitute.
European Women's Lobby (2012) *Brussels' Call 'Together for a Europe Free from Prostitution'.* Available from www.womenlobby.org/spip.php?article4374.
European Women's Lobby (2010) *Towards a Europe Free from All Forms of Male Violence against Women*, paper prepared by the EWL Centre on Violence against Women. Brussels: EWL.
EWL Factsheet (2016) *EWL Factsheet: Towards a Europe Free from all Forms of Violence against Women and Girls.* Available from www.ewl_factsheet_on_vaw_2016-final.pdf.
Finnemore, M. and Sikkink, K. (1998) 'International Norm Dynamics and Political Change', *International Organization*, 52(4): 887–917.
Fitzgerald, S. (2012) 'Vulnerable Bodies, Vulnerable Borders: Extraterritoriality and Human Trafficking', *Feminist Legal Studies*, 20(3): 227–244.
Gallagher, A. (2001) 'Human Rights and the New UN Protocols on Trafficking and Migrant Smuggling: A Preliminary Analysis', *Human Rights Quarterly*, 23(4): 975–1004.
Greenhill, B. (2010) 'The Company You Keep: International Socialization and the Diffusion of Human Rights Norms', *International Studies Quarterly*, 54(1): 127–145.
Greenwood, J. (2010) 'Regulating NGO Participation in the EU; a de-facto Accreditation system built on 'Representativeness', in J. Steffek and K. Hahn (eds) *Evaluating Transnational NGOs: Legitimacy, Accountability, Representation.* Basingstoke: Palgrave Macmillan, pp. 200–219.
Halley, J. (2006) *Split Decisions: How and Why to Take a Break from Feminism.* Princeton, NJ: Princeton University Press.
Hochschild, A. (2005) *Bury the Chains: Prophets and Rebels in the Fight to Free an Empire's Slaves.* New York: Houghton Mifflin.
Holton, R. (2005) *Making Globalisation.* Basingstoke: Palgrave MacMillan.
Honeyball, M. (2014) *Sexual Exploitation and Prostitution and its Impact on Gender Equality*, Report to European Parliament Committee on Women's Rights and Gender Equality, avaialble at www.europarl.europa.eu/sides/getDoc.do?pubRef=-//EP//TEXT+REPORT+A7-2014-0071+0+DOC+XML+V0//EN.
Honeyball Buzz, The (2012) 'A Europe Free of Prostitution?', *Blog of Mary Honeyball MEP*, 7 December, available from, https://thehoneyballbuzz.com/tag/criminalising-prostitution/.
ICRSE (2014) *560 NGOs and 94 Researchers Demand Members of European Parliament to Reject Ms Honeyball Report*, available at, www.sexworkeurope.org/news/general-news/560-ngos-and-94-researchers-demand-members-european-parliament- reject-ms-honeyball.
Jordan, A. (2002) *Complete Guide to the UN Trafficking Protocol.* Available from La Strada International: http://lastradainternational.org/doc-center/1916/the-annotated-guide-to-the-complete-un-trafficking-protocol.
Jordan, J. (2007) *Josephine Butler.* London: Bloomsbury Academic.
Katzenstein, K. (1996) *The Culture of National Security: Norms and Identity in World Politics* . New York: Colombia University Press.
Keck, M. and Sikkink, K. (1998) *Activists Beyond Borders: Advocacy Networks in International Politics.* Ithaca, NY: Cornell University Press.

Krasnodębska, M. (2014) 'Socialization as a Power Discourse: Conceptualizing the Eastern Enlargement of Western International Institutions', *Poznan University of Economics Review*, 14(3): 7–22.

Krieg, S. (2009) 'Trafficking in Human Beings: The EU Approach between Border Control, Law Enforcement and Human Rights', *European Law Journal*, 15(6): 775–790.

Limoncelli, S. (2010) *The Politics of Trafficking: The First International Movement to Combat the Sexual Exploitation of Women*. Stanford, CA: Standford University Press.

Marcovich, M. (2002) *Guide to the UN Convention of 2 December 1949 for the Suppression of the Traffic in Persons and of the Exploitation of the Prostitution of Others*. Available from www.catwinternational.org/Content/Images/Article/119/attachment.pdf.

Milivojevic, S. and Pickering, S. (2013) 'Trafficking in People, 20 Years On: Sex, Migration and Crime in the Global Anti-Trafficking Discourse and the Rise of the 'Global Trafficking Complex'', *Current Issues in Criminal Justice*, 25(2): 585–604.

Munck, R. (2008) 'Globalisation, Governance and Migration: an Introduction', *Third World Quarterly*, 29(7): 1227–1246.

O'Brien, E., Hayes, S. and Carpenter, B. (2013) *The Politics of Sex Trafficking: A Moral Geography*. Basingstoke: Palgrave MacMillan.

Raymond, J. (2002) 'The New UN Trafficking Protocol', *Women's Studies International Forum*, 25(5): 491–502.

Raymond, J. (1998) 'Prostitution as Violence against Women: NGO Stonewalling in Beijing and Elsewhere', *Women's Studies International Forum*, 21(1): 1–9.

Reimann, D. (2006) 'A View from the Top: International Politics, Norms and the Worldwide Growth of NGOs', *International Studies Quarterly*, 50(1): 45–68.

Risse, T. (2000) '"Let's Argue!": Communicative Action in World Politics', *International Organization*, 54(1): 1–39.

Soderlund, G. (2013) *Sex Trafficking, Scandal and the Transformation of Journalism: 1885–1917*. Chicago, IL: University of Chicago Press.

TVPA (2000) *Trafficking Victims Protection Act*. Available from US Department of State: http://www.state.gov/j/tip/laws/.

UN (1949) *Convention for the Suppression of the Traffic in Persons and of the Exploitation of the Prostitution of Others*. Available from www.ohchr.org/Documents/ProfessionalInterest/trafficpersons.pdf.

UNODC Ninth Session (2000) *Ad Hoc Committee on the Elaboration of a Convention against Transnational Organized Crime*, Feb–March 21–3, A/AC.254/4/Add.3/Rev.6:. Available from www.unodc.org/unodc/en/treaties/CTOC/background/session9.html.

UNODC Second Session (1999) *Ad Hoc Committee on the Elaboration of a Convention against Transnational Organized Crime Vienna*, 8–12 March, Proposals and Contributions Received from Governments, available from www.unodc.org/unodc/en/treaties/CTOC/background/Session2.html.

UNODC (2000) *United Nations Convention on Transnational Organized Crime and the Protocols Thereto*. Available from United Nations Office on *Drugs* and Crime: www.unodc.org/documents/treaties/UNTOC/Publications/TOC%20Convention/TOCebook-e.pdf.

UNWomen (1995) *The United Nations Fourth World Conference on Women*, Platform for Action: Violence against Women Diagnosis, available from www.un.org/womenwatch/daw/beijing/platform/violence.htm#object3.

Van Kersbergen, K. and Verbeek, B. (2007) 'The Politics of International Norms: EU Subsidiarity and the Imperfect Competence Regime of the European Union', *European Journal of International Relations*, 13(2): 217–238.

Wooditch, A. (2011) 'The Efficacy of the TiP Report: A Review of Evidence', *Criminal Justice Policy Review*, 22(4): 471–493.

Wylie, G. (2016) *The International Politics of Human Trafficking*. London: Palgrave MacMillan.

2 From contested to consensus

Swedish politics on prostitution and trafficking

Yvonne Svanström

Introduction

In 2010 a change in the legislation on purchasing sexual services was discussed in the Swedish parliament. There was, more or less, consensus on the proposal to increase the maximum penalty for buying sexual services from six months to one year's imprisonment. Of those parliamentarians present all voted for the proposal – regardless of party colour. Only one dissenting voice demanded the repeal of both the legislation on sexual services and on procuring. That MP argued that sex workers were not helped by the legislation, 'the only thing that has been on the agenda are your moralizing assumptions about having sex' (Riksdagsprotokoll (hereafter RP) 2010/11:101, Anf. 32).[1] However, what he also asked highlighted a change evident in party lines since the initial law was adopted in 1999:

> One can wonder about the changed attitudes of the parties. Around ten, twelve years ago, when the legislation was discussed, many parties, among those the Moderates and the Liberals were against the legislation […] During the ten years until now the legislation has not been evaluated. Still the parties have changed their opinion. On what grounds?
>
> (RP 2010/11:101, Anf. 32)

The main focus in this chapter is to analyse that political change in relation to the purchasing of sexual services, which has gone from being a contested arena to one of consensus among the political parties in Sweden. Arguably this consensus has been achieved because during the years since the legislation on sexual services was passed, prostitution has been subsumed under the issue of trafficking. On trafficking the political parties were from the start more or less in agreement, with consensus enabled by the embedding of the question in the larger issues of human rights, rather than the issue of male demand (which was central to the 1999 law).

This chapter first traces the evolution of the Swedish sex purchase ban of 2000. The politicisation of male demand in prostitution seemed new at the time, but needs to be placed in a longer historical context to illustrate the roots of turning towards the demand side of prostitution.

Although the time frame in this article is longer, including information from the early twentieth century and onwards until 2015, the parliamentary debates together with government actions during the years after the legislation will be the main focus.[2] During that period the state changed its colours from a Social Democratic-led government (1998–2006) to a coalition government (the Alliance) formed by the Moderates (Conservatives) and liberals (the Liberals, the Centre Party and the Christian Democrats) (2006–2014), some of which initially voted against the legislation. The eventual political consensus in support of the legislation will be explained against the framework of ideas of securitisation and governance feminism (Halley *et al.* 2006), as they have related to prostitution policies over the last decade.

Situating the Swedish welfare state

Sweden is a comparatively large country, but with a small population (9.5 million inhabitants), mostly centred on four large cities, where the capital Stockholm incorporates the majority with around 1 million in the city, and 2 million in the county. Sweden has been characterised as a typical Social Democratic welfare state, although its initial development was achieved through a settlement between the Social Democratic Party and the then Farmers' Party in the 1930s. By the 1950s Sweden had transformed from being mainly rural to a predominantly industrial welfare state. The welfare model was redistributive and tax financed, aimed at levelling out income inequalities and 'decommodifying' citizens by giving them a degree of immunisation from the market in the form of certain social benefits, which in many cases were flat rate benefits. Equality, solidarity and universalism underpinned the Swedish model, in combination with leaving wage negotiations and labour market relations to collective bargaining between peak level organisations of employers and workers, with little state intervention. The model was developed when Swedish society was relatively homogenous and during the so-called 'golden years' in Swedish economic development (Esping-Andersen 1990).

The Swedish welfare state is interventionist, reaching out into the lives of individuals in a manner viewed as paternalistic by some. Still, apart from the attempt at decommodifying its citizens, the Swedish welfare state has also had 'defamilialising' aspects; women in relationships do not have to depend on a male breadwinner, since social entitlements are individually rather than family based. Comparisons with some other European countries show how entitlements such as social security, sickness benefits, pensions, parental benefits/leave are individually based or flat rate benefits, and not based on family earnings (Sainsbury 1996). The women's and left movements' activities also paved the way for increased day-care and the participation of women in the paid labour force increased from the late 1960s.[3]

Therefore the Swedish – and Nordic – welfare states have been termed 'state feminist' and 'women friendly', where women can depend on the state rather than on a male partner. Thus, there are high levels of trust in the state and 'the history of the welfare states and their gender profile make Nordic women likely to view the state as a partner' (Skilbrei and Holmström 2013: 30). However, Ruth Lister has pointed to the 'half full' and 'half empty' analysis of the Nordic welfare state: although a majority of women are in the labour market in Sweden, the labour market is segregated according to gender and women are mainly employed in low-paid jobs in the public sector. Lister also points explicitly to the challenge of ethnic diversity that faces the welfare state, where immigrant women have difficulties in actually entering the labour market and when they do they make up the majority of part-time workers in largely low-paid jobs (Lister 2009; Vedin 2015).

Although avoiding the economic crisis of the 1970s longer than many other countries, change came. Increased immigration created a less homogenous society and the economic crises in the 1990s caused mass unemployment and demands for retrenchment in state welfare. The response from the state entailed deregulating markets and privatisation. In a general sense this has weakened the social security system, but Lundberg and Åmark argue that a new kind of welfare state has arisen, mixing public and private welfare solutions (Lundberg and Åmark 2001).

It is within this context of 'state feminism' that evolving debates about prostitution in Sweden must be understood. As this next section will demonstrate the shift over time towards framing prostitution as an issue of gender inequality and the push for a criminal justice approach emphasising punishing the buyers of sexual services, is understandable in this wider frame.

The history of prostitution and the state

For centuries, Sweden had harsh legislation on extra-marital sex, in some cases punishable by death. However, as in many other European countries prostitution was regulated for a major part of the 1800s and into the 1900s. Swedish regulation differed from the model country, France, by never including brothels as part of the system. Instead procuring and organising brothels was criminalised. The system was abandoned in 1919, after eight years of public inquiry.[4] The inquiry was preceded by protests organised by different women's movements (as in other European countries), which petitioned both government and local authorities to abolish regulation. In many of these petitions and public speeches the curbing of male demand and the rights of women were on the agenda (Svanström 2006a: 211). However, later in the process, these organisations became less radical in their tactics and conservative morals came to the forefront, reflecting an image that was preserved and reused in late twentieth and twenty-first century media debates concerning contemporary organisations.[5]

For a long period after 1919 prostitution evoked little public interest. It was regulated under the vagrancy legislation, which was subject to some discussion and a number of public enquiries during the 1920s-1940s. Some of the different proposals from these enquiries concerned prostitution, and were criticised from organisations within the autonomous women's movement, such as the old liberal women's organisation, the Fredrika Bremer Association. These organisations pointed to the demand side as an explanation for prostitution, and criticised the fact that men could avoid punishment (Svanström 2006b: 148). The first time the demand side was articulated in parliament was in the 1950s. During debate on a government proposal, a liberal woman MP stated that the government bill misunderstood the grounds for prostitution, since the 'primary reason for this phenomenon is, however, the demand side, and as long as society refrains from trying to reach the customers through information, it is highly probable that any action against the women will be useless'. She later proposed that a special public inquiry should look into prostitution and 'reaching customers' but no such inquiry was undertaken (Svanström 2006b: 155).

The 1960s was a period of liberal attitudes towards sexuality, which by the mid-1970s had been substituted by what was termed a commercialisation of sexuality. A public commission on sexual crimes that suggested decreasing the penalty for certain sexual crimes was published in 1976 and was severely criticised by different women's organisations. They demanded a new commission and a separate commission to investigate prostitution. Prostitution was centred on the larger cities, and in Malmö (Sweden's then third largest city) the municipality wanted to investigate connections between different establishments and illegal gambling, drugs, illegal alcohol, procuring and handling of stolen goods (Månsson 2012: 117). The report argued that sexuality had been commercialised and suggested the criminalisation of both buyers and sellers in order to facilitate social work and the provision of help for prostitutes (Månsson and Larsson 1976). The report had an enormous impact on a national level and was often referred to in parliamentary bills and debates during the latter part of the 1970s. Child prostitution and child pornography and the connections to the black market were high on the agenda. The commercialisation of sexuality and of society was seen as part of the explanation for prostitution. In civil society different women's organisations – both from the first and second wave – were involved in discussing and debating prostitution from a feminist perspective, increasingly demanding criminalisation of the customer (Erikson 2011: 69–70; Svanström forthcoming). Thus, although not such a cohesive approach, the idea of targeting the demand side of prostitution in Sweden was not entirely new when it surfaced in parliament in a comprehensive manner in the late 1980s.

Neo-abolitionism: prostitution as structural gender oppression

When the 1976 report proposing to decrease the penalty for certain sexual crimes was discarded, two other commissions were appointed, one of them to investigate prostitution. That commission aimed to map the prevalence of child and youth prostitution, and the reasons for prostitution. Further, prostitution's connection to drugs and sex clubs had to be investigated. The commissioner should have no restrictions in ' … proposing the actions that the investigation gives reason for.' However, it was noticed that for a long-term change, social work rather than criminalisation would probably be most efficient (Official report of the Swedish government (SOU) 1981:71, 32). The commissioner argued for more preventive social work to fight prostitution in the long run. To criminalise prostitution was not an option; although criminalisation might work as a deterrent in the long run it would be problematic in the short term. Criminalising only buyers was not discussed (SOU 1981:78, 144–45). A government bill followed the proposal from the commissioner: it would be prohibited to organise public pornographic shows (in effect putting so called sex-clubs out of business) and state economic support for preventive work against prostitution would be supplied (Proposition 1981/82:187, 1–4).

Another state commission on prostitution was appointed in 1993, by a coalition government of the right and liberal parties. It had been preceded by a number of party bills and bills from individual members of parliament for over a decade. During the period 1983–93 more than fifty party and member bills concerning prostitution were proposed, and of those about thirty proposed the criminalisation of the purchase alone. The latter came from representatives of all parties (except the Moderate Party), sometimes both men and women from the same party, sometimes only women, but never groups of men alone. There was also a cross-party bill in support of criminalising the purchase, signed by the women's lobby in all parties (except the Moderate Party). A cross-party bill was a unique political action within parliament and illustrates the unity among the women MPs on this question. In general, the question was debated and promoted by the women MPs rather than the men (Svanström 2004a).

In the 1980s-1990s, then, prostitution was formulated as a problem of (male) demand rather than as a general social question. The commissioner was tasked to map out the prevalence of problems of prostitution and to suggest social improvements. She was also 'without prejudice' to look into criminalisation as a possible method to use against prostitution (SOU 1995:15, 251). The idea of gender equality impregnated the report but less focus was put on the commercialisation of society or the economic reasons for prostitution. However, the framing was in a liberal vein, and the report from the commissioner proposed criminalising both parties since in a gender equal society it would be remarkable to criminalise only one. It was argued that criminalisation would work as normative legislation and a deterrent for both parties in prostitution. However, the proposals in the report were criticised severely, both in the referral process, in parliament and in the media.

After a change of government, the Social Democratic government presented a bill in 1998. It was mainly based on suggestions from another public commission appointed by the government, investigating harsher legislation concerning rape, violence against women and sexual harassment. The bill also treated prostitution, and in so doing suggested that the government saw prostitution, sexual offences and violence against women as interrelated.

Social and outreach work were to continue and knowledge production regarding prostitution was to increase. The most controversial proposal was to penalise the purchase of sexual services alone. When the bill and the report from the committee of legal affairs were presented in parliament the debate was intense. The division was between arguments that could be referred to as symbolising the individual and structural divide (Halley *et al.* 2006). Opponents argued that the legislation would be difficult to uphold, prostitution would go underground and make things worse for women. Supporters argued that prostitution was proof of the gendered and structural subordination of women in society, which had to be counteracted (Svanström 2004a). The then Social Democratic Minister for Gender Equality stated:

> We think prostitution is one of the worst expressions of the unequal distribution of power between men and women and that this not only affects the prostitutes or those who buy the services of prostitutes, but the entire society. We are convinced that this will change attitudes and decrease violence in society. That is why we propose a criminalisation of the sex-buyers. We are convinced that it will also decrease prostitution. […] For me it is obvious that women and men have unequal power in society and that this also matters concerning prostitution, rape, women beating, genital mutilation and everything else that systematically affects women.
>
> (RP 1997/98:114, Anf. 109)

The minister's arguments were in line with the arguments from women's lobbyists in parliament over the previous ten years. Radical feminist arguments had been heard in the debate – mostly from women but also from men within all parties except the Moderates. Their arguments focused on men's abuse of women through prostitution, and prostitution as degrading to all women in society. As a woman MP from the Christian Democrats stated, 'through criminalizing the buyers of prostitution society indicates that the gross violation and degradation of women that prostitution entails is unacceptable' (RP 1992/93:45, Anf. 186). However, later in the debate the Christian Democrats favoured criminalising both parties because, 'a point of departure has to be that grown human beings have full legal capacity and also take responsibility for what they do, regardless of being women or men' (RP 1997/98:114 Anf. 11).[6] Despite opposition from Moderates, Liberals and Christian Democrats the legislation was voted through with the support of the Social Democrats, the Left, the Green Party and the Centre Party (RP 1997/98:115, 4§, Mom. 16).

Prior to the passing of the legislation, the media ran several articles covering the debate between supporters and opponents of the law, often framed as a battle between middle class feminists and sex workers (Svanström 2004a: 239–41). This debate continued after the legislation passed, but how the legislation was implemented was now also on the agenda, with information sought on numbers of arrests, convictions, and the effect on women and clients. The legislation had strong support in society; a public poll in 2001 showed that 80 per cent supported the legislation (Engström and Olsson 2001: 4). Criticism from both advocates and opponents of the legislation mainly concerned the patriarchal views still evident in the justice system. For instance, it was pointed out that sex buyers were often awarded undue consideration in court. When prosecutors charged sex buyers at the same time as charging someone for procuring, judges suggested that 'sex buyers should not have to be pilloried alongside' procurers. Calls for appearance for questioning in connection with cases were sent to the person's place of work rather than to their home address as is customary (Svanström 2004b: 12). This was commented on in the media, with special focus on trafficked women because, 'while used women have been forced to tell what they have been subjected to in detail, the court seems almost embarrassed to have to incommode a man that has bought sex' (Svanström 2004b: 312–13).

In parliament, the debate on prostitution faded compared to the intense debate before the legislation passed. Subsequent debates were performed in a changed legal environment and those arguing were, for the most part, reactive rather than proactive. Bills from opposing parties demanded the repeal of the legislation (Motion 2000/01:Ju716) or an evaluation of the same (RP 2002/03:70, Anf. 63). MPs for the Christian Democrats continued to present bills wanting to criminalise both parties for the next five years (for example, motions 2001/02 JuU:10; 2002/03:JuU5; 2003/04:Ju313; 2004/05:Ju484; 2005/06:Ju394), but there were also demands from the same party to promote the Swedish legislation in the EU to counteract legalisation of prostitution elsewhere (RP 2001/02:25, Anf. 24, 2001/02:34, Anf. 4). This has led some researchers to point out that the legislation on sexual services can be seen as a question of national self-promotion, where the Swedish nation promotes and defends its gender equality position internationally (Gould 2001; Kulick 2003; Tham 2001: 417). Eduards argues, however, that although used in this manner by the Swedish state it cannot be interpreted as the ambition of the women's organisations (both within parliament and autonomous groups), whose initial ambition was to change focus from policing prostitution as a question of women in prostitution, to a focus on male demand (Eduards 2007; Erikson 2011). The shift from seeing prostitution as a question for social policy to a question for criminal justice can also be seen as a shift in responsibility: from society to the individual sex buyer (Erikson 2011).

After debating and presenting bills for a number of years, a report from the Council on Legislation on penal questions from 2004–05 was presented and debated in parliament. The report mentioned that the government indicated that the legislation on sexual services might be evaluated in an upcoming inquiry of the criminal code on sexual crimes and thus discarded the request for a special inquiry. However, in the vote on the report a majority of the MPs voted for the reservation demanding an evaluation (RP 2005/06:102, 12§). One was planned for 2006. By that time however, the Moderates – the erstwhile adamant opponents of the legislation – were in government and had changed their position,

> We have, since the introduction of the legislation, also seen that there have been different reports on when it has been successful or not. However, the latest is that it actually works rather well and has been a help to the police. A couple of years ago, the Moderate Party took the position that the legislation should stay, we have advantages from it.
>
> (RP 2006/07:63, Anf. 16)

Notably, arguments from the Moderates connected the legislation to policing and 'law and order' rhetoric. In that context the turnaround by the Moderates – and other ambivalent parties – is hardly surprising. While gender equality arguments were still heard in the parliamentary debates, they did not have the same reach as in the 1990s. Power structures and solidarity among women were seldom mentioned in the argumentation. Instead the debate took place in the context of criminal justice concerns rather than social policy. The legislation meant a turn from social work as the main way of counteracting prostitution to a criminal focus. This shift was further legitimated as prostitution was subsumed under questions of trafficking, as will be explained below.

Parliamentary debates pre and post 2000: changing discourse

Looking at the parliamentary discussions on prostitution in the 1990s, and the initial proposal regarding the criminalisation of sexual services, there are initially very few arguments for tying prostitution and sex trafficking together. Indeed, during the decade before the passing of the legislation on selling sexual services, trafficking was very seldom on the agenda, and hardly ever in connection to the purchase of sexual services. Of the around 40 party bills placed before the parliament pertaining to sexual services only two, from the Left party, mentioned trafficking. However, these bills used the Swedish word 'trade in humans' as a concept to refer to prostitution as such, not trafficking (Motion 1990/91:Ju614; 1991/92:Ju605). In parliament it was not until the legislation was actually to be voted on that the connection between the coming legislation and trafficking was made, in an answer from the Minister of Gender Equality to an MP on whether the legislation could work as a deterrent to 'the import of prostitution'. The minister answered, '[…] I think so. I am convinced of it. We should be leading in questions of gender equality like we are now. Trafficking of women between countries increases all the time. I think criminalization is a way to counteract that' (RP 1997/98:114, Anf. 11). The government proposal mentioned trafficking, but little space was given in the document. It was stated that the trade in sexual services had developed into an international industry during the last decades, and although this was of little extent in Sweden there were indications of an increase, so:

> … to take this step is an important marker towards other countries to show our stance in this question. It may also be supportive for the groups in different countries, working against prostitution. Through criminalization

> the interest from different groups or individuals to expand organized prostitution in Sweden should also decrease.
>
> (Proposition 1997/98:55, 103)

However, the only tangible proposal concerning trafficking pertained to the 1997 EU Council of Ministers' declaration to prevent and fight trafficking in women. As the declaration required member states to have a national rapporteur regarding trafficking, the government appointed the Swedish National Police Agency to the role (Proposition 1997/98:55, 50). Thus, it was not until after passing the legislation on sexual services that the discourse in parliament, and in proposals from the government, quite markedly turned. Prostitution as a single issue disappeared or was subsumed in the larger question of trafficking.

This change in parliamentary debate was obviously EU-prompted, and surfaced against the backdrop of the UN Palermo Protocol and intensified collaboration within the EU. In 1998 the government appointed a committee to investigate sexual crimes and related issues. It included investigating whether the Swedish legislation concerning trafficking in women had to be changed as a result of intensified EU collaboration. The Government Official Report from 2001 stated that although the joint application of several of the existing paragraphs in the existing legislation might cover the crime of trafficking, there was still a need for new legislation (SOU 2001:14, 457). The government proposed that if a trafficked person was under 18 years of age, the crime would always be trafficking (regardless of consent), whereas if the person was older it had to be coerced. The crime of trafficking for sexual purposes would be in effect even if the person had been aware of prostitution being part of the deal, and where she or he had no other option but to submit (Proposition 2001/02:124, 22).

When the legislation on the criminalisation of the purchase of sexual services was discussed in 1998, the debate was intense and lengthy with members from all parties participating. When the new legislation on trafficking for sexual purposes was debated in May 2002 the discussion was short: there was one MP from the Green Party debating with the Social Democratic Minister in charge. The MP argued against coercion being part of the crime, not least since it was contradictory to the legislation regarding sexual services, where the purchase was a crime regardless of the person's consent. The legislation was voted through, with only the Green Party against it (Svanström 2004a: 308–09).

Interestingly enough, this paradoxical contradiction in approaches to legislation did not produce an echo in parliament or in the media. However, the clashing legislative approaches were picked up in the 2004 proposal to broaden the crime of trafficking. Until then the Swedish law had only criminalised trafficking for sexual purposes, but now the crime of trafficking was renamed trafficking in human beings and broadened to encompass trafficking for sexual purposes, for the removal of organs, for compulsory conscription or in forced labour. The penalty increased from a maximum of two to six years' imprisonment (Proposition 2003/04:111). This was prompted by the ratification of the UN Convention in 2004. The proposal argued that trafficking in human beings was a complex problem, concerning questions of 'human rights such as children's rights, the fight against organised crime, questions of migration, gender equality, poverty and social, economic and political differences within and between countries' (Proposition 2003/04:111, 9). The proposal noted that in the light of the principle that underpinned the legislation concerning sexual services – coercion did not have to be part of the picture. Any new legislation should really cover 'all measures that are aiming for the usage of someone in prostitution or for other sexual purposes regardless of whether improper means had been used' (Proposition 2003/04:111, 58). The same proposal stated that the legal issues were complex and needed to be further investigated.

This contradiction between legislation on trafficking and on sexual services never became a topic in parliament. Instead the debate focused on the possibility of permanent residence, hospital care and support for trafficking victims and also the possibility of sentencing those buying sexual services from trafficked women for rape (RP 2003/04:120, Anf. 45, 47, 48, 56). Permanent residence for victims of trafficking was, for example, one issue that took up much parliamentary time on this general issue of trafficking. In general, when in opposition political parties tended to favour the granting of permanent residence for victims. However, those in government were more wary, opposing the issue in terms of avoiding measures that might incentivise irregular migration. For instance, the Social Democratic Minister and MPs from the party argued that to award permanent residence from the start would contribute to trafficking, rather than the opposite (RP 2003/04:85, Anf. 115, 122). Although this position was criticised by several MPs, the Minister of Justice said, 'I can briefly say that still one has to be careful with that kind of measure (permanent residence), which might almost be an incentive to come here and prostitute oneself' (RP 2000/01:34, Anf. 52)

The issue of permanent residence seemed to have been a comfortable question to have to the forefront when in opposition, but neither the Social Democratic nor the Alliance government made any changes in that direction. Rather, in practice, the reverse happened. In 2013, a Social Democratic MP presented a written question to the Conservative Minister of Justice regarding whether prostitution was enough grounds for deportation (Skriftlig fråga 2013/14:201). The background was a case in Gothenburg, where the police had deported a woman in connection to a case of trafficking for sexual purposes according to the Aliens Act. The men had been sentenced to procuring and trafficking (Göteborgs tingsrätt, mål B 8184–11). The woman who was to be deported had contacted the Prostitution Group (a council run outreach group), and asked whether this was correct. The group made a complaint to the Parliamentary Ombudsman on her behalf (Redogörelse 2013/14:JO1, 353–57). The Ombudsman came to the conclusion that the decision was right, based on the legislative history preceding the act (Prop. 1979/80: 96, SOU 1979:64, 134). The Prostitution Group pointed out that in this case the victim was made responsible for the crime that she had been subjected to (Dahlborg *et al.* 2012).

What is evident is that in the parliamentary discussions concerning trafficking from around 2003 there is an astounding consensus between the parties, which is also commented upon in parliament. Recurring statements from MPs from opposing parties refer to 'consensus', and 'being in agreement' about the issues at hand, while debating the particulars. There was also consensus on framing trafficking as a human rights issue, discussing trafficking in terms of migration control and as treating prostitution and trafficking together, since prostitution could never be voluntary (RP 2002/03:70, Anf. 60, 72, 82, 2002/03:111, Anf. 156, 2002/03:46, Anf. 32, 2002/03:50, Anf. 35, 2003/04:82, Anf. 27, 2005/06:102, Anf. 102, 2009/10:43, Anf 18).

It was not until 2010 that the Alliance government presented new trafficking legislation, where the prerequisite of the trafficker taking control over the victim was abolished, as was the provision that a crime had to be on the statute books in a country where it was committed as well as Sweden to be prosecutable (Betänkande 2009/10:JuU33; Proposition 2009/10:152). While eradicating the clash between the legislation on sexual services and trafficking, the parliamentary debate on the proposal mainly concerned whether the government had done enough on the issue, during its six months as chair of the EU Council of Ministers during the autumn of 2009. The former Minister of Justice from the Social Democrats opened the debate and talked about 'four lost years' when the Alliance government could have made a difference regarding its involvement and lobbying on these questions (RP 2009/10:121, Anf. 95). Still, the question of trafficking did not seem to be high on the agenda. The former Minister of Justice left the chamber after his declaration, and an MP from the Christian Democrats noted, 'when we gaze on the audience in the chamber there are nine persons from the Alliance and three persons from the opposition. I also think this is a sign of the weight that is invested in this kind of debate' (RP 2009/10:121, Anf. 105).

A significant pattern evident in the parliamentary debate during the years after passing the legislation on sexual services was that regardless of differences in opinion on the legislation on prostitution, there was, more or less, consensus that prostitution and trafficking had to be treated together. The demand side of trafficking for sexual purposes was in focus, and connected to Swedish legislation; curb the demand side and trafficking in women for sexual purposes would diminish. However, on a general level there was also a changed focus on how these discussions were framed. The earlier, quite outspoken gender equality (and feminist) framing regarding prostitution was gradually weakened and a human rights perspective came to the forefront resulting in a subsuming of the gender equality argument, now only occasionally surfacing. The quest for sharper punishments was adamantly asserted by all parties, as was the ambition and desire to promote the 'Swedish model' in Europe.

The final test – everybody's favourite legislation

In 2008, after being in government for one and a half years, the conservative/liberal Alliance government launched a public investigation into the effects of the sex purchase legislation. The terms of reference for the investigation affirmed the presupposition that the legislation should be kept, its goal was to evaluate and investigate how the legislation had worked in practice, and its effects on prostitution and trafficking in Sweden. It was also to evaluate the effects on those 'selling sexual services" (SOU 2010:49, 49). The investigation was part of the government's action plan against prostitution and trafficking (Regeringens skrivelse 2007/08:167). It was noted that these phenomena were 'serious obstacles against social equality, and equality between the sexes and the victims' possibilities to come into possession of their human rights [… and] the government emphasizes that measures have to be undertaken from a judicial, social and gender equality perspective' (SOU 2010:49, 56).

In 2010 the evaluation was published, concluding that the legislation had had a positive effect on prostitution and trafficking but that the combination of criminal justice and social work, in terms of tackling the problem, was of utmost importance. Besides establishing a national centre against prostitution and trafficking, the report proposed increasing the maximum penalty for imprisonment from six months to one year for particularly serious cases. During the public consultation process, the report received both acclaim and criticism from the different organisations and agencies.

The government's response followed within the year and it adopted the penalty proposal but not to establish a national centre. In parliament, compared to the debates during the promulgation of the law in 1998, there was an astounding consensus between the opposition and the governing parties, both sides using more or less the same arguments. The opposition wanted to abolish the demand for dual criminality for sexual services bought abroad, which was not, in fact, in the government's proposal, and wanted an increased effort from the government to promote the legislation and its connection to working against trafficking in the EU. The Social Democrats stated that:

> One has to make clear that prostitution and trafficking in human beings have strong connections. Active measures from the Swedish government internationally give good opportunities to influence other nations within the EU to adopt the idea of criminalizing the purchase of sexual services.
> (RP 2010/11:101, Anf. 1)

The same formulation was also used by the government, for example in the words of a Christian Democrat, 'the connection between prostitution and trafficking in human beings is clear. For me it is evident that trafficking is best fought by fighting prostitution. The Swedish sex purchase legislation is a statement of the kind of society we want' (RP 2010/11:101, Anf. 4). Moreover when defending their work in the EU, the government claimed that, 'under the presidency [of the EU we] worked very hard to communicate the Swedish point of view. We have been clear […] that the Swedish sex purchase legislation should be exported' (RP 2010/11:101, Anf. 6). A Moderate MP stated, 'I want to establish that us Moderates think that the criminalisation of the purchase of sexual services is a good thing. It is very good for the single, exposed, often a woman, and good to note that society does not condone prostitution' (RP 2010/11: 101, Anf. 17).

Thus, there was consensus in parliament. Parties which voted against the legislation in 1998 now embraced it as their own. The gender equality argument was subsumed in the larger discussion on the merits of the legislation and its possibilities of changing attitudes in the EU. Both government and opposing parties were in agreement on the legislation and increasing the penalty. The only dissenting voice demanding repeal (quoted at the beginning of this chapter) was the last speaker in the debate. The change from a contested question in the late 1980s to a matter of agreement 25 years later can perhaps be seen as remarkable, but is less so when placed in a larger context described in this chapter. Below I draw together the main themes evident in this process.

Conclusion

Providing an extended time frame for examining the debates on prostitution and state governance reveals a number of perspectives that a shorter time frame cannot. Firstly, the abolitionist approach, pointing to the demand side of prostitution, has a long tradition within Swedish politics. This is found within autonomous groups such as the early women's movement, feminist groups during the second wave, and among women's lobby groups in party politics. There is a clear pattern of mostly women arguing for criminalising the customer from as far back as early twentieth century. They criticised the power structures in society to which women were subordinated, and claimed that prostitution was the one of the most obvious examples of those structures. Secondly, the longer view also reveals the change in political discourse after the neo-abolitionist legislation prohibiting the purchase of sexual services was initially adopted. In the new millennium prostitution became framed differently: focus turned from prostitution *within* the nation towards trafficking for sexual purposes *through* the nation. As others have pointed out, this means that questions regarding prostitution are discussed against a framework of international law and the agendas of international organisations.

History shows us that the politicisation of male demand in prostitution resurfaced in the late 1970s and intensified in the early 1990s leading into the legislative process. The politicisation took place before Sweden entered the European Union, but the legislation was introduced after Swedish membership in 1995. The change towards debating trafficking came with the new UN protocol in 2000. In effect, trafficking can perhaps be seen as a political non-issue until after entering the EU. It was absent in the parliamentary and lobbying process promoting the abolitionist legislation, which was framed as changing norms regarding female subordination within the nation. Trafficking was only vaguely incorporated in proposals as an adjustment to EU directives. In the ensuing debates, however, there is a turn towards Europe and an outspoken wish to promote the neo-abolitionist legislation as a way to counteract trafficking. However, as has been pointed out, the government's use of the legislation for self-promotion should not be mistaken as the goal of the women's lobby groups. Yet, the interpretation of prostitution as a structural subordination of women in society has undoubtedly been weakened. In contrast to earlier versions of abolitionism and neo-abolitionism up until the 1990s, where male power structures and prostitution were interconnected, the post-legislative debate had less of this. Although a gender equality perspective was present, it was less outspoken and prostitution was subsumed in the larger question of trafficking and human rights. The change of venue from a perspective of national male demand to international and global trafficking where the Swedish legislation could make a difference seems to have enabled political consensus on a once controversial issue.

The general change from a social policy to a criminal policy focus concerning prostitution, as pointed out by a number of scholars, must be seen as enhanced by the discursive change from a national focus to an international, or a European, focus in the understanding of the law more generally. Regardless of a number of public inquiries' recommendations to increase social support or knowledge about prostitution, different governments chose to provide only a budget for policing. In this political and social environment, it is also possible for former adversaries of neo-abolitionism to embrace the legislation. Conservatives rarely point towards gender equality arguments in their support of the legislation but, rather, point to the advantages of using police efforts and the law's role in bolstering this outcome. This kind of framing of the debate points to the larger question of securitisation which, it must be said, is absent in Swedish government or parliamentary documents where the human rights argument is stressed.

Paradoxically, the legislation on trafficking, in many instances, was contradictory to the legislation on sexual services. However, had the national legislation on sexual services overridden the legislation on trafficking, the legislation may have been less restrictive concerning possibilities of (permanent) residence – an issue in parliament promoted by several parties, but never acted on in practice. There is a discrepancy between government promotion of the different legislations and its efforts in practice, and between different layers of practitioners regarding prostitution and trafficking – the political level, the judicial level and the police and social work level. In a unanimous acceptance of the neo-abolitionist approach, but with less backing in practice and a perhaps diluted content, the legislation can be used to symbolically promote Swedish liberal gender equality norms rather than as a radical questioning and overturning of patriarchal sexual standards.

Notes

1 The motion was preceded by a motion the year before and by an article in one of the evening papers demanding the same thing (Motion 2010/11:Ju249; Federley and Jakobsson, 2010). The MP, Fredrik Federley, has been called 'the bad boy of the Centre Party and its foremost headliner' (Eriksson, 2015).

2 The main material was accessed through the database Rixlex at www.riksdagen.se/sv/Dokument-Lagar/ using Swedish truncated keywords equivalent for prostitution, sexual services, sex purchase, trafficking [prostitution, sexköp, sexhandel, könsköp, könshandel, människohandel, trafficking]. For the period September 1999–September 2014 this rendered 127 records of proceedings in the Chamber where the topic was of importance, 10 proposals from the government, 15 reports and statements of opinion from the parliamentary committees, 4 Swedish Government Official Reports. Additional materials for the period 1989–1998 encompass 29 Records of proceedings and 48 Parliamentary motions. The period 1989–2002 was already sampled with the same keywords for work undertaken for earlier articles (Svanström 2004a, 2004b).

3 It has been pointed out that because of Sweden being dominated by mainly agricultural small-scale industry well into the 1930s, many married women have 'always' had a high participation in the labour force, working alongside their husbands in agriculture. This, although not argued in this chapter, I think is of fundamental importance when it comes to *not* seeing prostitution as work in Sweden (Svanström, forthcoming).

4 The Swedish state relies heavily on public commissions for making political decisions. These can be differently structured but are always appointed by the government.

5 In the late 1970s a number of organisations joined together fighting prostitution and pornography through open debates, meetings and pamphleting. These were often portrayed as being moralistic in character. More recently organisations like ROKS (Riksorganisationen för kvinnojourer och tjejjourer i Sverige – an organisation working with battered women), are portrayed as being radical feminist and moralising over prostitution. After a controversial television documentary in 2005, where representatives of the organisation were heard referring to men as animals, a number of members left the organisation. The documentary was heavily criticised in other media and also sentenced for being biased in the Granskningsnämnden (The Review Board) within the Myndigheten för Press Radio och TV (Authority for Press, Radio and Television). The documentary was termed 'Könskriget' ('Gender wars') and was aired on Sveriges Television (Swedish Television) on May 15 and 22, 2005.

6 However, the party was split as the women's lobby had earlier signed a motion to the contrary. In the ensuing vote, however, they did not vote for the proposal but abstained from voting, thus following the party line.

References

Dahlborg, K. *et al.* (2012) 'JO gör Brottsoffren till Brottslingar', *Göteborgs-Posten*, 24 November.

Eduards, M. (2007) *Kroppspolitik: Om Moder Svea och andra Kvinnor*, Stockholm: Atlas Akademi.

Engström, A. and Olsson, L. (2001) 'Starkt Stöd för Skärpt Sexlag, *Svenska Dagbladet*, February 4.

Erikson, J. (2011) *Strider om Mening: En Dynamisk Frameanalys av den Svenska Sexköpslagen*, Uppsala: Uppsala Universitet.

Eriksson, G. (2015) 'Federley: Dags att Släppa Beröringsskräck med SD', *Svenska Dagbladet*, September 24.

Esping-Andersen, G. (1990) *The Three Worlds of Welfare Capitalism*, Cambridge: Polity Press.

Federley, F. and Jakobsson, P. (2010) 'Samhället har Svikit Svenska Sexarbetare', *Aftonbladet*, September 7.

Gould, A. (2001) 'The Criminalisation of Buying Sex: the Politics of Prostitution in Sweden', *Journal of Social Policy*, 30(3): 437–456.

Halley, J. E., Kotiswaran, P., Shamir, H. and Thomas, C. (2006) 'From the International to the Local in Feminist Legal Responses to Rape, Prostitution/Sex Work and Sex Trafficking: Four Studies in Contemporary Governance Feminism', *Harvard Journal of Law and Gender* 29: 335–423.

Kulick, D. (2003) 'Sex in the New Europe: The Criminalization of Clients and Swedish Fear of Penetration', *Anthropological Theory* 3(2): 199–218.

Lister, R. (2009) 'A Nordic Nirvana? Gender, Citizenship, and Social Justice in the Nordic Welfare States', *Social Politics*, 16(2): 242–278.

Lundberg, U. and Åmark, K. (2001) 'Social Rights and Social Security: The Swedish Welfare State, 1900–2000', *Scandinavian Journal of History*, 26(3): 157–176.

Månsson, S.-A. (2012) 'Kön, Sexualitet och Socialt Arbete: Återblick på Ingången till ett Forskningsfält', *Socialvetenskaplig Tidskrift*, 2.

Månsson, S.-A. and Larsson, S. (1976) *Svarta Affärer. Utredning om Vissa Klubbars och Näringsställens Sociala Betydelse och Struktur*, Malmö: Socialförvaltningen.

Sainsbury, D. (1996) *Gender, Equality and Welfare States*, Cambridge: Cambridge University Press.

Skilbrei, M.-L. and Holmström, C. (2013) *Prostitution Policy in the Nordic Region: Ambiguous Sympathies*, Farnham: Ashgate.

Svanström, Y. (forthcoming) *From Prostitution to Sexual Services: Changing Concepts within the Swedish Social and Political Economy in the 20th Century.*

Svanström, Y. (2006a) *Offentliga Kvinnor: Prostitution i Sverige 1812–1918*, Stockholm: Ordfront

Svanström, Y. (2006b) 'Prostitution as Vagrancy: Sweden 1923–1964', *Scandinavian Journal of Criminology and Crime Prevention*, 7(2): 142–163.

Svanström, Y. (2004a) 'Criminalising the John: a Swedish Gender Model?' in J. Outshoorn (ed.) *The Politics of Prostitution: Women's Movements, Democratic States, and the Globalisation of Sex Commerce*, Cambridge: Cambridge University Press.

Svanström, Y. (2004b) 'Handel med Kvinnor: Debatten i Sverige och Nederländerna om Prostitution och Trafficking' in C. Bergqvist and C. Florin (eds) *Samtiden i Framtiden. ett Jämförande Perspektiv på Framtidens Könsrelationer*, Stockholm: Institutet för Framtidsstudier.

Tham, H. (2001). 'Law and Order as a Leftist Project? The Case of Sweden', *Punishment & Society*, 3(3): 409–426.

Vedin, U. (2015) *Etablering i Skuggan av Hög Arbetslöshet: Skillnadsskapande och Migrationseffekter*, Stockholm: Landsorganisationen i Sverige.

Public papers

Riksdagsprotokoll (Protocols from the Chamber)

1992/93:45, 1997/98:114, 1997/98:115, 2000/01:34, 2001/02:25, 2001/02:34, 2002/03:46, 2002/03:50, 2002/03:70, 2002/03:111, 2003/04:82, 2003/04:85, 2003/04:120, 2005/06:102, 2006/07:63, 2009/10:43, 2009/10:121, 2010/11:101

Motioner (Motions)

1990/91:Ju614; 1991/92:Ju605, 2000/01:Ju716, 2001/02: JuU10; 2002/03:JuU5; 2003/04: Ju313; 2004/05:Ju484; 2005/06:Ju394, 2010/11:Ju249

Skriftliga Frågor (Written questions)

2013/14:201 Prostitution som grund för avvisning

Betänkanden (Committee reports)

Betänkande 2009/10:JuU33 Förstärkt straffrättsligt skydd mot människohandel

Regeringens Propositioner (Government proposals)

1979/80:96 med förslag till ny utlänningslag, m. m.
1981/82:187 om vissa åtgärder mot prostitutionen
1997/98:55 Kvinnofrid
2001/02:124 Straffansvaret för människohandel
2003/04:111 Ett utvidgat straffansvar för människohandel
2009/10:152 Förstärkt straffrättsligt skydd mot människohandel

Regeringens Skrivelse (Government report)

Handlingsplan mot prostitution och människohandel för sexuella ändamål. Regeringens skrivelse 2007/08:167

Statens Offentliga Utredningar (SOU) (Official reports of the Swedish government)

Prostitutionen i Sverige SOU 1981:71
Könshandeln SOU 1995:15
Ny utlänningslag SOU 1979:64
Sexualbrotten – Ett ökat skydd för den sexuella integriteten och angränsande frågor SOU 2001:14
Förbud mot köp av sexuell tjänst. En utvärdering 1999–2008 SOU 2010:49

Justititieombudsmannen (The Parliamentary Ombudsmen)

Redogörelse 2013/14:JO1, 353–57

Göteborgs tingsrätt (The Gothenburg District Court)

Göteborgs tingsrätt, mål B 8184–11. Redogörelse 2013/14:JO1, 353–57.

3 The Netherlands

Analysing shifts and continuities in the governing of sexual labour

Silke Heumann, Sara Vida Coumans, Tamar Shiboleth and Marieke Ridder-Wiskerke

Introduction

When the Netherlands lifted the ban on brothels and pimping in 2000, it became a symbol of a 'liberal' approach to sex work[1], and the 'model case' for an alternative to the abolitionist model introduced in Sweden two years earlier (Bernstein 2007: 145). Today, however, in the Netherlands legalised sex work has come under increasing political and social pressure. Neo-abolitionist measures have found their way into public discourse and policy interventions within and despite a context of legalised sex work. This makes the 'Dutch case' particularly interesting and distinctive. How was that possible? What has helped neo-abolitionist discourses to gain traction in the Dutch context? How are they shaping law and policy interventions aimed at the sex industry and with what implications?

In this chapter we try to address this question by tracing the public debates, legislation and policies around sex work and trafficking in the past two decades. We unpack their rationale in light of the broader changes in the political climate and reflect on their consequences in terms of sex workers' labour and human rights.

The first section addresses the contradictory currents that have historically shaped Dutch debate around sex work and trafficking and maps out the concerns and rationale that informed the lifting of the ban on brothels in 2000, which in part explain its contradictory effects. The second section discusses current attempts to reform national legislation on sex work, introducing elements of neo-abolitionism. We focus particularly on the ongoing debates to increase the legal age for sex work and the criminalisation of clients of non-registered sex workers. The third section offers an overview of the main national and international agents promoting neo-abolitionism in the Netherlands.

The 2000 lifting of the ban on brothels and its implementation: concerns, rationale and effects

To understand the different and contending currents shaping Dutch policy towards the sex industry it is good to situate them in the context of historical debates around sex work and trafficking and how they related to each other.

In general, it is known that the emergence of trafficking concerns in the late nineteenth century (known as 'white slavery') was based on an assumed link between sex work and trafficking and characterised by the goal of abolishing sex work (Doezema 1999; Outshoorn 2005; De Vries 1997, 2005). In the Netherlands, the influence of the abolitionist movement led to the introduction of the 'Morality Laws' in 1911 that established a ban on brothels and the prohibition of 'traffic in women' (De Vries 2005). De Vries (2005: 53–53) suggests that a main argument used to justify the prohibition of brothel keeping was that brothels represented the necessary counterpart for trafficking and that a ban necessarily would curb trafficking. However, described more as a 'symbolic victory over vice', the legislation was vaguely formulated and barely enforced (De Vries 2005: 54). In practice, throughout the twentieth century, a rather pragmatic policy prevailed that has been characterised as one of 'regulated tolerance' (in Dutch: Gedoogbeleid) (Brants 1998). Though sex workers themselves were not criminalised, they continued to be stigmatised as 'fallen' or 'sinful' women, or as 'psychiatrically disturbed' in the 1950s and 1960s, as well as victims of poverty (Outshoorn 2012: 234).

The growth of the sex industry in the 1970s that created an influx of foreign sex workers to cover the growing demand, led to a re-emergence of debates around sex work and trafficking in the early 1980s (Outshoorn 2004b). Within the feminist movement, closely connected to the state through the Office for Emancipation, discussions emerged in the early 1980s around violence against women in relation to sex work, from the perspective of women's right to self determination (De Vries 1999; Outshoorn 2004a: 185–186; 2004b: 169–170). Out of these debates emerged the first attempt in the mid-1980s to distinguish voluntary from forced sex work, with the goal of improving the sex workers' position (De Vries 1999: 149; Outshoorn 2004b: 169). De Vries points towards how, as in the nineteenth century, trafficking figured centrally in the discussion around 'prostitution', but this time the argument was reversed, in that lifting the ban on brothels was proposed to fight trafficking (De Vries 1999: 148–148). Outshoorn (2000: 169) notes that there was no strong abolitionist lobby during the 1980s. Sex work had never been a salient issue in Dutch second wave feminism and even though the discussions were framed in terms of sexual violence and sexual domination, legalisation was seen as the best solution to address violence and abuse. At the same time Orthodox Protestantism, prominent during nineteenth century abolitionism, had lost power in the context of 1970s secularisation (Outshoorn 2000). Another powerful actor pushing to lift the ban on brothels was the Association of Dutch Municipalities; however its main concern was less the empowerment of sex workers and more the possibility of getting a tighter grip on the sex industry to safeguard public order (Outshoorn 2004b).

Outshoorn shows how since the 1980s a discourse around the legalisation of sex work crystalised out of multiple concerns: feminist concerns around women's rights and women's oppression, conservative concerns around public order, 'morality' and women's 'dignity', and concerns around migration into the sex industry that conflated trafficking and migrant sex work. This convergence led to a 'split' image of the 'prostitute in which, on the one hand, Dutch sex workers were presented as modern and emancipated, and, on the other hand, migrant women as exploited and trafficked' (Outshoorn 2001: 485; Outshoorn 2012: 242; Outshoorn 2014: 171). This double discourse is crucial to understand the rationale of the law reform at the turn of the century.

In 1987, the bill to lift the ban on brothels (known as the 'Repeal Bill') passed the parliament (the 'Tweede Kamer') under a government coalition of Christian Democrats (CDA) and centre-right Liberals (VVD). The Liberals strongly supported the bill and among Christian Democrats, even though morally against sex work, a pragmatic attitude prevailed. The bill, however, was put on hold in the senate (the 'Eerste Kamer') because of the need to revise trafficking legislation first in order to ensure consistency (Outshoorn 2004b: 169–170).

The Trafficking Bill was originally drafted to match the Repeal Bill, which meant that foreign sex workers were not automatically declared as trafficked. However, in 1989 a new Cabinet formed, consisting of a coalition of Christian Democrats (CDA) and Social Democrats (PvdA) (Outshoorn 2000). Hirsch Ballin, a fervent abolitionist from the CDA became Minister for Justice and opposed both the Repeal Bill and the proposed Trafficking Bill. He introduced radical amendments, effectively eliminating the distinction between forced and voluntary prostitution when 'third world women' were involved, and introducing the possibility for municipalities to ban prostitution on a local level (Outshoorn 2004: 170; Haveman and Wijers 1993: 21–23). This proposal was very controversial and heavily debated, but finally approved in parliament with the reluctant vote of the PvdA.

When both laws were discussed in the Senate in 1992 they encountered strong opposition, especially towards the proposals introduced by Minister Hirsch Ballin. The Repeal Bill was stopped and the Trafficking Bill was approved in 1993 in a heavily amended version that only included a few changes: a more specific definition of trafficking; the introduction of gender neutral language (from 'trafficking in women' to 'human trafficking') and an increase in penalties for trafficking (Outshoorn 2001, 2004, 2005).

The proposal to repeal the ban on brothels was revisited in 1997 by a new government coalition composed of social democrats (PvdA), centre right liberals (VVD) and left liberals (D66) (Outshoorn 2001: 482). This government, known as the 'Paars' (Purple) Cabinet, presented a favorable political context for the legalisation of sex work due to the absence of Christian parties (Outshoorn 2004b: 169). Both the PvdA and VVD supported legalisation, which was passed in parliament in 1999 and came into effect the subsequent year.

What drew most public attention during the law reform process was the legalisation of sex work through lifting the brothel ban. In practice, however, legal sex work was only possible under very specific conditions: in the licensed sector and by sex workers above the age of 18, with legal residence. Moreover, this legalisation went hand in hand with enforcement of regulation and of legislation against the non-legal sector (Daalder 2007). These more restrictive aspects of the law reform received little attention.

The official goals of the repeal of the ban on brothels were:

- "Control and regulation of the exploitation of prostitution.
- Improvement in the fight against involuntary prostitution.
- Protection of minors from sexual abuse.
- Protection of the position of prostitutes."

(Eerste Kamer 1999/2000: n.p., authors' translation)

The stated rationale was that decriminalisation of sex work would help free sex work from prostitution-related crime; forms of prostitution that involved violence or abuse or where minors were involved were to receive higher penalties (from one to six years). In addition there was an expectation that 'the regulation of and introduction of a separation between forbidden and unforbidden forms of prostitution will improve the legal position and work conditions of prostitute' (Eerste Kamer 1999/2000: n.p.).

Not visible in this formulation, yet explicitly debated and built into the law reform was the fact that persons without a legal residence permit were deliberately excluded from participating in the legal sector. This became clear in the government handbook published in October 1999 to train local authorities in the implementation of the law. A stated aim was: 'the reduction of the extent of prostitution by illegals (persons without valid residence permit)' (Ministerie van Justitie and Ministerie van Binnenlandse Zaken en Koninkrijksrelaties 1999: 10, authors' translation). The possible undesirable side effect of pushing illegal forms of sex work more underground was acknowledged in the handbook, yet seen as a 'necessary price to pay for regulation and control' (Ministerie van Justitie and Ministerie van Binnenlandse Zaken en Koninkrijksrelaties 1999: 12).

Legalisation was not only pushed by sex workers rights activists, but fuelled by Dutch pragmatism, characterised by a strong regulation and harm reduction approach, and the expectation that it would increase visibility of criminal practices and assist in fighting trafficking (Dutch Ministry of Foreign Affairs 2012; Hubbard *et a.* 2008: 141–142; Outshoorn 2001, 2004b; Ridder-Wiskerke and Aggleton 2014: 16). So, 'in no way should the Dutch legalisation of brothels be interpreted as a libertarian move: it is a policy to bring prostitution activities to the surface, in order to make for better control by the authorities' (Outshoorn 2004b: 175). In consequence many people in the sex industry experienced a tightening of state policing and control. Understanding this rationale, as well as the split image created between EU sex workers and migrant sex workers, helps to understand the apparently contradictory effects of the policy in the decade after legalisation.

The gradual encroachment on legal sex work after legalisation

It seems ironic that the implementation of the 2000 law pushed ever-larger sectors of the sex industry into illegality. Some of its negative effects became visible immediately and were closely connected to the law's formulation, while others were a result of its local implementation. An immediate effect of the law reform, due to the exclusion of sex workers without residency from the legal sector, was that two thirds of sex workers moved from a situation of 'regulated tolerance' into total illegality, effectively pushing them out of the brothels in the city centres to the (initially still) 'tolerated' areas of street sex work, and, following a crack down, into further invisibility (Aalbers and Deinema 2012: 135).

The 2000 law also included a decentralised model of sex work governance, giving the 441 municipalities considerable discretion in brothel licensing. Most have their own protocols, (some don't have any) prescribing how to deal with sex establishments resulting in confusion for sex workers, clients and law enforcement (Shiboleth 2015: 31). This opened the door to more restrictive policies at the municipal level and created big disparities between different cities (Wagenaar *et al.* 2013). For example in Utrecht it is illegal for sex workers to receive their clients at home while not in Rotterdam. Municipalities have also introduced their own sanctions for clients of specific kinds of sex work. For example, the city of Rotterdam closed all its red light districts and street sex work zones in 2005 making street sex work illegal (for both sex workers and clients), while sex workers do not need a license for home-based sex work (Shiboleth 2015: 32). In the city of Amsterdam, from the late 1990s, there was a growing interest in gentrifying the city centre and after legalisation, the city council started retracting licenses and buying up property in the red light district (Aalbers and Deinema 2012: 135).

Wagenaar *et al.* (2013) note a significant decrease in the licensed prostitution sector following legalisation. Between 2000 and 2012, the number of clubs decreased from approximately 800 to 360–370, and licensed windows from 2096 in 1999 to 1466 in 2009 (Wagenaar *et al.* 2013: 31–32). This continued after the extension of the Public Administration Probity Screening Act (known as the BIBOB Act) in 2011. Originally introduced in 2003, this act made it possible to withdraw licenses on the sole basis of suspicion of illegal activities. After its extension it was applied extensively to the sex industry (Daalder 2007: 15; Wagenaar *et al.* 2013). Though these authors identify other factors that have likely contributed to this decrease, such as the increase in internet and home-based sex work, stricter rules, regulations, and enforcement also contributed to the reduction (Wagenaar *et al.* 2013: 32 and 51), documented also by Hubbard *et al.* (2008). For instance at the time of legalisation, the estimated number of sex workers in Amsterdam was 8000–10,000, and by 2008 there were only 1500 working in licensed premises (Hubbard *et al.* 2008: 147). The others are likely to have been pushed into illegality, making it unsurprising that abuses in the sex industry have not been effectively curbed.

A major flaw of the law reform is that sex workers' rights were actually not central and only addressed through 'protectionist' arguments, which did not translate into proper labour rights (Wagenaar *et al.* 2013). Sex workers' rights became marginal and the state decided that labour relations between sex workers and employers were a 'private' issue. In the end, big businesses profited because a) they were better able to comply with licensing requirements and costs and b) they had lawyers to undermine sex workers rights, by denying and legally challenging the labour relations between them and sex workers, arguing that the latter were 'independent', thereby allowing evasion of tax and sex workers' labour rights. Sex workers were, hence, not protected as employees, but neither did they have the labour rights that other independent entrepreneurs had. Even basic things like opening a bank account and getting a mortgage are difficult for sex workers (Wagenaar *et al.* 2013; Siegel 2015). Daalder (2007) and Wagenaar *et al.* (2013) conclude that legalisation did not improve or strengthen the sex workers' position and the latter show that this has specifically to do with the lack of tools that sex workers were given in these reforms to increase their bargaining position.

While one of the goals of legalisation was to improve the fight against trafficking by distinguishing between legal and illegal forms of sex work, what defines legality is not, in the first place, a question of consent versus coercion. Coercion occurs in the licensed sector while undocumented migrant sex workers are not necessarily coerced yet are automatically situated in the illegal sector. So the line between legal and illegal does not follow the line of abuse or labour exploitation with sex worker's rights at the centre, but is determined by migration policies, age protectionism, and municipal gentrification policies.

Hubbard *et al.* (2008), in a comparative study of Sweden, Netherlands and the UK argue that, despite very different choices in law reform, the three countries shared considerable common ground in their concern with national sovereignty in the context of globalisation and migration and in the projection of these anxieties upon the 'prostitute body'. In all three cases, new legislation was used to eliminate particular spaces of sex work (Hubbard *et al.* 2008: 149), particularly street sex work. Hence, despite claiming to do so, none of the models has contributed to gender justice. Rather they have produced new spaces of exclusion and marginality (Hubbard *et al.* 2008).

To explain how different models produce such similar results, Scoular (2010) distinguishes between a narrow focus on the legal/policy framework and a broader Foucauldian conception of governmentality to incorporate a broad range of local agents governing sex work based on shared neoliberal notions of individual responsibility and respectability. This idea is useful in understanding the contradictory outcomes of the 2000 law reform. The decentralised model of governance that it relies on has allowed space for the emergence of neo-abolitionist interventions through local governance practices, even while the national law remains unchanged (Wagenaar, Altink and Amesberger 2013). But by 2008 national law also started to come under pressure.

Current reforms: growing neo-abolitionist tendencies

Throughout the decade following legalisation, there was a growing consensus that it did not bring about its expected effects of, depending on the perspective:

securing 'public order'; effectively fighting trafficking, or improving sex workers' social position and labour rights.

Though there were different ideas about what had gone wrong and how to remedy it, the argument that legalisation had not only failed to curb trafficking but had enabled it, gained increasing support. This shift became more visible in the discussion around a possible reform of the national legislation.

Since 2003, there have been discussions among individual sex workers' activists and sex work allies like Aids Fonds and the Rode Draad about the need for a uniform national legislation ('*kaderwet*' or 'framework law') to a) address the adverse effects of the decentralised system; b) make the rules and the licensing process more transparent; and c) regulate sex workers' labour rights.[2] Such new law was also needed to respond to the changes in the sex industry. More sex workers were working from online platforms and via online escort agencies, which were not regulated. In 2007 the Sex Workers' labour union, De Rode Draad, entered conversations with different ministries about a National Prostitution Law.

However, by 2008, the spirit of the law reform had changed considerably, under the influence of the Christian parties (Christian Democrats and Christian Union)[3] and the increasing dominance of abolitionist and neo-abolitionist discourses. Hirsch Ballin (CDA), who again became Minster of Justice, played an important role in the shift to a more restrictive model.

By 2009, the emphasis of the proposed law reform had changed from 'Kaderwet' (with emphasis on the intended uniform legal framework), to 'Law Regulating Prostitution and Preventing Abuses in the Sex industry' ('Wet Regulering Prostitutie and voorkoming van misstanden in de seksindustrie').[4] It was officially introduced to Parliament by Minister Hirsch Ballin and the Minister for Home Affairs and it included crucial elements of neo-abolitionism. Among other things proposed were:

- the introduction of a nationwide licensing policy for sex businesses
- the right of municipalities to define a limit to licenses including the 'null optie': the right to refuse licenses altogether if they have a strong 'public order argument'
- a compulsory registration of sex workers into a central database
- compulsory ID for sex workers
- an increase of the legal minimum age for sex workers from 18 to 21 years
- the criminalisation of clients of unregistered sex workers

(Wagenaar *et al.* 2013; Outshoorn 2005, Dutch Rijksoverheid 2009)

When Ivo Opstelten (VVD) became the Minister for Justice in 2010 the first round of debate over a new national prostitution law took place in the Dutch parliament. The proposed law encountered strong criticism in relation to sex workers' rights to privacy and to the efficacy of criminalising clients, voiced by (anti-abolitionist) feminists like the Association for Women and Law 'Clara Wichmann', sex workers' rights and privacy rights activists. The compulsory ID for sex workers was removed from the initial law as there was too much opposition, but the compulsory registration remained[5] (Eerste Kamer der Staten Generaal 2011).

Despite its controversial nature, the law was approved by the Dutch Parliament on 28 March 2011 with the support of all parties, except the Green Party (Groen Links) and the Left Liberal Party (D66)[6]. This marked an important shift in the positions of key political actors. While the Christian parties (CDA and Christen Unie) have always been predominantly abolitionist, the right liberal party (VVD) and the Social Democrats (PVDA) were supportive of liberalisation during the 1990s and early 2000s (Outshoorn 2004).

The Senate however, opposed the law and after two years of debates, postponements and communications between it and the Minister of Justice, in 2013 it solved the problem through a 'novelle' – a sort of amendment that split the law into two. This was an initiative of politicians from the Green Party, together with the D66 and the Socialist Party (SP) and allowed the removal of controversial aspects for later discussion, while the aspects that enjoyed consensus could be approved. This was welcomed because the introduction of a nationwide licensing policy had been awaited with some urgency. The 'novelle' was introduced again to the parliament in January 2014 and was still under discussion at the time of writing (May 2016).[7]

The removal of these aspects of the law seemed an important success from the perspective of sex workers' rights. However several problematic aspects remained. Firstly, the increase of age from 18 to 21, and the 'nuloptie' – the right of a municipality to reject licenses altogether – remained. Secondly, the proposal seeking client criminalisation was subsequently re-introduced by members of parliament from the Christian Union, the Social Democrats and the Socialist Party as a separate law reform in 2014.

These last two proposals – the increase of sex workers' age and client criminalisation – are used here to exemplify the growing pressures for neo-abolitionist measures in the Dutch system. When proposed in 2009 the main argument justifying the age increase was that young people possess less *weerbaarheid* (resilience); that is skills to protect themselves based on their life experience and the possibility of economic independence (Coumans forthcoming). While this appears to be a dominant way of approaching young people's decision-making, it moves away from a human rights-based approach and ignores young people's agency and evolving capacities to make life choices (Cook and Dickens 2000: 14; Bourdillon 2006: 1202; Coumans forthcoming). Agency and protection should not be treated as mutually exclusive but as complementary.

The propensity to control young people's sexuality and, in particular, that of young sex workers can be understood as a gendered control process (Coumans 2014: 37) related to the tendency of positioning the sex worker as a female body and the client as a male body. The sex worker is viewed as the opposite of an ideal representation of femininity, which is a young, innocent, pure, female body, that must be kept away from this 'pollution' as long as possible (Douglas 1966). This explains the desire to increase the legal minimum age from 18 to 21, though the general age of consent is 16, and the role it plays in the incremental introduction of neo-abolitionism (Coumans 2014: 37).

Initially part of the proposal was to criminalise sex workers under the age of 21. This was dropped in April 2015 by the Minister for Justice, following advice from the *Nationale Rapporteur voor Mensenhandel*[8], that it would increase the vulnerability of young sex workers. The proposal to criminalise clients and brothels for involvement in sex work of those under 21 years is still standing (NRC 2015).[9]

Being a client is not against the law in the Netherlands, still there are some exceptions in which their penalisation is possible. Clients who use the services of sex workers under eighteen can be penalised according to article 248b of the Criminal Code (Daalder 2007: 40). This would change to 21 if the increase in age is approved and would make clients responsible for identifying the age. Clients and sex workers alike have argued that this is problematic. Sex workers would have to show their official identification documents, including private information such as their real name and clients would have to recognise fake documents. As mentioned earlier, sex workers' privacy concerns prevailed and the proposal of compulsory identification was dropped.

But attempts to increase the responsibilities of clients by criminalising paying for sexual services continue to gain traction. There is a strong lobby for the implementation of a new bill drafted in 2014 based on the report, 'Regulation of Prostitution and Abuses in the Sex Industry' (Lindenberg 2014), which would make paying for sexual services of forced sex work punishable by law.[10] The proposal (article 173g) was introduced on 25 November 2014, by the Christian Union, PvdA and the SP. It proposes an addition to Article 173f on Human Trafficking to criminalise clients who 'engage in sexual acts' with somebody of whom they 'knew or could reasonably have suspected' was a victim of trafficking under penalty of a maximum of six years imprisonment.[11]

According to Segers, the frontrunner of the Christian Union, evident signals of coercion are, 'sex workers who are forced to work from containers for very low income, sex workers who work with three bulky Bulgarian men keeping watch at the door, and/or sex workers who are covered with bruises' (cited in Shiboleth 2015: 32). However, research consistently shows that coercion can be found in every sector of the sex industry (Bovenkerk and Pronk 2007; Van de Bunt 2007; Kiemel and ten Kate 2007; Staring 2007) and the signs of coercion are not as obvious as those described by Segers. Shiboleth (2015: 17) argues that for clients 'it is difficult, or even impossible, to distinguish between voluntary and forced prostitutes'.

In October 2015, the difficulty in identifying forced sex work led to a proposal to amend the law, dropping the phrase 'could reasonably have suspected'.[12] A similar formulation however was brought back in a proposed amendment in April of 2016 that substitutes the sentence with 'had serious reasons to suspect' trafficking.[13] This proposal was finally approved on 31 May 2016 by the parliament with the support of all major parties, including the Christian Parties, the Social Democrats, the Socialists and the Green Party.[14] It has yet to be discussed and approved by the Senate.[15]

So why this increasing focus on criminalising clients? Despite the fact that the commercial value of sex is well known, paying for sexual services is still branded as taboo and stigmatised (Shiboleth 2015: 118). Clients are portrayed as people of immoral behaviour by the media, politicians and lobbyists, evident in both the name given to clients (*hoerenloper*[16]) and the discourse equating prostitution with human trafficking and clients with rapists. Although the sex industry can be considered a high risk sector for labour exploitation, not all sex workers are trafficked, a nuance that often gets lost in public discourse, and which clients are feeling the effects of (Shiboleth 2015).

Meanwhile, as the debate around national legislation evolves, municipalities continue to develop and apply their own protocols on how to deal with sex establishments, which include several problematic policies. For instance, Amsterdam and Utrecht are implementing compulsory registration. In 2013 Utrecht closed down the Zandpad, its window prostitution boats, in the name of anti-trafficking measures with a tremendous impact on sex workers who had nothing to do with trafficking and were not consulted in that decision (Siegel 2015)[17]. Amsterdam, the first municipality in the Netherlands to do so, approved an increase in the legal minimum age for sex workers from 18 to 21 in 2015. So while the national law reform process is advancing slowly, in practice, policies are becoming more restrictive.

These reforms are relevant because in a context in which sex work is still legal, they make it possible for the State to intervene in the sex industry, under the banner of 'anti-trafficking' measures. The combination of these measures create the reality for a large sector of the sex industry that comes very close to one in which sex work is not legal: police raids, closing down of brothels, policing and punishing of clients and, consequently, increasingly precarious work conditions and livelihoods for sex workers.

The non-licensed sector becomes 'illegal' and conflated with exploitation and human trafficking, creating a legitimate field of intervention for anti-trafficking policies. The Dutch approach to trafficking – though legitimised through a human rights discourse – has been criticised for failing to effectively protect victims (Musto 2010). Rather, it prioritises migration control and the prosecution of international criminal networks over the human rights of victims, and focuses on exiting from the sex industry and the repatriation of victims. Drawing on Bernstein's work, Musto calls it the 'Dutch protectionist carceral paradigm' (Musto 2010: 386–387). This approach has gained prominence internationally precisely in the context of proliferation of neo-abolitionism and has been widely criticised for its ineffectiveness in curbing trafficking and labour exploitation in the sex industry (Crowhurst, Outshoorn and Skilbrei 2012; Crowhurst 2012; Bernstein 2010; Heumann *et al.* 2016; Baye and Heumann 2014; Outshoorn 2014).

Considering the EU wide offensive of anti-trafficking polices (see Chapter 1 of this volume), neo-abolitionist politics seem likely to succeed even in a country that, a decade ago, was a symbol of liberalism and 'tolerance'. A number of key constituencies are pushing more neo-abolitionist agendas. Political parties have been mentioned above, but they are part of a wider nexus of agents and it is to this that the next section turns in order to explain the contemporary relevance of neo-abolitionism in the Netherlands.

Agents of neo-abolitionism

It is clear that the motivations behind Dutch law were always mixed and contradictory. Seeking to control the sex industry rather than promoting workers' rights and the localisation of Dutch politics create dynamics towards abolitionist measures. It is clear that some political parties are swayed but there are also civil society and regional/European forces that are pushing the neo-abolitionist agenda in the Netherlands with the increasing degree of success evidenced by the new local and national legal measures described above. Some of these will be addressed below.

International pressures

According to Kulick (2003) the success of the neo-abolitionist model in Sweden was a result of a ten-year strong lobby of the abolitionist feminist movement that managed to frame sex work as a form of violence against women. This converged with a moral agenda of conservative politicians who wanted to send a clear message to society that buying sexual services is not acceptable. Kulick also points towards the fear of 'invasion' by mainly Eastern European women, after Sweden joined the EU, with the resultant opening of borders to other member states.

As testified throughout this book, Sweden has engaged in systematic efforts to 'export' their model to other European countries, through direct lobbying in individual member countries as well as through the European Union. An official Swedish report (SOU 2010: 29) evaluating the Swedish 1999 law, describes paying for sexual services as 'shameful and unacceptable' and reveals the intent to send this message to the rest of the world even though the report cannot conclude that the law has resulted in a reduction of prostitution in Sweden (SOU 2010: 35–36). Relatedly, there is no indication that closing down legal zones for sex work has resulted in a reduced number of clients in the Netherlands but rather, as we saw, has resulted in clients looking for illegal alternatives in which everyone involved is less visible (Shiboleth 2015). Nevertheless, as the Swedish model has become hegemonic within the EU, the Netherlands is under pressure (together with Germany and Austria) to align its policy and anti-prostitution lobbies, such as the civic initiative Exxpose, to mobilise Dutch civilians to agree with neo-abolitionism, inspired by the Swedish model.

According to Outshoorn (2005: 144) the reform of trafficking legislation in the EU, and also in the Netherlands, was also a result of UN and EU lobbying in member states which found expression in the (UN) Palermo Protocol and also within regional organisations such as the Organization for Security and Co-operation in Europe (OSCE).[18]

Similar trends are observable on the level of the European Parliament and Council, such as the European Commission Directive 2011/36/EU that established that 'all member states should take necessary measures to appoint a national rapporteur and to take steps to translate the EU directives into national legislation' (Wijers 2015) and forced member states to align their national policies to EU guidelines. Dutch anti-trafficking legislation was reformed in 2013 with explicit reference to the pressure to implement the EU directives.[19] In terms of civil society agents, as noted in other chapters in this book, the European Women's Lobby played a significant role in promoting neo-abolitionist policies embedded in its program on violence against women.[20] The European Women's Lobby is strongly dominated by Sweden, Norway, France and the UK, all countries with neo-abolitionist movements[21]. The Dutch representation of EWL, Nederlandse Vrouwen Raad (NVR), does not agree with these objectives. However it has not been able to change the direction of EWL policy. In addition it is under considerable pressure to change its position. In October 2015 the NVR organised an 'Expert meeting on Dutch Prostitution policy in the European Context' and subsequently sent a letter to the Parliament affirming its opposition to neo-abolitionism and reiterating its support for the Dutch policy (NVR 2015). However, when talking about voluntary sex work they refer to women above 21, hence not explicitly opposing the increase in age. The role of EU-level activism on the issue was evident in the role played by the Honeyball Report (see Chapter 1), which figured prominently in the parliamentary debates around client criminalisation in the Netherlands during 2014.

Political parties

On a national level the Christian parties (the CU and CDA) have historically been agents of abolitionism (Outshoorn 2012) and played a crucial role in shifting the proposal for national law reform towards a more restrictive framework, including 'nulloptie', the registration of sex workers, increase in age and client criminalisation. These parties operate mostly from a moral perspective on sex work but have increasingly drawn on discourses of sex work as violence against women.

Notable, however, is that the secular parties that in 2000 supported the legalisation of sex work have either changed their positions or are internally divided around the issue. The VVD and some members of the PvDA support abolitionist measures. Lodewijk Asscher (PvdA) at that time Alderman in Amsterdam, stated in 2011, 'we should stop considering prostitution to be normal, most of the time it is just human trafficking' (Trouw 7 October 2011). On 5 November 2012 he became the Minister for Social Affairs and his department is responsible for improving the position of sex workers nationally. In 2010 Gert Jan Segers from the CU and Mirthe Hilkens from the PvdA visited Sweden to learn more about the 'Swedish Model'. Although the Green Party rejected the 'Wet Regulering Prostitutie', the closing of the Red Light District in the municipality of Utrecht in 2013 was ordered by a mayor from this party.

Political parties' support for neo-abolitionist measures is partly linked to a moral agenda, in which it is difficult to distinguish between neo-abolitionist feminist and conservative frames: both conflate sex work with trafficking and hence an extreme form of violence against women. It is also linked to an anti-immigration agenda, as has already been established by previous authors (Wagenaar *et al.*. 2013; Outshoorn 2012). More generally, Crowhurst, Outshoorn and Skilbrei (2012) note that the increase in punitive measures towards the sex industry is also part of a more general trend towards law-enforcement and criminal approaches to social problems observable across different EU members.

Influences on public opinion

The media also played an important role in the shift towards neo-abolitionism. From 2000 onwards, the extensive publicity on trafficking and the 'lover boy panic' gradually changed public opinion and has led to a 'renewed discourse about young female victims which eclipsed the image of the modern consenting sex worker' (Outshoorn 2012: 242).

In 2004 Linda Terpstra and Anke van Dijk[22] published a book based on ten stories of service users of their organisation who were victims of 'loverboys', *Loverboys, een Publieke Zaak: Tien Portretten.* Terpstra and van Dijk are founding members of the women's shelter, Fier Fryslan, and support a number of other neo-abolitionist initiatives including exit programs. Together with Lou Repetur from the organisation 'Pretty Woman', a support organisation for young women regarding 'relationships and sexuality', they garnered considerable media attention, claiming that countless young girls were lured into sex work (Repetur 2005)[23]. It is interesting to note that the media constantly re-used the same sources giving the impression of a big problem, when the story derived from a couple of sources only (Burger and Koetsenruijter 2008).

In 2005, Ruth Hopkins, another strong critic of legal sex work published her book *Ik Laat je Nooit Meer Gaan*, in which she follows the trail of a woman from Albania, through the Ukraine to the Netherlands (Hopkins 2005). The author had written several articles on this topic since the early 2000s, including in the feminist magazine Opzij. Prior to publishing her book, she wrote a critical article about the Amsterdam red light district (known as the 'Wallen') on 1 October 2005 in the NRC Handelsblad where she outlined how 'traffic in women' had not been reduced since the ban on brothels was lifted in 2000. Her book created public distress and policy makers were asked why nothing was done about these issues. In 2008 she also wrote about one of the worst cases of human trafficking in the red light district by means of storytelling, though without capturing the country's huge variety in the sex industry nor suggesting solutions to the problem of trafficking.[24]

In 2008, 'Schone Schijn' was published, a report that showed that there was human trafficking within the licensed sectors of the sex industry and the 'Sneep' case – involving a large trafficking network operating in the legal sector – was covered widely in the media (KLPD 2008). Since then, sex work has increasingly been equated with criminality and human trafficking (Siegel 2015: 33–34). The trafficking scandals and the sensationalist media attention they received (Wagenaar *et al.* 2013) spurred the legitimacy of the neo-abolitionist lobby.

Finally, the framing of the debate about increasing the minimum age for sex workers was strongly influenced by a book that received much public attention: *Puberbrein* (2009). This book was written by Huub Nelis and Yvonne van Sark from Young Works, a Dutch organisation focused on youth communication and youth culture. Of the book's intent, one of the authors stated, 'we have written this book because we think that adults overestimate young people, as if they know everything through the Internet about sex, alcohol and drugs – and from the age of 12 we expect young people to deal with this by themselves. We think that young people need more structure and support' (van Sark, YouTube 2009). The argument presented in this book reinforces the idea of adult intervention into children's and young people's lives (Cole and Durham 2007: 8) and has shaped the debate on sex work to the extent that the increase of age is basically not an issue of great controversy any more.

A significant sector of Dutch feminists continues to be supportive of a legal and regulatory regime of sex work. National neo-abolitionist actors however are fuelled by the international influences from Sweden, the UN and the EU. In addition, what explains the traction of neo-abolitionist policies is their convergence with multiple state interests in relation to immigration control, public order and urban gentrification. Here, the media played an important role in shifting public opinion by giving space to often sensationalist accounts on human trafficking thereby contributing to the conflation between trafficking and sex work in the public imagery.

Conclusions

In this chapter we traced the way in which neo-abolitionist policies have entered the Dutch policy arena despite its regime in which sex work is legal under certain conditions.

We argued that, in order to understand the current resonance of neo-abolitionism in the Netherlands, we have to look at the concerns that fuelled the 2000 legalisation of sex work and its explicit goals: namely the concern around trafficking of women into the sex industry and the desire to control the sex industry. These goals created the grounds for an implementation that would encroach on the space for sex workers to exercise their work legally.

But current anti-trafficking policies are not only or simply a continuity. In 2000, public opinion and policy makers were much more on board with the idea that sex work can and should be seen as any other work and have equal rights. Today the discourse has shifted much more to one that is more and more explicitly targeting the legal sector of prostitution, arguing that legalisation has not curbed trafficking, that abuses take place in the legal sector and that prostitution needs to be controlled more thoroughly (Nationaal Rapporteur 2007, 2012 , 2013).

Since 2000, the political climate in the Netherlands, as in other European countries, has changed. The changes include the increasing power of the political right, including right wing neo-populism spreading anti-immigrant sentiments; the growth of EU with its effect on migration patterns and on the implementation of neoliberal economic policies manifest in processes of state securitisation, criminal justice approaches to 'social problems' and tightening of immigration laws and border control. All these factors have been identified as strongly shaping the policies and realities governing sex work and 'trafficking' both in the Netherlands and elsewhere (Bernstein 2007, 2010; Crowhurst, Outshoorn and Skilbrei 2012; Janssen and Hovener 2010; Wagenaar *et al.* 2013; Outshoorn 2012: 242; Wagenaar and Altink 2012: 285).

In a context in which sex work remains legal, and a total reversal of legalisation is unlikely to gain sufficient political support, the policies that have been implemented can be characterised as a systematic encroachment on the legal space for sex work by a consistent narrowing of the boundaries of what constitutes legal prostitution. There has been a gradual encroachment on space, demand, supply and sex worker's organisations representation. While this encroachment was first implemented through a set of scattered, uncoordinated local governance practices at the municipal level, there is currently an attempt to bring about law reforms on a national level that will further reduce the legal space for sex work. The resulting growth of the non-licensed sector, together with its criminalisation and conflation with exploitation and human trafficking, leads to the constitution of a legitimate and growing field of intervention for neo-abolitionist politics.

Notes

1 In this chapter we use the term 'sex work' and not 'prostitution'. The former recognises sex work as work; characterised by extremely variable labour conditions; the latter derives from views that regard it as inherently violent and exploitative, (Bernstein 1999; Heumann *et al.* 2016; Vanwesenbeeck 2001;). When specific references are made to the Dutch proposal 'Wetsvoorstel Regulering Prostitutie en Bestrijding Misstanden Seksbranche', for consistency purposes we refer to prostitution.

2 http://sekswerkerfgoed.nl/de-wet-regulering-prostitutie/.

3 www.rijkso'verheid.nl/documenten/brieven/2008/05/16/brief-tweede-kamer-p rostitutiebeleid.

4 www.rijksoverheid.nl/actueel/nieuws/2009/04/24/kabinet-wil-prostitutie-reguleren-en-m isstanden-tegengaan.

5 Nederlands Dagblad (ND) (2011) 'Opstelten Ziet af van Pasje Prostituees', ND 10 Feb 2011 www.nd.nl/nieuws/politiek/opstelten-ziet-af-van-pasje-prostituees.228356.lynk. Vereniging voor Vrouw en Recht 'Clara Wichmann' (VVR) (2009): 'Commentaar Wetsvoorstel Prostitutiewet' (32 211), 1 December 2009. www.vrouwenrecht.nl/2009/12/01/commentaar-wetsvoorstel-prostitutiewet-32-211-1-december-2009/.

6 Eerste Kamer der Staten Generaal. 'Wet regulering prostitutie en bestrijding misstanden in de seksbranche' (Wetvoorstel 32.211) www.eerstekamer.nl/wetsvoorstel/32211_wet_regulering_prostitutie, last accessed 24 Sep 2015)

7 Update: In the end the 'novelle' was only approved by the parliament two and half years later, on 21 June 2016 and at the time of the copyediting of this paper (August 2016), still has to go through the Senate: www.eerstekamer.nl/wetsvoorstel/33885_novelle_wet_regulering, last accessed 20 August 2016.

8 Ministerie van Veiligheid en Justitie (2015) Positie prostituees beneden 21 jaar versterkt Nieuwsbericht, 20 Juli 2015. www.rijksoverheid.nl/ministeries/ministerie-van-veiligheid-en-justitie/nieuws/2015/07/20/positie-prostituees-beneden-21-jaar-versterkt.

9 www.nrc.nl/nieuws/2015/07/20/prostituees-onder-21-toch-niet-strafbaar.

10 www.sp.nl/sites/default/files/initiatiefwet_memorievantoelichting.pdf. Accessed on 8 March 2016.

11 www.eerstekamer.nl/wetsvoorstel/34091_initiatiefvoorstel_segers. Accessed 20 August 2016.

12 www.eerstekamer.nl/behandeling/20151015/amendement_van_de_leden_van_oosten/document3/f=/vjyainv6u4re.pdf.

13 Tweede Kamer der Staten Generale 2016, Amendement van het Lid van Tongeren, Kamerstuk 34 091, Nr. 12, Vergaderjaar 2015–2016.

14 Tweede Kamer der Staten Generale 2016, Voorstel van wet van de leden Segers, Volp en Kooiman tot wijziging van het Wetboek van Strafrecht en het Wetboek van Strafrecht BES, houdende de invoering van de strafbaarstelling van misbruik van prostitué(e)s die slachtoffer van mensenhandel zijn (Wet strafbaarstelling misbruik prostituees die slachtoffer zijn van mensenhandel), Kamerstuk 34091, Gewijzigd voorstel van wet, 31 mei 2016.

15 www.eerstekamer.nl/wetsvoorstel/34091_initiatiefvoorstel_segers. Accessed 20 August 2016.

16 Translates as the pejorative term 'whorewalker'.

17 In the meanwhile the municipality of Utrecht has agreed to open a 'New Zandpad' in Overvecht, a neighbourhood in the outskirts of the city, in buildings constructed by the municipality. (www.utrecht.nl/ondernemen/prostitutie/het-nieuwe-zandpad/voorgeschiedenis/). 'Sex Workers Denounce the Increase in Rent Prices' (https://utrechtkrijgtspijt.wordpress.com/2016/07/13/hoge-huur-nieuwe-zandpad-leidt-tot-uitbuiting/).

18 OSCE (nd) 'Combating Trafficking in Human Beings', www.osce.org/secretariat/trafficking.

19 www.eerstekamer.nl/wetsvoorstel/33309_implementatie_richtlijn.

20 EWL political demands www.womenlobby.org/EWL-political-demands-1954?lang=en.

21 EWL (2011) 'About the Campaign', www.womenlobby.org/-about-the-campaign-?lang=en.

22 The same authors and organisation also published a series of other books on youth prostitution, including: *Publiek Geheim: Jeugdprostitutie* (2004); *De Betovering Verbroken: Methodiek en Aanpak Meisjesprostitutie* (2006).

23 See also www.prettywoman-utrecht.nl/faq/.

24 Hopkins, R. (2008). 'Jij Werkt nu Voor Ons.' Retrieved from www.nrc.nl/handelsblad/2008/05/31/jij-werkt-nu-voor-ons-11547669.\

References

Agustín, L. (2007) *Sex at the Margins: Migration, Labour Markets and the Rescue Industry*, London amd New York: Zed Books.

Aalbers, M. B., and Deinema, M. (2012). 'Placing Prostitution: The spatial–sexual order of Amsterdam and its growth coalition'. *City*, 16(1–2): 129–145. http://doi.org/10.1080/13604813.2012.662370.

Baye, E. and Heumann, S. (2014) 'Migration, Sex Work and Exploitative Labour Conditions: Experiences of Nigerian Women in the Sex Industry in Turin, Italy, and Counter-Trafficking Measures', *Gender, Technology and Development*, 18(1): 77–105.

Bernstein, E. (2010) 'Militarized Humanitarianism Meets Carceral Feminism: The Politics of Sex, Rights and Freedom in Contemporary Anti-trafficking Campaigns', *Signs: Journal of Women in Culture and Society*, 36(1): 45–71.

BernsteinE. (2007) *Temporarily Yours: Intimacy, Authenticity, and the Commerce of Sex*, Chicago, IL and London: University of Chicago Press.

Bernstein, E. (1999) 'What's Wrong with Prostitution – What's Right with Sex Work – Comparing Markets in Female Sexual Labor', *Hastings Women's Law Journal*, 10(1): 91–117.

Bourdillon, M. (2006) 'Children and Work: A Review of Current Literature and Debates', *Development and Change*, 37: 1201–1226.

Bovenkerk, F. and Pronk, G. J. (2007) 'Over de Bestrijding van Loverboymethoden', *Justitiële Verkenningen*, 33(7): 82–95.

Brants, C. (1998) 'The Fine Art of Regulated Tolerance: Prostitution in Amsterdam', *Journal of Law and Society*, 25(4): 621–635.

Burger, J. P. and Koetsenruijter, A. W. M. (2008) 'Nieuws over Loverboys Komt uit een Klein Kaartenbakje. Inhoudsanalyse van Berichtgeving in Nederlandse Nieuwsmedia (1995–2005)', retrieved from https://openaccess.leidenuniv.nl/handle/1887/20063.

Cole, J. and Durham, D. L. (2007) *Generations and Globalization: Youth, Age, and Family in the New World Economy*, Bloomington, IN: University of Chicago Press.

Cook, R. and Dickens, B. M. (2000) 'Recognizing Adolescents' 'Evolving Capacities' to Exercise Choice in Reproductive Healthcare', *International Journal of Gynaecology and Obstetrics: the official organ of the International Federation of Gynaecology and Obstetrics*, 70(1): 13–21.

Coumans, S. V. (2014) 'How Age Matters', *ISS Working Paper Series/General Series*, 588: 1–51.

Coumans, S. V. (forthcoming) 'Bodies, Brains and Age: Unpacking the Age Question in the Dutch Sex Work Debate', in R. Huijsmans (ed.) *Generationing Development: A Relational Approach to Children, Youth and Development*. Basingstoke and New York: Palgrave Macmillan.

Crowhurst, I. (2012) 'Caught in the Victim/Criminal Paradigm: Female Migrant Prostitution in Contemporary Italy', *Modern Italy*, 17:4, 493–506, DOI: 10.1080/13532944.2012.707000

Crowhurst, I., Outshoorn, J. and Skilbrei, M. L. (2012) 'Introduction: Prostitution Policies in Europe', *Sexuality Research and Social Policy*, 9(3): 187–191.

Daalder, A. (2007) *Prostitution in the Netherlands since the Lifting of the Brothel Ban*. Den Haag: Boom Juridische Uitgevers.

De Vries, P. (2005). '"White Slaves" in a Colonial Nation: the Dutch Campaign Against the Traffic in Women in the Early Twentieth Century', *Social & Legal Studies*, 14(1): 39–60. http://doi.org/10.1177/0964663905049525.

De Vries, P. (1999) 'De Ketenen van de Blanke Slavin en het Belastbare Inkomen van de Sekswerkster', in R. Holtmaat and G. C. J. J. van den Berg (eds) *Eeuwige Kwesties: 100 Jaar Vrouwen en Recht in Nederland.* Jubileumuitgave van Nemesis, Tijdschrift over Vrouwen en Recht. Deventer: W. E. J. Tjeenk Willink, pp. 140–153.

De Vries, P. (1997) *Kuisheid voor Mannen, Vrijheid voor Vrouwen. De Reglementering en Bestrijding van Prostitutie in Nederland, 1850–1911.* Hilversum: Uitgeverij Verloren.

Doezema, J. (1999) 'Loose Women or Lost Women? The Re-emergence of the Myth of White Slavery in Contemporary Discourses of Trafficking in Women', *Gender Issues*, 18(1): 23–50.

Douglas, M. (1966) *Purity and Danger: An Analysis of Concepts of Pollution and Taboo.* London: Routledge.

Dutch Ministry of Foreign Affairs (2012) 'Dutch Policy on Prostitution. Questions and Answers2012', retrieved from: www.minbuza.nl/binaries/content/assets/minbuza/en/import/en/you_and_the_netherlands/about_the_netherlands/ethical_issues/faq-prostitutie-pdf–engels.pdf-2012.pdf.

Dutch Rijksoverheid (2009) 'Memorie van Toelichting: Bijlage van Wetsvoorstel Regulering Prostitutie en Bestrijding Misstanden Seksbranche' (a webpage of Rijksoverheid), retrieved from www.rijksoverheid.nl/onderwerpen/prostitutie/documenten-en-publicaties/kamerstukken/2009/11/11/memorie-van-toelichting.html.

Eerste Kamer der Staten Generaal (2011) 'Regels Betreffende de Regulering van Prostitutie en Betreffende het Bestrijden van Misstanden in de Seksbranche' (Wet regulering prostitutie en bestrijding misstanden seksbranche – Gewijzigd voorstel van wet), Kst 32211 A, Den Haag, retreived from www.eerstekamer.nl/behandeling/20110329/gewijzigd_voorstel_van_wet_6.

Eerste Kamer (1999/2000) Opheffing Algemeen Bordeelverbod (25.437): Hoofdlijnen. www.eerstekamer.nl/wetsvoorstel/25437_opheffing_algemeen#p2.

Haveman, R. and Wijers, M. (1993) 'Wetgeving: Vrouwenhandel en Exploitatie van Prostitutie', *Nemesis: Tijdschrift over Vrouwen en Recht*, March/April: 21–23. www.tijdschriftnemesis.nl/_pdf/1993_2.CV.pdf.

Heumann, S., Siegmann, K.A. and Empower Foundation (2016) 'Towards New Perspectives on Labour Precarity and Decent Work for Sex Workers', in K. Biekart, W. Harcourt and P. Knorringa (eds) *Exploring Civic Innovation for Social and Economic Transformation*, London, New York: Routledge, pp. 168–191.

Hopkins, R. (2005) *Ik Laat je Nooit Meer Gaan.* Breda: De Geus.

Hubbard, P., Matthews, R., and Scoular, J. (2008) 'Regulating Sex Work in the EU: Prostitute Women and the New Spaces of Exclusion', *Gender, Place and Culture*, 15(2): 137–152. http://doi.org/10.1080/09663690701863232.

Janssen, M. and Hovener, V. (2010) 'De Publieke Vrouw: Zelfstandig Ondernemer of Slachtoffer?', *Lover*, 1 June 2010. www.tijdschriftlover.nl/politiek_en_maatschappij/de_publieke_vrouw___zelfstandig_ondernemer_of_slac.

KLPD (2008) *Schone Schijn: de Signalering van Mensenhandel in de Vergunde Prostitutiesector.* Driebergen: Dienst Nationale Recherche.

Kiemel, J., and ten Kate, W. (2007) 'De Programmatische Aanpak van Mensenhandel en Mensensmokkel', *Justitiële Verkenningen*, 33(7): 96–106.

Kulick, D. (2003) 'Sex in the New Europe: The Criminalization of Clients in Swedish Fear of Penetration', *Anthropological Theory*, 3(2): 199–218.

Lindenberg, K. (2014) *Prostituant en Strafrecht: Quickscan van de Strafrechtelijke Verantwoordelijkheden van de Prostituant bij Mensenhandel en Minderjarigheid.* Groningen: Rijksuniversiteit Groningen.

Ministerie van Justitie; Ministerie van BinnenlandseZakenenKoninkrijksrelaties (1999) *Handboek Lokaal Prostitutiebeleid, Deel 1: De Opheffing van het Algemeen Bordeelverbod*. Den Haag: VNG Uitgeverij.

Musto, J. L. (2010) 'Carceral Protectionism and Multi-Professional Anti-Trafficking Human Rights Work in the Netherlands', *International Feminist Journal of Politics*, 12(3–4): 381–400. http://doi.org/10.1080/14616742.2010.513107.

Nationaal Rapporteur MensenhandelenSeksueelGeweldtegenKinderen (2007) *Mensenhandel: Vijde Rapportage van de Nationaal Rapporteur*. Den Haag: BNRM.

Nationaal Rapporteur MensenhandelenSeksueelGeweldtegenKinderen (2012) *Mensenhandel. Jurisprudentie Mensenhandelzaken 2009–2012. Een Analyse*. Den Haag: BNRM.

Nationaal Rapporteur MensenhandelenSeksueelGeweldtegenKinderen (2013) *Mensenhandel: Negende Rapportage van de Nationaal Rapporteur*. Den Haag: BNRM.

Nelis, H. and Sark, Y. (2009) *Puberbrein*. Kosmos Uitgevers.

NRC (2015) 'Prostituees onder 21 toch niet Strafbaar' retrieved from www.nrc.nl/nieuws/2015/07/20/prostituees-onder-21-toch-niet-strafbaar.

NVR (Nederlandse Vrouwenraad) 2015. Verslag expert meeting Nederlands Prostitutiebeleid in Europese context. www.nederlandsvrouwenraad.nl/html/index.php?paginaID=2761, accessed 20 August 2016.

Outshoorn, J. (2000) 'Legalizing Prostitution as Sexual Service: the Case of the Netherlands', Conference Paper, European Consortium for Political Research (ECPR) Joint Sessions, University of Copenhagen, Denmark, 14–19 April, https://ecpr.eu/Filestore/PaperProposal/8cededd9-302d-4870-8d0b-618c34524ef4.pdf.

Outshoorn, J. (2014) 'The Contested Citizenship of Sex Workers: The Case of the Netherlands', in C. R. Showden and S. Majic (eds) *Negotiating Sex Work: Unintended Consequences of Policy and Activism*. Minneapolis, London: University of Minnesota Press, pp. 171–194.

Outshoorn, J. (2012) 'Policy Change in Prostitution in the Netherlands: From Legalization to Strict Control', *Sexuality Research and Social Policy*, 9(3): 233–243.

Outshoorn, J. (2005) 'The Political Debates on Prostitution and Trafficking of Women', *Social Politics*, 12(1): 141–156.

Outshoorn, J. (2004a) *The Politics of Prostitution: Women's Movements, Democratic States and the Globalization of Sex Commerce*. Cambridge: Cambridge University Press.

Outshoorn, J. (2004b) 'Pragmatism in the Polder: Changing Prostitution Policy in the Netherlands', *Journal of Contemporary European Studies*, 12(2): 165–176. http://doi.org/10.1080/1460846042000250873.

Outshoorn, J. (2001) 'Debating Prostitution in Parliament: A Feminist Analysis', *European Journal of Women's Studies*, 8(4): 472–490.

Repetur, L. (2005) 'Pretty Woman: Van Risicomeiden Tot (ex-)Prostituees', *Maatwerk*, 6(5): 46–48. DOI 10.1007/BF03070521.

Ridder-Wiskerke, M. and Aggleton, P. (2014) 'Lifefstyle, Work or Easy Money? Male Sex Work in the Netherlands Today', in P. Aggleton and R. Parker (eds) *Men Who Sell Sex: Global Perspectives*. London: Routledge, pp. 15–26.

Scoular, J. (2010) 'What's Law Got to Do with It?' *Journal of Law and Society*, 37(1): 12–39.

Shiboleth, T. (2015) *Being a 'John'. A Client's Perspective on Paying for Pleasure*. The Netherlands: Wolf Legal Publishers.

Siegel, D. (2015) *Het Zandpad – Closing Brothels or Closing Eyes? Utrechtse Sekswerkers na de Sluiting van het Zandpad*. Den Haag: Boom Lemma Uitgevers.

SOU (2010) En Utvärdering1999–2008. Betänkande av Utredningen om utvärdering av Förbudet mot Köp av Sexuell Tjänst [with English summary]. Stockholm (SOU 2010: 49). sweden.gov.se/content/1/c6/14/91/42/ed1c91ad.pdf.

Staring, R. (2007) 'Handelaars in Vrouwen: Achtergronden en Werkwijzen', *Justitiële Verkenningen*, 33(7): 50–63.

Van de Bunt, H. G. (2007) In het Hart van de Vergunde Sector', *Justitiële Verkenningen*, 33(7): 78–81.

Vanwesenbeeck, I. (2001) 'Another Decade of Social Scientific Work on Sex Work: A Review of Research 1990–2000', *Annual Review of Sex Research*, 12(1): 242–289. http://doi.org/10.1080/10532528.2001.10559799.

Wagenaar, H. and Altink, S. (2012) 'Prostitution as Morality Politics or Why It Is Exceedingly Difficult To Design and Sustain Effective Prostitution Policy', *Sexuality Research and Social Policy*, 9: 279–292.

Wagenaar, H., Altink, S. and Amesberger, H. (2013) *Final Report of the International Comparative Study of Prostitution Policy: Austria and the Netherlands*. Platform 31, the Hague. Retrieved from http://lastradainternational.org/lsidocs/Prostitution_policy_report.pdf.

Wet Regulering Prostitutie en Bestrijding Misstanden Seksbranche www.eerstekamer.nl/wetsvoorstel/32211_wet_regulering_prostitutie.

Wijers, M. (2015) 'Purity, Victimhood and Agency: Fifteen years of the UN Trafficking Protocol', *Anti-Trafficking Review*, 4: 56–79, www.antitraffickingreview.org.

YouTube (2009) 'Introductie Puberbrein Binnenstebuiten', *Puberbrein Website*. Retrieved from www.puberbrein.nl/_index.php?parentId=3.

4 Strange confluences

Radical feminism and evangelical Christianity as drivers of US neo-abolitionism

Crystal A. Jackson, Jennifer J. Reed and Barbara G. Brents

Introduction

In this chapter we explore the politics of neo-abolitionism in the United States. Neo-abolitionism is the newest incarnation of the movements to abolish prostitution, exemplified by model legislation from Sweden that criminalises the buyer of sex but not the seller. The beginnings of abolitionism in the United States can be traced to feminist efforts in the 1830s through to the passage (in 2000) and subsequent revisions of the Trafficking Victims Protection Act (TVPA). What has distinguished abolitionist efforts in the United States at the turn of both the nineteenth and twentieth centuries has been the parallel activism of feminists and conservative religious organisations.

This chapter will explore similarities and differences between these two surges in anti-prostitution advocacy to illustrate the shift from abolitionism to neo-abolitionism in the United States. First we discuss the original surge as nineteenth century US women's groups joined with religious moral reformers to campaign for anti-prostitution laws. This first prostitution abolition movement drew parallels between abolishing the African slave trade and slavery in the US and efforts to abolish prostitution of free women. We then discuss late 1900s abolitionism and its turn to neo-abolitionism *after* anti-prostitution feminists, Christian evangelicals, and the political right created a coalition to pass the Trafficking Victims Protection Act (TVPA) in 2000. Today, neo-abolitionist politics in the US is couched in public concerns about a growing market economy commodifying more aspects of life, middle class concerns about race and immigration, feminist concerns about male sexual exploitation of women, conventional religious beliefs about proper gender roles, virtue, the family and sexual morality, and neoliberal ideologies which blame individuals rather than structures for social problems (see Bernstein 2007, 2010; Hoang and Parreñas 2014; Kerodal, Freilich and Galietta 2015; Kleemans 2011; Koken 2010; Sanders 2009; Weitzer 2011, 2014; Zhang 2009, 2012; Zimmerman 2012).

The TVPA and its subsequent reathorisations during conservative political administrations helped institutionalise neo-abolitionism in the United States and extend the reach of neo-abolitionist policies internationally. Neo-abolitionist frames have been embraced by politicians, some feminists, faith-based communities, social service workers, and policing organisations across the country. Their collective focus on punitive and protectionist criminal justice initiatives (rather than preventive social protection) to human trafficking echoes broader neoliberal governance trends in the US toward increased surveillance and criminalisation of people of colour, poor people, and transgender identified individuals (Bernstein 2010, 2012; Lerum 2014).

History of US prostitution regimes and feminist prostitution reform

Anti-prostitution reform in the US today reflects longstanding politics of race, class, gender and religion that began to play out against prostitution in the US as early as the 1830s. Prostitution in the US, like Europe, was not a distinct offence through the 1800s. Laws instead sought to maintain social order, targeting poor individuals and 'loose' women for night-walking, vagrancy, disorderly conduct or lewdness. Brothels were regulated by public nuisance laws, which meant neighbours' complaints could shut them down (Luker 1998; Lucas 1995).

Early in the nineteenth century, a coalition of women's organisations and clergy came together in the social purity movement to fight individual immorality, equally including prostitution and alcohol consumption. One tactic included 'rescuing' fallen working class women from lives of ruin and instructing them in middle class rules of piety, respectability and family (Pivar 2002). Later in the century, during what historians call the 'first wave' of feminism in the United States, these reformers focused more directly on prostitution through 'new' abolitionism, a reference to nineteenth-century American anti-slavery abolitionism. Many first wave feminists drew on their own experiences fighting the African slave trade, ending slavery in the US and fighting for the rights of Black men to vote as they fought for women's voting rights from the late 1800s-1920. For some of these first wave feminists, fighting for women's freedom by abolishing prostitution and like evils seemed a parallel cause. Some of these feminist organisations joined with the purity crusaders to fight red light districts appearing in increasingly crowded cities in the late 1800s, and were later joined by the medical profession seeking to fight venereal disease (Halley *et al.* 2006; Pivar 2002).

Several elements are important in understanding the place of feminism in these prostitution reform movements and abolitionism in the United States. First, feminists at the turn of the twentieth century (as now) were not united in their stance against prostitution. Many associated with socialist and anarchist movements of the time and fought for women's sexual liberty, rejecting institutions, including marriage, that held women and men to reproductive sex as the only appropriate avenue for sexual expression and supported the right to sell sex (Laite 2012).

Second, early feminist organisations who opposed prostitution were not successful in passing anti-prostitution policies using a women's rights or equality frame until joined by other moral, gendered or racially motivated groups. Foreshadowing the focus on male behaviour in contemporary neo-abolitionism, feminist groups pushed for a 'single moral standard' of sexual piety and devotion to family *for men* as the path to women's full equality. They succeeded in passing laws raising the age of consent and some rape reform. It was not until they joined male physicians and public health reformers in the social hygiene movement that they succeeded in passing policies extending the state's reach to patrolling dance halls and roadhouses for promiscuous and unhealthy sexual behaviour of both sexes (Luker 1998). By the start of World War I, however, with pressure from the military, social hygienists decided to support prophylaxis and treatment for male soldiers in fighting venereal disease as opposed to punishing promiscuous behaviour, effectively ending that organisation's efforts in fighting for a single moral standard (Luker 1998).

That said, laws against prostitution specifically did not emerge until another concern inspired action – the reaction against a large immigration wave in the early 1900s. Mimicking a similar panic in Europe in the 1880s, social purity- and social hygiene-inspired journalists stoked fears of innocent young white women sold into slavery by sexually uncontrollable and criminally inspired immigrant men. Women's bodies were situated as tools of citizen-building and as pillars of familial patriotism to be protected. This white slavery panic resulted in the nation's first (and only) prostitution-related law in 1910, the Mann Act, criminalising the transportation of individuals from one state to another for the purpose of prostitution (Donovan 2006; Lucas 1995).

This collection of values and coalitions that included anti-immigration, feminist and public health reformers helped push through a number of state level laws aimed at eliminating red light districts, punishing third parties involved in transporting or tolerating prostitution. Contrary to what the original feminist activists sought, laws criminalised prostitutes and framed them as diseased, immoral or delinquent.

Third, then, these early abolitionist movements individualised and feminised prostitution, helping to frame prostitution as problem of women's individual morality and character rather than a problem of patriarchal power and women's equality (Brents and Sanders 2016; Luker 1998). They codified individual prostitutes as both victims and offenders, their crime a problem of individual malleability, or self-control and morality. Campaigns against women with loose morals inspired unprecedented surveillance of working class young girls, including public recreation in saloons and dance halls, seeing them as both victims and offenders. Third parties were criminalised under pandering and pimping laws as they were seen as threats to the individual prostitute's self-determination. In this feminisation and individualisation of prostitution, male prostitutes, while small in number, disappeared completely from the characterisation of the 'problem' of prostitution. By the end of World War I, almost every state in the union had made prostitution illegal.

Fourth, it wasn't until the tail-end of the second wave feminist movement in the 1970s and 1980s that US feminists successfully made prostitution an issue of women's rights. Early 1900s conflicts about women's sexual rights solidified into the 1980s 'sex wars' between, on one hand, pro-sex feminists and sex worker rights movements who saw women's sexual rights as including the right to sell sex versus, on the other hand, abolitionist radical feminists who saw prostitution and pornography as male domination over female sexuality writ large, akin to slavery and violence.

Although radical feminist opposition to the sexualisation of culture in general and sexual commerce in particular resonated briefly with the conservative, religious right on pornography, it wasn't enough to forge political alliances during the 1980s. Groups such as Focus on the Family, Concerned Women for America, and the Moral Majority remained opposed to broader goals of women's empowerment, and fought feminists on reproductive rights and abortion. And feminists remained unwilling to support the institutions of patriarchal, heterosexual marriage (Bernstein and Jakobsen 2010). It was tricky for abolitionist-leaning feminists to find common ground with conservative, religious organisations, even if they agreed that prostitution was problematic.

Sex trafficking, feminism and the religious right

What catapulted prostitution control back onto the national public agenda at the turn of the twenty-first century was the reemergence of concerns over sex slavery, now called 'sex trafficking,' as a global social concern. Just as 'white slavery' fears gripped the US at the turn of the twentieth century, now at the turn of the twenty-first century sex trafficking fears gained attention at the same time as immigration re-entered the media (Doezema 1999). While concerns over trafficking began as a fight against international organised crime in both sex and non-sexual labour, by 2010 a significant shift occurred as trafficking became a 'woman's' issue, and the federal government focused on local women (citizens and non-citizens alike) forced by individuals to sell sex. Neo-abolitionism emerged in this context in a way that simultaneously incorporated the women's rights framing of the earlier feminist sex wars with the conservative sexual politics of the religious right. Two movements helped bring sex trafficking and neo-abolitionism into the limelight: radical feminist anti-prostitution activists and Christian evangelicals. In this next section we discuss the reasons for this shift and the rise of neo-abolitionism.

By the late 1980s, abolitionist radical feminists seemed to be losing the fight against prostitution and pornography. Globally, sex worker rights movements made significant gains as a number of countries around the world began to decriminalise prostitution, including the Netherlands and parts of Australia. Sex worker organisations were active in international conferences on criminal trafficking in labour and sex work and were making gains in making sex worker rights part of the anti-criminal trafficking agenda. While not successful in changing prostitution laws in the US, the pro-sex and sex worker rights movement was slowly growing as the sex industry was becoming more mainstream in an increasingly sexually liberal climate (Brents and Sanders 2010).

In 1988, Women Against Pornography (WAP), one of the key anti-prostitution radical feminist organisations in the 1970s sex wars, made a strategic change of direction. Laura Lederer, one of the founders of WAP and of Take Back the Night,[1] helped fund and organise a 1988 conference that defined trafficking as 'globalised prostitution' and urged feminists to shift the fight from their focus on domestic censorship of pornography to international sex trafficking. They could shift the attack away from the sex lives of Western feminists to humanitarian concerns over third world women. This strategy was a way to respond to anti-censorship, sex worker-inclusive feminists (sometimes referred to as sex positive feminists) who critiqued anti-pornography efforts as essentialist and simplistic, and even sexist for stigmatising women's labour, and pitting women against women.

Through this conference, Lederer convinced activists that they could frame sex worker rights activists as protecting themselves while poor women in other countries were being exploited. Lederer joined with WAP leaders, Janice Raymond and Doris Leidholdt, and in 1988 created the Coalition against Trafficking in Women (CATW) and WAP eventually faded as an organisation. A few years later, Lederer founded The Protection Project as a campaign under CATW to specifically address sex trafficking internationally. Other organisations emerged in the early 1990s to fight sex trafficking and prostitution using this frame. Many of these organisations, including Equality Now, shared members on their boards of directors. This laid the foundation for what would become neo-abolitionist feminism in the United States (Soderlund 2005, Bernstein 2007, 2010; Milivojevic and Pickering 2013).

At the same time, these anti-pornography/anti-prostitution feminists were joined, and in some ways eclipsed by, faith-based anti-trafficking organisations (Soderlund 2005). During the 1990s, Christian evangelical organisations began investing resources to fight international 'human rights' violations through UN agencies, finding common ground with a range of groups on issues such as the environment, HIV/AIDS and sex trafficking. For the Christian groups, this interest in trafficking reflected a new strategy to stand apart from the divisive domestic politics of leaders like Jerry Falwell and the Moral Majority during the 1970s and 80s. These largely white evangelical Christian groups embraced a conservative sexual politics. They saw a wide variety of social ills that could be solved through the promotion of traditional gender roles, anti-abortion activism, opposition to premarital sex and early moral training. But they took a 'leftward sweep' in articulating these concerns through the language of social justice and women's rights (Bernstein 2007, 2010; Bernstein and Jakobsen 2010).

As Evangelicals for Social Action founder, Ron Sider, said, the anti-trafficking movement's focus on sexual violation does 'fit with the evangelical concern for sexual integrity' (Shapiro 2004). They came to the fight against trafficking by focusing on rescue, in which they positioned powerless third world women as needing protection from 'bad men' (Bernstein 2007, 2010; Bernstein and Jakobsen 2010, Shapiro 2004). Their goal of abolishing prostitution could not be clearer. As a spokesperson for Concerned Women for America wrote in 2005, 'the UN blames social and economic disparities for fostering trafficking,' but 'the demand for prostitutes is the driving force behind sex trafficking,' a demand which the United States Congress is 'working to end' (Berman 2006: 276).

Unlike in the 1970s and 1980s, these two groups, radical feminist organisations and Christian Evangelicals, now worked in tandem. Feminist abolitionists subsumed their fight for women's equality in other arenas to support the heterosexual middle class family and a reformed moral asexuality. They did not challenge the gender norms embodied within conservative religious morality. The work of abolitionist feminist and evangelical religious groups led to the creation of the main piece of contemporary abolitionist legislation in the United States, the Trafficking Victims Protection Act (TVPA) of 2000. In the next section, we will discuss the development of the TVPA, and how it has come to provide institutional support for neo-abolitionist end-demand politics.

Institutionalising neo-abolitionism: the Federal Trafficking Victims Protection Act

No law has done more to provide institutional support to the neo-abolitionist movement than the Trafficking Victims Protection Act (TVPA) of 2000. The TVPA has institutionalised the ideology and provided a material support for anti-prostitution advocacy and narrowed the fight against international labour trafficking to a punitive approach to both domestic and international sex trafficking. Moreover, the TVPA helped propel the US into a major role internationally through funding anti-sex trafficking efforts.

The genesis of the TVPA began in the mid-1990s, when President Clinton oversaw the creation of a President's Interagency Council on Women (PICW), headed by Madeline Albright and Hillary Clinton as co-chairs, to spearhead the administration's trafficking efforts (Stolz 2005). While centralising this into a 'woman's office', the efforts reflected left-liberal trafficking frames involving NGOs concerned with human rights, migrant labour protections, and the trafficking of women and men for a wide range of labour (including agriculture and domestic work). These groups were less concerned with whether prostitution was legal or not. However, these concerns about broad trafficking issues were quickly and quite successfully 'captured' by feminist abolitionists who had been absorbed into the anti-trafficking efforts of Christian evangelicals and well-placed Christian conservative Republican Congressional leaders (Chuang 2010; Berman 2006; Bernstein 2007, 2010) as we describe below.

The creation of this coalition is often credited to moral entrepreneur Michael Horowitz, a Fellow at the conservative Hudson Institute, who had just successfully spearheaded the International Religious Freedom Act, which passed in 1998. That bill, forged of a left–right coalition of human rights and religious NGOs (including Amnesty International and Human Rights Watch), granted US agencies power to sanction nations and to protect individuals defined as being persecuted on account of their religion (Bromfield and Capous-Desyllas 2012; Stolz 2005; Bernstein 2007, 2010).

Horowitz saw trafficking as a 'natural follow-up' to this bill, and worked with Representative Chris Smith (Republican-Washington) to write a bill modeled on the same approach, empowering the US to sanction governments seen as complicit in trafficking (Ragan 2013, Soderlund 2005). Three general groups were brought together in this new coalition. First, the trafficking coalition included a wide range of religious groups: newly formed evangelical religious NGOs (for example, the International Justice Mission), conservative religious groups founded in the 1980s (Family Research Council and Focus on the Family), long time religious NGOs (the National Association of Evangelicals, the Southern Baptist Convention), and even left leaning NGOs such as the Religious Action Center of Reform Judaism. Second, the coalition also included politically connected moral conservatives such as William Bennett, the former Education Secretary and Drug Czar under the Reagan administration, and Chuck Colson, convicted Watergate conspirator, former Nixon administration attorney and born-again Christian. These moral conservatives were finding new political power under an increasingly reactionary Republican US Congress. The third group brought into this coalition included feminist neo-abolitionists, primarily Laura Lederer of the Protection Project and CATW, Jessica Neuwirth of Equality Now, and eventually, Gloria Steinem from the National Organization for Women (NOW) (Stolz 2005; Chapkis 2003).

The feminist abolitionist agenda would have failed without this relationship with religious groups, and it changed the tenor of feminist arguments. Gone were the disagreements over abortion. Former anti-pornography crusader Laura Lederer bridged the two organisations, saying that the religious organisations brought a 'biblical mandate to the women's movement' and that feminist abolitionists 'would not be getting attention internationally otherwise' (Soderlund 2005; Chuang 2010; Weitzer 2007). In 2002 she became an evangelical Christian herself. This new coalition of abolitionists kept their goal of abolishing prostitution subtle in discussions with left-leaning Clinton administration officials, and instead articulated an explicit goal to end trafficking. While representatives from CATW, and the growingly vocal Donna Hughes, did not hide their desire to abolish prostitution, one informant involved in TVPA discussions told Bromfield and Capous-Desyllas (2012: 256), 'We all knew what we were about [in favour of abolishing prostitution] but we weren't ever having these discussions out loud'. Given this approach, the later conflation of trafficking and all sexual labour as one and the same, rather than different phenomena requiring different legislative solutions, is not surprising.

With support of this coalition of three disparate groups, Republican House Representative Chris Smith introduced 'The Freedom from Sexual Trafficking Act of 1999' (HR 1356) which reflected the perspectives of conservative and religious interests. It had a narrow focus on sexual trafficking and prostitution, defined voluntary prostitution as trafficking, provided for new and increased criminal penalties for sex trafficking, and, in so doing, ignored labour trafficking and male victims of any kind of trafficking. At the same time, liberal Democratic Senator Paul Wellstone introduced a bill called 'The International Trafficking of Women and Children Victim Protection Act' (S 600) that reflected the Clinton Administration's definition of trafficking as forced or coerced labour in the sex, garment, food service, domestic service and agricultural industries, and focused on preserving the autonomy of workers (Stolz 2005).

Fearing that the Wellstone bill's definition of trafficking limited to 'force, fraud, coercion and deception' might prevail as these bills were heard and compromises negotiated in Congress, powerful conservatives and faith-based organisations viciously attacked the Clintons in a number of prominent op-eds in newspapers. President Clinton had been embroiled in a high profile sex scandal with a White House intern. Seeing a political weak spot, Republican conservatives William Bennett and Chuck Colson did not attack the trafficking bills in Congress, but rather accused the Clinton Administration, the PICW and its co-chair Hillary Clinton, of supporting a change in trafficking definitions in UN protocols (similar to the 'force, fraud and coercion' language in Wellstone's bill) that they claimed legitimised prostitution and hardcore pornography. Groups from the right and left, from NOW and Planned Parenthood Federation of America to the Ethics and Religious Liberty Commission, Campus Crusade for Christ, Institute on Religion and Democracy, and the right wing Heritage Foundation, protested with letters and op-eds claiming that the bill weakened protections against women and girls. A *New York Post* article attempted to link Clinton with prostitutes, labeling the PICW the 'Hooker' Panel for weakening international laws protecting women and children (Stolz 2005).

The Trafficking Victims Protection Act (TVPA) was passed in 2000 as a compromise and constituted a blending of the two bills, one conservative (Smith), one liberal (Wellstone). The TVPA created a new federal crime of trafficking with stiff penalties (similar to the conservative Smith bill) and provided special visas to foreign nationals found (through a fairly strict set of criteria) to be victims of trafficking. The bill created the Office to Monitor and Combat Trafficking in Persons within the State Department to monitor and sanction governments that did not take steps to eliminate trafficking. The original bill was hazy in its general definition of trafficking, but limited visas to those who experienced only severe trafficking induced by force, fraud, or coercion, or any person under 18 years of age found to perform commercial sex.

While happy with the law generally, abolitionist feminists were not happy with limiting trafficking to forced labour, and believed that the Clinton Administration did not go far enough in institutionalising their view that no prostitution was voluntary and that all prostitution should be defined as trafficking (Weitzer 2007). With the entry of a new, more conservative president in 2001, anti-prostitution feminists did not remain unhappy for long.

Neo-abolitionists transform the TVPA

The election of born-again Christian President George W. Bush in 2001 (elected with unprecedented support from an increasingly political evangelical Christian base) allowed unrivalled access of faith-based organisations into federal government. These organisations and their abolitionist feminist allies took over TVPA administration and subsequent amendments, and secured for their agenda a large proportion of federal funds and foreign policy access, thus institutionalising the material basis of what would become neo-abolitionism (Weitzer 2007). In what follows, we highlight a number of such organisations and the inter-related networks of key players to illustrate the takeover of the neo-abolitionist approach to prostitution in the US. This approach a) explicitly conflated trafficking and prostitution by arguing that all prostitution is coercive and violent against women, and that any sexual labour is ripe for trafficking, b) demanded aggressive criminalisation of prostitution and trafficking, particularly targeting men seen as victimising women, c) prioritised efforts against sex trafficking over other forms of labour trafficking and d) expanded the scope of the bill to include domestic and international trafficking. In so doing, prostitution was further feminised and individualised – women were situated as victims in need of protection, a discourse that resonates with normative gender ideology.

The Bush Administration appointed anti-prostitution feminist leaders and conservative Christians to key positions in the TVPA offices. For example, former Women against Pornography now CATW and Protection Project founder Laura Lederer was hired in 2001 as Senior Director for Global Projects on Trafficking in Persons at the US Department of State (Weitzer 2007) and from 2002–2009, as Senior Advisor on Trafficking in Persons in the State Department. Horowitz and Colson reportedly strong-armed Bush aide Karl Rove into appointing John Miller, former three-term Republican Congressman from Washington and head of a think tank pushing creationism in public schools, to take over the State Department's Office to Monitor and Combat Trafficking in Persons in 2002 (Soderlund 2005). As head of that Office from 2002–2006, Miller worked closely with faith-based and feminist organisations including CATW to establish an 'abolitionist outpost' in the State Department. As Miller commented to a *New York Times* reporter in 2003 about these neo-abolitionists, 'They're consumed by this issue. I think it's great. It helped get the legislation passed, it helped spur me. I think it keeps the whole government focused' (quoted in Weitzer 2007: 460).

Miller's office institutionalised the view that 'sex work' was 'slavery', effectively silencing both advocacy groups and social services engaging in domestic and international harm reduction efforts around prostitution (Bernstein and Jakobsen 2010, McKelvey 2004, Shapiro 2004, Weitzer 2007). It also created the Trafficking in Persons (TIP) Reports that are published annually. The TIP Reports evaluate foreign countries' efforts to fight trafficking and place each country onto one of three tiers. Countries that are deemed Tier Three are not doing enough, according to the US government, to fight trafficking. This includes, 'whether the government of the country has made serious and sustained efforts to reduce the demand for (A) commercial sex acts; and (B) participation in international sex tourism by nationals of the country' (US Department of State 2011).

In the US, federal policies such as the TVPA must be periodically 'reauthorised' by a new vote in Congress. This vote determines any changes to the language of the Act, and also approves funding, support, and directives. Subsequent reauthorisations of the TVPA accomplished two outcomes that further institutionalised the neo-abolitionist approach and silenced opposition, 1) they directed more and more funding to neo-abolitionist groups, and 2) further narrowed the definition of trafficking to domestic sex trafficking with a focus on ending demand. Originally, 'trafficking' assistance focused on coercion in connection to the movement across nation-state borders. Subsequent reauthorisations institutionalised the concept of *domestic* trafficking (within a nation-state, of citizens or non-citizens) meaning resources and support could be directed within the US as well as internationally.

Through the funding redirected in these reauthorisations, the US has spent an estimated $771 million between 2001 and 2010 on domestic and international anti-trafficking efforts (Siskin and Wyler 2013: 57). The bulk of these funds went to organisations which espoused a neo-abolitionist stance (Chuang 2010). Among the organisations receiving funding from the US State Department, Justice Department and Department of Health and Human Services, are prominent neo-abolitionist feminist organisations such as CATW, Protection Project, SAGE (Standing against Global Exploitation) and faith-based organisations (Catholic Conference of Bishops, Salvation Army, International Justice Mission, World Vision and Shared Hope International) and their allies around the world (Soderlund 2005).

In 2003, TVPA insiders were able to limit funding to outsider organisations through an 'anti-prostitution loyalty oath' attached to the President's Emergency Plan for AIDS Relief (PEPFAR). The 'loyalty oath' prohibited the use of US funds for programs that promote, support or advocate 'the legalisation or the practice of prostitution' or for organisations that did not have a policy that explicitly opposes prostitution. This prevented funds being allocated to health services for 'known prostitutes'. Administration officials credited Donna Hughes, who has a PhD in genetics and is a University of Rhode Island Women's Studies Professor, with helping identify international organisations in receipt of funds who were believed to be 'supporting prostitution', including groups providing HIV/AIDS services.

PEPFAR's anti-prostitution loyalty oath also impacted federal research grants for scholarship. Research funding on human trafficking from the US Department of Justice (DOJ), Office of Justice Programs (OJP), and National Institute of Justice (NIJ) has been disproportionately awarded to neo-abolitionist and anti-prostitution groups. Many scholars have criticised research about the extent of sex trafficking used by anti-prostitution and neo-abolitionist groups in policy advocacy citing poor data sources, unverifiable global generalisations as well as muddy definitions of trafficking (see critiques by Chuang 2014, Fitzgerald 2015b, Hoang and Parreñas 2014; Kerodal, Freilich and Galietta 2015, Kleemans 2011, Lerum and Brents 2016; Weitzer 2011, 2014; Zhang 2009, 2012). In 2006, the US Government Accountability Office (GAO) distanced itself from its own widely cited 2003 and 2004 international estimates and TIP reports citing weak methods, data gaps and discrepancies and concluding that country-level data are generally not reliable or comparable (US GAO 2006; Fedina 2015; Heineman, MacFarlane and Brents 2012).

The second outcome embedded in TVPA reauthorisations was to further narrow the focus of anti-trafficking efforts toward voluntary prostitution and to turn attention to the 'demand' for prostitution. This turn to 'end demand' policy solidified the neo-abolitionist approach, and these groups used newfound funding and attention to focus on passing new legislation at the federal and state levels. In 2005, leading neo-abolitionist feminists and religious activists came close to passing a national bill criminalising demand, the 'End Demand for Sex Trafficking Bill' (HR 2012). The bill would have required federal measures to combat commercial sexual activities including lap dancing, pornography and legal brothel prostitution. The bill was referred to a subcommittee for consideration in June of 2005, and died from lack of action. But several of its provisions were incorporated into the 2005 TVPA reauthorisation. The most important was to shift attention from international trafficking (where proponents were having trouble finding actual victims, Brennan 2008) to, instead, target domestic traffickers and customers. The focus now went to 'domestic trafficking' and child sexual exploitation where anyone under age 18 who sold sex in the US was defined as a trafficking victim. This move allowed a host of criminal justice efforts to focus on combating domestic commercial sex acts, less thinly veiled as trafficking, and has, arguably, done little to help youth (Young Women's Empowerment Project 2012; Bernstein 2010).

In 2005 alone, the TVPA allocated $50 million for law enforcement and social service agencies to focus their activities on demand for commercial sex in the United States. It appropriated $25 million for state and local law enforcement agencies to educate, investigate, and prosecute persons who purchased commercial sex acts and $10 million for NGOs to assist citizens and permanent residents who were victims of both sex trafficking and severe forms of trafficking. Today, at least 47 states in the US have such 'demand reduction' programs related to prostitution (Showden and Majic 2014). Thus the TVPA helped institutionalise a powerful neo-abolitionist approach in the US largely through empowering key neo-abolitionist organisations and furthering local law enforcement efforts against prostitution demand. However, neo-abolitionists were not able to get national end demand legislation and as we will see, since the Bush years there have been important challenges to the neo-abolitionist stronghold on prostitution policy and discourse. In the following section, we delineate current neo-abolitionist trends and efforts.

Neo-abolitionism in the United States: present and future

Since George Bush left the US presidency in 2009, neo-abolitionist rhetoric coming from the federal government has lessened, largely because neo-abolitionist groups no longer have the same access to government. But the movement certainly has not gone away. Below we discuss the long-lasting effects of the TVPA on the neo-abolitionist movement. We offer seven examples of what neo-abolitionism looks like today, including fractures in the stronghold of neo-abolitionism where social justice efforts have fought back.

First, for example, the anti-prostitution loyalty oath in PEPFAR was overturned for US based organisations in 2013 and for foreign organisations receiving US funds in 2015, finally removing a decade of restrictions and lack of access to funds. This win was the result of multiple organisations and governments showcasing how the oath negatively impacted their abilities to provide basic services to marginalised communities. However, US funds still cannot be used for specific programs that are perceived as promoting prostitution (for example, a sex workers' rights organisation). Additionally, the ideology behind the oath has had a profound effect on service provision, disproportionately continuing financial support for neo-abolitionist NGOs and limiting other organisations' abilities to do research and provide HIV services.

Second, the millions of dollars allocated under the TVPA go largely to criminal justice and related social services efforts, keeping anti-prostitution and anti-sex trafficking efforts well funded. Today, many domestic and international organisations rely on TVPA monies to keep staffing levels and to maintain their programs. This is what scholar Laura Agustín refers to as the 'rescue industry' (2007), a well-established, multi-organisation industry with over a decade of TVPA funding supporting anti-sex trafficking efforts. These trafficking dollars have helped fund the rise of a number of well-organised, well-funded neo-abolitionist organisations like the Polaris Project and Demand Abolition.

Polaris Project is a federal non-profit organisation with religious roots (see Weitzer 2013) that receives substantial US government funding. Since 2007 Polaris Project has maintained a National Human Trafficking Resource Center Hotline used to gather statistics on human trafficking with a focus on sex trafficking (Polaris Project n.d.). These statistics are based on calls made to report a tip about potential cases (which has now expanded to include webform, email, and textline versions). Even though no follow up is done to verify the credibility of reports, hotline data is used to promote harsher prostitution legislation (Reed 2013).

In 2010, Demand Abolition played a key role in a US planning meeting that served as a foundation to combat demand for commercial sex (see Abt Associates Inc. 2010). Several stakeholders convened in Cambridge, Massachusetts to strategise a large scale, long-term national campaign. Demand Abolition has since begun funding public awareness around 'National Day of Johns Arrests' that were conceived of in 2011 by the Sheriff of Cook County,

Illinois, Thomas Dart. This includes replicating thousands of 'johns schools' DVDs and distributing them to police departments nationwide. According to the Demand Abolition website, these DVDs aim 'to deter men from purchasing sex by educating them about the harms and consequences of prostitution on themselves, on the people they purchase, and on the community' (Hunt Alternatives n.d.). In early 2015 during one such two-week US-wide sting operation that targeted sex buyers and coincided with the Super Bowl, 570 would-be sex purchasers were arrested and 23 men were taken into custody on charges of pimping, trafficking or promoting prostitution (Alter 2015).

Interestingly today, however, some of the anti-prostitution language has shifted from incarceration to social services as the best way to combat sex trafficking and end prostitution. Recently in the US, the rescue industry has grown to include the 'treatment industrial complex', with mandatory 'alternatives to incarceration', often under threat of jail or imprisonment for both clients and sex workers who choose not to participate (Chen 2015, Ray and Caterine 2014). Now, in addition to an established 'prison industrial complex', women arrested for soliciting may find themselves in one of the new 'Trafficking Intervention Courts'. Judges mandate 'johns schools' for men (clients who have been arrested) and a range of alternatives to incarceration for women (who are arrested on a prostitution charge). While john's schools were first implemented in the 1990s, there has been an increase in using these alternatives to jail for men who are arrested for soliciting prostitution and who are first time offenders. According to Chen (2015), although on the face, such programmes seem to make 'corrections' less punitive, 'they maintain the political framework of 'redeeming' bad people, rather than dismantling anti-social systems'. While shifting the consequences of an arrest from prison to programs offered by public and private NGOs, the focus on 'treating' their problems as a result of individual behaviours still shifts attention away from a lack of living wage jobs or wider economic inequalities (Chen 2015; Ray and Caterine 2014; Sered 2015).

Fourth, because of a decline in social service funding generally over the last 20 years, neo-abolitionism has contributed to a landscape where state and local governments must compete for federal anti-sex trafficking funding to support social programs generally. Across the country, law enforcement and social services in a variety of regions now clamour to be identified as the next 'sex trafficking hotspot'. In fact, almost every state in the union, and numerous cities within those states, have been identified as a trafficking hotspot by some combination of governments at the federal, state and local levels, who, along with social service stakeholders, identify a mix of infrastructure (e.g. international airports, major highways, major ports) and geography (proximity to major cities like Los Angeles or a shared international border with Mexico or Canada) as justification.

Fifth, the lasting impact of the TVPA is evident in changes to state laws. The neo-abolitionist organizations like Demand Abolition have helped fund and promote a number of state level anti-trafficking bills that increase penalties for individuals accused of sex trafficking. The definitions of trafficking vary from state to state and often are quite vague (Reed 2015).

Further, neo-abolitionism has led to the re-branding of many criminal and criminalized activities as trafficking. This narrows the ways in which we could potentially situate prostitution as a complex and varied criminal justice issue. In 2015 the federal government passed the Justice for Victims of Trafficking Act. This comprehensive neo-abolitionist inspired bill situates any buyer of sexual service to be one-and-the-same as a trafficker, as noted by sex worker activists themselves (D'Adamo 2015). Because the bill is so new, states and localities are figuring out how to interpret the directives and what implementation looks like.

Finally, neo-abolitionism within the United States has begun to be challenged by activists, sex workers, and academics. The consequences of the TVPA and its subsequent reauthorisations are continually challenged. For example, the growth of the US anti-sex trafficking movement has served to mobilise resistance from sex workers. Growing out of sex worker rights organising efforts from the 1970s, activists like Carol Leigh and Robin Few have helped bring a younger generation of sex workers activists into a number of new and existing organisations. Their work since the TVPA is often entrenched in neo-abolitionist debates, engaging in critiques of the conflation of trafficking and consensual prostitution, challenging the assertion that sex work is inherently violent at the same time as fighting for recognition, fighting for visibility and freedom from state violence (Jackson 2016).

Groups include the Sex Workers Outreach Project (SWOP-USA and local chapters), Helping Individual Prostitutes Survive (HIPS) in Washington, DC, Red Umbrella Project in New York City and St James Infirmary in San Francisco. They all provide outreach to sex workers, engage in public education, and advocate for change. Numerous organisations also offer outreach and assistance to people who have engaged in the sex trade for survival, like Women with a Vision in New Orleans that addresses HIV/AIDS in communities of colour with a focus on African-American women, and Streetwise and Safe in New York City who assist homeless LGBTQ youth of colour (Lerum *et al.* 2012, Majic 2011). In addition, scholarly research has greatly expanded and, despite the lack of – or great difficulty in – accessing federal research funds, a growing number of feminist and non-feminist academics conduct research on the complexities of sexual labour, the intersectional realities of prostitution, and the collateral damage of anti-trafficking policies (see Brents *et al.* 2012; Chuang 2014; Hoang and Parreñas 2014; Kerodal, Freilich and Galietta 2015; Lerum and Brents 2016; Kleemans 2011; Weitzer 2011, 2014; Zhang 2009, 2012).

The hardline in criminalising prostitution to end trafficking may be softening. On 4 March 2015, the non-profit organisation Erotic Service Providers Legal, Education and Research Project (ESPLERP) filed a federal lawsuit to challenge the criminalisation of prostitution in the state of California. The lawsuit argued that banning prostitution is unconstitutional because it violates the US Constitutional First Amendment by hindering the right of adults to engage in consensual, private activities (Burke 2015). In 2016, three female lawmakers introduced bipartisan legislation to decriminalise prostitution in the state of New Hampshire. The legislators cited the global human rights organisation Amnesty International's August 2015 recommendation that governments across the world decriminalise all aspects of consensual prostitution (Brown 2016). And while women are permitted to work in licensed brothels only in particular rural counties, the state of Nevada has managed to maintain the only current legal model for prostitution in the US (Brents, Jackson and Hausbeck 2010).

Conclusion

This chapter charted the evolution of abolitionism to neo-abolitionism in the United States. Neo-abolitionism undoubtedly achieved many of its advocates' aims in the last decades with lasting impact but as indicated above, while the 'rescue industry' and 'treatment industrial complex' deploy anti-prostitution tactics, the shiny façade of neo-abolitionism may be cracking. On one hand, the neo-abolitionist focus on individual victims and individual perpetrators has been a key component of neoliberal culture and politics, rebranding various social problems connected to poverty, migration and labour rights as individual moral problems while expanding the criminal justice system (and now social services) to increase monitoring and control of marginalised populations (Bernstein 2012; Chuang 2014; Brennan 2008). While sex worker rights movements cast prostitutes as responsible, self-sufficient, sex *work*ers, neo-abolitionist movements and their military humanism and carceral feminism (Bernstein 2010) have placed the prostitute back into the category of victim (Fitzgerald 2015a). On the other hand, the sexual politics of neoliberalism are contradictory, and it remains to be seen how the political power of religious, feminist (pro- and anti-prostitution), and conservative groups will continue to impact prostitution politics in the United States.

Note

1 Take Back the Night is an annual anti-violence against women event, usually raising awareness of sexual assault. Early TBTNs were often women-only marches and vigils, sometimes protesting pornography or other forms of sexual labour as symbols of violence against women. Today, TBTN is common on college campuses as a way to raise awareness of sexual assault and other forms of gendered violence.

References

Abt Associates Inc. (2010) *Developing a National Action Plan for Eliminating Sex Trafficking: Executive Summary*. Cambridge, MA: Hunt Alternatives Fund. Available at: www.demandabolition.org/wp-content/uploads/2011/07/Abt-executive-summary-De

veloping-a-National-Action-Plan-for-Eliminating-Sex-Trafficking.pdf. Accessed 17 February 2016.

Agustín, L. M. (2007) *Sex at the Margins*. London: Zed Books.

Alter, C. (2015) 'Over 570 Arrested in Super Bowl Sex Traffic Sting', *TIME*. Available at: http://time.com/3692993/super-bowl-sex-traffic-sting/. Accessed 21 December 2015.

Berman, J. (2006) 'The Left, the Right, and the Prostitute: The Making of US Anti Trafficking in Persons Policy', *Tulane Journal of International and Comparative Law*, 14(2): 269–293.

Bernstein, E. (2012) 'Carceral Politics as Gender Justice? The "Traffic in Women" and Neoliberal Circuits of Crime, Sex, and Rights', *Theory and Society*, 41(3): 233–259.

Bernstein, E. (2010) 'Militarized Humanitarianism Meets Carceral Feminism: The Politics of Sex, Rights, and Freedom in Contemporary Anti Trafficking Campaigns', *Signs: Journal of Women in Culture and Society*, 36(1): 45–71.

Bernstein, E. (2007) 'The Sexual Politics of the "New Abolitionism"', *Differences: A Journal of Feminist Cultural Studies*, 18(3): 128–151.

Bernstein, E. and Jakobsen, J.R. (2010) 'Sex, Secularism and Religious Influence in US Politics', *Third World Quarterly*, 31(6): 1023–1039.

Brennan, D. (2008) 'Competing Claims of Victimhood? Foreign and Domestic "Victims" of Trafficking in the United States', *Sexuality Research and Social Policy*, 5(4): 45–61.

Brents, B., Beer, S., Bernstein, E., Choo, H. Y., Cook, D., Hoang, K., Joseph, L., Lerum, K., Lakkimseti, C., Mattson, G., Scull, M. and Wu, T. (2012) 'Sex Work and Trafficking Workgroup Working Paper', in M. Bernstein (ed.) *Crossing Boundaries, Workshopping Sexualities, proceedings of Sociology of Sexualities, Assessing the State of the Field*, pp. 34–38. Available at: www.asanet.org/sectionsex/documents/miniconferencepapers/workingpapers.pdf. Accessed 27 June 2015.

Brents, B. G., Jackson, C. A. and Hausbeck, K. (2010) *The State of Sex*. New York: Routledge.

Brents, B. G. and Sanders, T. (2016) 'The 'Victim and Offender and Discourse' in the Debates and Policy on Prostitution and Sex Work', in T. Sanders (ed.) *Oxford Handbook of Sex Offenses and Sex Offenders*. New York: Oxford University Press.

Brents, B. G. and Sanders, T. (2010) 'Mainstreaming the Sex Industry: Economic Inclusion and Social Ambivalence', *Journal of Law and Society*, 37(1): 40–60.

Bromfield, N. F. and Capous-Desyllas, M. (2012) 'Underlying Motives, Moral Agendas and Unlikely Partnerships: The Formulation of the US Trafficking in Victims Protection Act through the Data and Voices of Key Policy Players', *Advances in Social Work*, 13(2): 243–261.

Brown, E. N. (2016) 'Prostitution Decrim Debated by New Hampshire Lawmakers', *Reason* Available at: http://reason.com/blog/2016/02/01/prostitution-decriminalization-debated-i. Accessed 8 February 2016.

Burke, C. (2015) 'Inside the Groundbreaking Lawsuit that Could Decriminalize Sex Work in California', *The Daily Dot*. Available at: www.dailydot.com/opinion/california-sex-workers-bill-decriminalization/. Accessed 12 February 2016.

Chapkis, W. (2003) 'Trafficking, Migration, and the Law: Protecting Innocents, Punishing Immigrants', *Gender & Society*, 17(6): 923–937.

Chen, M. (2015) 'How Prison Reform Could Turn the Prison-Industrial Complex into the Treatment-Industrial Complex', *The Nation* Available at: www.thenation.com/article/how-prison-reform-could-turn-the-prison-industrial-complex-into-the-treatment-industrial-complex/. Accessed 20 December 2015.

Chuang, J. (2010) 'Rescuing Trafficking from Ideological Capture: Prostitution Reform and Anti-Trafficking Law and Policy', *University of Pennsylvania Law Review*, 158(6): 1655–1728.

Chuang, J. (2014) 'Exploitation Creep and the Unmaking of Human Trafficking Law', *The American Journal of International Law*, 108(4): 609–649.

D'Adamo, K. (2015). No Victim, No Problem: The JVTA In *Practice. Tits and Sass.* Available at http://titsandsass.com/no-victim-no-problem-the-jvta-in-practice/. Accessed 25 August 2015.

Doezema, J. (1999) 'Loose Women or Lost Women? The Re-emergence of the Myth of White Slavery in Contemporary Discourses of Trafficking in Women', *Gender Issues*, 18(1): 23–50.

Donovan, B. (2006) *White Slave Crusades: Race, Gender, and Anti-vice Activism, 1887–1917*. Urbana and Chicago: University of Illinois Press.

Fedina, L. (2015) 'Use and Misuse of Research in Books on Sex Trafficking: Implications for Interdisciplinary Researchers, Practitioners, and Advocates', *Trauma, Violence and Abuse*, 16(2): 188–198.

Fitzgerald, J. (2015a) 'Celebrity and the Spectacle of the Trafficking Victim', *Tits and Sass* available at http://titsandsass.com/celebrity-and-the-spectacle-of-the-trafficking-victim/. Accessed 15 February 2016.

Fitzgerald, J. (2015b) 'How the Government and Christian Lobby Quashes Real Research on Sex Workers', *Pacific Standard*. Available at: www.psmag.com/politics-and-law/government-christian-lobby-quashes-real-research-on-sex-workers. Accessed 15 February 2016.

Halley, J. E., Kotiswaran, P., Shamir, H. and Thomas, C. (2006) 'From the International to the Local in Feminist Legal Responses to Rape, Prostitution/Sex Work, and Sex Trafficking: Four Studies in Contemporary Governance Feminism', *Harvard Journal of Law and Gender*, 29(2): 335–423.

Heineman, J., MacFarlane, R. and Brents, B. G. (2012) 'Sex Industry and Sex Workers in Nevada', in D. M. Shalin (ed.) *The Social Health of Nevada: Leading Indicators and Quality of Life in the Silver State*. Las Vegas, NV: UNLV Center for Democratic Culture. Available at: http://cdclv.unlv.edu/mission/index.html. Accessed 26 June 2015.

Hoang, K. K. and Parreñas, R.S. (eds) (2014) *Human Trafficking Reconsidered: Rethinking the Problem, Envisioning New Solutions*. New York: International Debate Education Association Press.

Hunt Alternatives (n.d.) *National Day of Johns Arrests*. Cambridge, MA: Demand Abolition. Available at: www.demandabolition.org/national-day-of-johns-arrests/. Accessed 15 December 2015.

Jackson, C. A. (2016). 'Framing Sex Worker Rights: How US Sex Worker Rights Activists Perceive and Respond to Mainstream Anti-Sex Trafficking Advocacy', *Sociological Perspectives*, 59(1): 27–45.

Kerodal, A. G., Freilich, J. D. and Galietta, M. (2015) 'The Efficacy of Sex Crime and Human Trafficking Legislations', *International Journal of Comparative and Applied Criminal Justice*, 39(2): 93–97.

Kleemans, E. R. (2011) 'Expanding the Domain of Human Trafficking Research: Introduction to the Special Issue on Human Trafficking', *Trends in Organized Crime*, 14(2–3): 95–99.

Koken, J. A. (2010) 'The Meaning of the "Whore": How Feminist Theories on Prostitution Shape Research on Female Sex Workers', in M. H. Ditmore, A. Levy and

A. Willman (eds) *Sex Work Matters: Exploring Money, Power and Intimacy in the Sex Industry.* London: Zed Books, pp. 28–64.

Laite, J. (2012) *Common Prostitutes and Ordinary Citizens: Commercial Sex in London, 1885–1960.* New York: Palgrave MacMillan.

Lerum, K. (2014) 'Human Wrongs vs. Human Rights', *Contexts* (Winter): 22–24.

Lerum, K. and Brents, B. G. (2016) 'Sociological Perspectives on Sex Work and Human Trafficking', *Sociological Perspectives,* 59(1): 17–26.

Lerum, K., McCurtis, K., Saunders, P. and Wahab, S. (2012) 'Using Human Rights to Hold the US Accountable for its Anti-Sex Work Agenda: The Universal Periodic Review and New Directions for US Policy', *Anti-Trafficking Review,* 1: 80–103.

Lucas, A. M. (1995) 'Race, Class, Gender, and Deviancy: The Criminalization of Prostitution', *Berkeley Women's Law Journal,* 10(1): 47–60.

Luker, K. (1998) 'Sex, Social Hygiene, and the State: The Double-Edged Sword of Social Reform', *Theory and Society,* 27(5): 601–634.

Majic, S. (2011) 'Serving Sex Workers and Promoting Democratic Engagement: Rethinking Nonprofits' Role in American Civic and Political Life', *Perspectives on Politics,* 9(4): 821–840.

McKelvey, T. (2004) 'Of Human Bondage', *American Prospect.* Available at: http://prospect.org/article/human-bondage. Accessed 11 February 2004.

Milivojevic, S. and Pickering, S. (2013) 'Trafficking in People, 20 Years On: Sex, Migration and Crime in the Global Anti-Trafficking Discourse and the Rise of the "Global Trafficking Complex"', *Current Issues in Criminal Justice,* 25(2): 585–604.

Pivar, D. J. (2002) *Purity and Hygiene: Women, Prostitution, and the "American Plan", 1900–1930.* Westport, CT: Greenwood Press.

Polaris Project (n.d.) *National Human Trafficking Resource Center (NHTRC).* Available at: https://polarisproject.org/national-human-trafficking-resource-center. Accessed 15 February 2016.

Ragan, T. (2013) 'Nevada Movement Draws the Line on Human Trafficking', *Las Vegas Review Journal.* Available at: www.reviewjournal.com/news/las-vegas/nevada-movement-draws-line-human-trafficking. Accessed 25 November 2015.

Ray, A. and Caterine, E. (2014) *Criminal, Victim, or Worker?: NYC Human Trafficking Intervention Courts' Impact on People in the Sex Trade.* Available at: http://redumbrellaproject.org/advocate/nyhtic/. Accessed 8 February 2016.

Reed, J. J. (2015) 'Sex Work and Sex Trafficking: Influencing State Policy on a Complex Social Issue', in S.K. White, J. White and K. Korgen (eds) *Sociologists in Action on Inequalities: Race, Class, Gender, and Sexuality.* London: Sage, pp. 124–129.

Reed, J. J. (2013) 'What Happens in Vegas ... Could Get You 10 Years to Life', *Voters Legislative Transparency Project (VLTP).* Available at: http://vltp.net/what-happens-in-vegas-could-get-you-10-years-to-life/. Accessed 28 December 2015

Sanders, T. (2009) 'Kerbcrawler Rehabilitation Programmes: Curing the "Deviant" Male and Reinforcing the "Respectable" Moral Order', *Critical Social Policy,* 29(1): 77–99.

Sered, S. (2015) 'Alternatives to Incarceration: Be Careful What You Wish For', *Truthout.* Available at: www.truth-out.org/opinion/item/29323-alternatives-to-incarceration-be-careful-what-you-wish-for. Accessed 20 December 2015.

Shapiro, N. (2004) 'The New Abolitionists' *Seattle Weekly.* Available at: www.seattleweekly.com/2004-08-25/news/the-new-abolitionists/. Accessed 20 December 2015.

Showden, C. and Majic, S. (2014) *Negotiating Sex Work: Unintended Consequences of Policy and Activism.* Minneapolis, MN: University of Minnesota Press.

Siskin, A. and Wyler, L. S. (2013) *Trafficking in Persons: US Policy and Issues for Congress*. Congressional Research Service. Available at: www.fas.org/sgp/crs/row/RL34317.pdf. Accessed 23 November 2015.

Soderlund, G. (2005) 'Running from the Rescuers: New US Crusades Against Sex Trafficking and the Rhetoric of Abolition', *NWSA Journal*, 17(3): 64–87.

Stolz, B. (2005) 'Educating Policymakers and Setting the Criminal Justice Policymaking Agenda: Interest Groups and the "Victims of Trafficking and Violence Act of 2000"', *Criminology and Criminal Justice*, 5(4): 407–430.

US Congress, House of Representatives (2008) *William Wilberforce Trafficking Victims Protection Reauthorization Act of 2008*. HR 7311. 110th Congress, 2008. Available at: www.congress.gov/bill/110th-congress/house-bill/7311. Accessed 1 December 2015.

US Congress, House of Representatives (2005) *Trafficking Victims Protection Reauthorization Act of 2005*. HR 972. 109th Congress. Available at: www.congress.gov/bill/109th-congress/house-bill/972. Accessed 1 December 2015.

US Congress, House of Representatives (2003) *Trafficking Victims Protection Reauthorization Act of 2003*. HR 2620. 108th Congress. Available at: www.congress.gov/bill/108th-congress/house-bill/2620. Accessed 1 December 2015.

US Congress, House of Representatives (2000) *Victims of Trafficking and Violence Protection Act of 2000, Division A: Trafficking Victims Protection Act of 2000*. HR 3244. 106th Congress. Available at: www.congress.gov/bill/106th-congress/house-bill/3244. Accessed 1 December 2015.

US Congress, House of Representatives (1999) *Freedom From Sexual Trafficking Act of 1999*. HR 1356. 106th Congress, 1999. Available at: https://www.congress.gov/bill/106th-congress/house-bill/1356. Accessed 1 December 2015.

US Congress, Senate (2013) *Violence Against Women Reauthorization Act of 2013, Title XII: Trafficking Victims Protection*. S 47. 113th Congress. Available at: www.congress.gov/bill/113th-congress/senate-bill/47. Accessed 1 December 2015.

US Congress, Senate (1999) *International Trafficking of Women and Children Victim Protection Act of 1999*. S 600. 106th Congress. Available at: www.congress.gov/bill/106th-congress/senate-bill/600. Accessed 1 December 2015.

US Department of State (2011) *Trafficking Victims Protection Act: Minimum Standards for the Elimination of Trafficking in Persons*. Trafficking in Persons Report 2011. Available at: www.state.gov/j/tip/rls/tiprpt/2011/164236.htm. Accessed 26 July 2015.

US Government Accountability Office (GAO) (2006) *Human Trafficking: Better Data, Strategy, and Reporting Needed to Enhance US Anti-Trafficking Efforts Abroad*. Report to the Chairman, Committee on the Judiciary and the Chairman, Committee on International Relations, House of Representatives GAO-6–825. Available at: http://www.gao.gov/products/GAO-06-825. Accessed 1 September 2015.

Weitzer, R. (2014) 'New Directions in Research on Human Trafficking', *The Annals of the American Academy of Political and Social Science*, 653(1): 6–24.

Weitzer, R. (2013) 'Popular Claims vs. Evidence-Based Conclusions in Human Trafficking', presented at *New Frontiers of the Dark Figure: Measuring Hidden Crimes*, Belfast, UK. Available at: https://sexworkresearch.wordpress.com/2013/07/08/popular-claims-vs-evidence-based-conclusions-in-human-trafficking/. Accessed 20 December 2015.

Weitzer, R. (2011) 'Sex Trafficking and the Sex Industry: The Need for Evidence Based Theory and Legislation', *Journal of Criminal law and Criminology*, 101: 1337–1370.

Weitzer, R. (2007) 'The Social Construction of Sex Trafficking: Ideology and Institutionalization of a Moral Crusade', *Politics & Society*, 35: 447–475.

Young Women's Empowerment Project (YWEP) (2012) *How Youth in the Sex Trade and Street Economy Are Turned Away from Systems Meant to Help Us & What We Are Doing to Fight Back*. Available at: https://ywepchicago.files.wordpress.com/2012/09/bad-encounter-line-report-2012.pdf. Accessed 8 February 2016.

Zhang, S. X. (2012) 'Measuring Labour Trafficking: A Research Note', *Crime, Law and Social Change*, 58(4): 469–482.

Zhang, S. X. (2009) 'Beyond the "Natasha" Story: A Review and Critique of Current Research on Sex Trafficking', *Global Crime*, 10(3): 178–195.

Zimmerman, Y. (2012) *Other Dreams of Freedom: Religion, Sex, and Human Trafficking*. Oxford: Oxford University Press.

5 The Irish parliament and prostitution law reform

A neo-abolitionist shoe-in?

Eilís Ward

Introduction

In February 2016, the government of the Republic of Ireland (hereafter Ireland) went to the polls, leaving suspended two pieces of legislation then making their way through the parliament. One, the *Criminal Law (Sexual Offences) Bill 2015*, primarily addressing child sexual abuse, contained new offences of paying to engage in sexual activity with a) a prostitute and b) a trafficked person. The bill proposed decriminalising the person selling sex.

Had the bill got over the line, Ireland would have become the fifth European jurisdiction to adopt this approach, signaling a radical shift in the state's prostitution regime that heretofore repudiated involvement in 'private' sexual arrangements between consenting adults even where money was involved. At the time of writing, the new government intended revisiting the bill and, given the consensus that had emerged, it is likely that the state will make good its intention to adopt a Swedish-style sex purchase ban (SPB).

This chapter is concerned with a particular stage in the law reform process that preceded the tabling of the bill in 2015: the public consultation process held by a parliamentary committee that, according to the Minister for Justice, Frances Fitzgerald, played a critical role in the bill's content (Dáil Éireann Debates 28 January 2016). Convinced by 'persuasive evidence' that the Swedish law reduced both prostitution and sex trafficking, the committee recommended the same, and endorsed the view that prostitution was a form of violence against women and unacceptable in a society committed to gender equality (HoO 2013).

The story of the legislation, however, began long prior to that consultation process. A pivotal point was a review of prostitution law initiated by the Justice Minister Alan Shatter in 2012 and important too was a sustained decade-long campaign, known as Turn off the Red Light (ToRL), whose singular focus was the adoption of Swedish-style legislation for Ireland (Kennedy 2012; Lyon 2013; Ward and Wylie 2014), echoing the global radical feminist neo-abolitionist movement (Weitzer 2010a).

In this chapter I argue that, by the time the Committee's work began, the political debate was, in fact, all but over. ToRL's representation of the problem of prostitution (and its solution), had already been internalised by the political elite such that the Committee process closed down consideration of the range of policy options set out by the government (DJE 2012), and served to institutionalise neo-abolitionist discourse already hegemonic in Irish society (Ward and Wylie 2014; FitzGerald and McGarry 2015). The power of that discourse played out in two significant ways. First, its valence rendered oppositional views vulnerable to accusations of 'pimp thinking': of being an apologist for pimps, brothel owners and the exploitation of women and children (Flynn 2016; Kennedy 2012). Second, in keeping with radical feminism's view, it provided an exclusively 'victim script' for those selling sex (Leahy 2013; Fitzgerald and McGarry 2015) in contrast to the complex reality of contemporary sex work including its relationship to migration (Agustín 2007). The discourse's normalisation of the oppressive paradigm of prostitution, and its uncompromised account of domination (Weitzer 2010b; Scoular 2004), is evidenced by the fact that, prior to the committee's task beginning, all political parties but one had *already* signed up to neo-abolitionism. An interesting exception, and somewhat solitary voice, was that of Minister Shatter who, as we will see, did not support neo-abolitionism but whose resignation, in time, cleared the way for his successor, a long-standing ToRL supporter, to move with the Committee's recommendations.[1]

This article is concerned then with the framing process surrounding neo-abolitionism's figuration in the Irish parliament culminating in the work of the parliamentary committee, the Joint Committee on Justice, Defence and Equality (JCJDE). By framing, it understands a process whereby, through frequent repetitions and confirmations of the radical feminist representation of sex work, inside and outside the house, certain practices of state were rendered possible and others unthinkable (Dunn 2009: 78). In this case, the 'truth claim' of ToRL advocacy, set out in what follows, rendered neo-abolitionism the only possible state approach and rendered other options, including for instance that legislative change might not be necessary, 'unthinkable'. Much of the ToRL's discursive power, it will be argued, rested on its own-commissioned research (Kelleher *et al.* 2009) that achieved 'monument' status and became a canonical text (Neumann 2009: 67) trumping any competing or critical voices.

The chapter firstly presents a brief history of feminist activism on prostitution in Ireland. It then traces the evolution of the law reform process with reference to pro Swedish-law motion in the Seanad (Upper House)[2], which, though lost, forced a government commitment to a review, leading to the JCJDE-led consultation. The chapter concludes by considering some implications of these events.

Before beginning, a reflexive note is required. Along with co-editor of this volume, Dr Gillian Wylie, I made both a written and an oral submission to the JCJDE consultation and was one of three academics invited to speak at a Department of Justice seminar held as part of that process, in October 2012. Throughout, our stance emerged from our scholarly expertise and was not allied to any organisational position (see Ward and Wylie 2014).[3]

Feminist activism and the sex trade

Irish feminist activism on the sex trade was salient during two historical moments: the suffragist period and during feminism's second wave of the 1970s and 1980s albeit without apparent engagement with either of the two legal changes that occurred viz: the *Criminal Law Amendment Act 1935* and the *Criminal Law (Sexual Offences) Act 1993*.

As in Great Britain, Irish suffragists took up the cause of prostitution though Luddy concludes that they utilised women's bodies for propaganda and political purposes (2007: 181) and, in keeping with the discourses of the times, found common cause with advanced nationalists for whom the (corrupt) British soldier was the problem. Following independence, the state reluctantly acknowledged native culpability in the continued 'social evil' of prostitution. Resonating with the condition of post-colonial social anxiety, Ireland underwent a moral panic, resulting in incarceration of the indigenous sexually errant population, exemplified by the attitude to prostitution in the *Criminal Law Amendment Act 1935*. Unambiguously prohibitionist, the Act sought to shut down the places of prostitution by punishing clients, prostitutes and brothel keepers more harshly. Moreover, legislators held fast to the concept of the 'common prostitute' (in practice, always a woman) that allowed prosecution solely on the opinion of a police officer (Ward 2010).

Prosecutions for prostitution-related crime dropped in the wake of the law but within a decade, rose again. By the 1960s, brothels were well established in parts of Dublin city, a function of the sex trade's adaptability, now shifting from largely on-street to off-street activity (Ward 2010). If prohibitionism's expected outcome was prostitution's banishment, it failed.

The attention paid by the second wave of the women's movement, in contrast, thoroughly repudiated the 'social evil' paradigm (Levine 1982; Gannon, 1985; Purcell 1985) and offered instead a gendered critique. Hence, a moment of dialogue opened up between sex workers and activists behind the goal of women's rights mediated by the response to the brutal murder of an ex-prostitute in 1971 which sparked a sex worker, Dolores Lynch, to propose a sex worker trade union. This ferment was powerfully captured later in a widely read ground breaking biography by a sex worker (Levine and Madden 1987). In time, the material needs of women in prostitution – namely integrated responses and coordinated exit strategies – were included in the report to government from the state feminist institution, the Second Commission on Women (Government of Ireland 1993: 181–2) although it had received just one submission specifically on prostitution (Dáil Éireann Debates Vol. 423, 24 June 1993). In response to the AIDS crisis, the state founded the Women's Health Project in 1991, a harm reduction service for drug-addicted women in prostitution.

Remarkably, prostitution was, however, entirely absent from parliamentary debates during these decades notwithstanding the implications of an 1981 Supreme Court ruling that had left the category of the 'common prostitute' unconstitutional, voiding overnight the state's main instrument for policing the law. It was 13 years before the state addressed the lacuna, ignoring meanwhile ameliorative recommendations from the Law Reform Commission (LRC 1985) and, in response to a European Court of Human Rights judgement, the government brought forward the *Criminal Law (Sexual Offences) Act 1993*, aimed at decriminalising homosexuality, but which included changes in prostitution law.

The most significant change introduced here was the removal of the 'common prostitute' offence, and at the same time, new crimes of kerb-crawling and managing prostitution were introduced and penalties for all prostitution-related crimes were increased (Ward 2010). Undoubtedly, this Act heralded greater liberalism on the part of the state in relation to both homosexuality and the act of prostitution. It broke with decades of prohibitionism and moved the state towards abolitionism, reflected in the prominence of harm reduction and public nuisance considerations in parliamentary debates. Connecting homosexuality with prostitution, parliamentarians argued that both belonged to categories of private sexual behaviour between consenting adults that were beyond the state's concern. For instance, they debated the definition of a brothel to ensure it excluded the family home of a prostitute (which was adopted) though a proposal to establish a Task Force on prostitution was ruled out of order (Dáil Éireann Debates 24 June 1993, Vol. 432). Moreover, the government professed no desire to criminalise the prostitute and refused a role in policing private sexual arrangements between consenting adults even when money exchanged hands. Its brief was with public manifestations of prostitution only (Seanad Éireann Debates Vol. 137: 262, 29 June 1993).

However, once the dust had settled, it became evident that the stated intention not to criminalise those selling sex was rhetorical only. As anticipated by parliamentarians exercised by the law's more 'draconian' criminal justice measures, arrests and prosecutions rose in the law's wake (Ward 2010). Underscoring its reliance on law enforcement, the state ignored the CSW's recommendations to address the social and economic factors pushing people into selling sex.

Notwithstanding this tension between law and practice, the repudiation of prohibitionism was unambiguous. Five years later, the state accepted that some women were in prostitution 'voluntarily and willingly' and reiterated its exclusive interest in the sex trade's more intrusive aspects (DJELR 1998). The possibility of regulationism was mooted (Ryan and Ward forthcoming). It had been proposed during the 1993 parliamentary debate[4] and proposed by on-street sex workers themselves (Haughey and Bacik 2000).

During these decades, however, as feminist organisations lobbied on domestic and sexual violence and as women's human rights became a powerful transformative tool (Connolly 2003; Reilly 2008), the sex trade remained peripheral to both feminist and national politics. The proposal to establish a prostitute's trade union went nowhere. That marginality was dramatically reversed upon the foundation of the Immigrant Council of Ireland (ICI) in 2001 and its long, slow crusade under the banner of the ToRL campaign. Established with financial assistance from the Religious Sisters of Ireland, an order of Catholic nuns, the ICI's intellectual originators and founding personnel came from the violence against women movement which had successfully embraced advocacy in the 1990s (Galligan 1998: 126). Its chief executive, for instance, was a former director of Women's Aid.

The ICI's early years were largely devoted to consensus building on the case for Ireland's adoption of Swedish-style legislation. Large membership organisations, such as youth groups and trade unions, the state-feminist organisation, the National Women's Council of Ireland, as well as political parties and local government authorities were successfully targeted to join the campaign. As an entity, ToRL itself remained marginal in the public imagination until the mid-2000s but by around 2010 it claimed at least 1 million supporters.[5] The campaign remained led by the ICI and later, co-led by Ruhama, a faith-based organisation that works with on-street prostitution, both of which became established as the authoritative voices on prostitution and sex-trafficking (Fitzgerald and McGarry 2015). A comprehensive evaluation of the campaign is beyond the reach of this chapter and, to date, little analysis of it exists. However, the following general points can be noted.

The ToRL needed to assert both a pressing need for legal reform and the appropriateness of a new paradigm, neo-abolitionism, to address that need. Sex work, linked to trafficking or as a discrete policy issue, was not heretofore on the domestic political agenda and Ireland's prostitution regime was not at the time under scrutiny. Whilst the state relied on criminal justice measures for regime effect, it did not frame the problem of prostitution as one of violence against women but of public order. Internationalisation of the sex industry had occurred (Ward 2010) and though migrant women were indeed showing up in the expanding escort service sector, the profile of sex-trafficked women was considered by the state to be, up to 2013, 'quite low': 44 suspected cases (Fitzgerald 2014). Data on trafficking of any kind, including for the purposes of sexual exploitation, was and remains problematic (Lyon 2013) and numbers produced each year by the state's Anti Human Trafficking Unity (AHTU) concern suspected victims only.

The campaign, however, moved forward in leaps forcing legal reform and creating a movement to do that upon the production of its own report, commissioned for the campaign by the ICI (Kelleher *et al.* 2009). The report's commitment to neo-abolitionism and to radical feminism's representation of prostitution, then growing in strength within the EU,[6] was clear and its canonical status in terms of truth claims about the nature of the sex trade in Ireland was swiftly established. The report's assertions, and notably, its conclusion that there were 1,000 women available for prostitution each day in Ireland, of whom 97 per cent were migrants, as we will see, became 'truths' about the sex trade and remained virtually uncontested, despite difficulties with its methodology and research methods (Ward 2013a; Ward 2013b).

Media coverage of prostitution, sex trafficking and the sex trade ballooned during these years (Ryan and Ward forthcoming). Campaign literature, press releases and media contributions rested on the representation of prostitution as a form of violence against women, caused by male power and a function of patriarchical power relations (O'Connor 2008; ToRL 2012) and, in keeping with neo-abolitionism internationally, was inextricably linked in a causal relationship with trafficking (Scoular 2004: 351). Building on its membership base, ToRL representation was iterated throughout all media from the late 2000s onwards through 'launches,' commentaries and other creative events.[7]

The media reiteration of the report's claims was replicated within the law reform process as we will see. I argue that ToRL moved comprehensively into the parliament in 2011 and created a 'regime of truth' (Dunn 2009: 86) to ensure that neo-abolitionism framed the state's understanding of prostitution.[8] It is to this process, leading up to the consultation, that I now turn.

Neo-abolitionism and parliamentary processes

If debates about the sex trade surrounding the 1993 law reform were largely contained in the parliament, the situation surrounding the 2015 law could not have been more different. In this section, however, I focus on the parliamentary process and attempt to trace the background and context for the consensual alignment that manifested itself prior to and during the JCJDE's work. The timeline of concern is structured around the first Senate motion in October 2011; the second motion in April 2012; the JCJDE consultation process (Winter 2012-Spring 2013); and its report in June 2013. The heads of the bill (*The Criminal Law (Sexual Offences) Bill*), which included the ban on sex-purchasing, was published in November 2014 and the bill itself the following year.

Central to the argument made here was the fact that long before the Minister for Justice empowered the JCJDE to explore the options facing the state for prostitution law reform, all the major parties except one, Sinn Féin,[9] and many independent parliamentarians, were already committed to the adoption of a Swedish-style regime. Most critically, both parties of the ruling coalition, Fine Gael and the Labour Party, supported a SPB from at least 2009[10] onwards and the Labour Party committed itself to legislating for an SPB in 2011 (*Irish Times* 3 February 2011). Once Fianna Fáil came on board that year, consensus was virtually intact. The position of Minister Shatter was indeed out of step with his Cabinet and governing coalition parties.

However, this chapter is concerned in principle with the framing of prostitution within the law reform process, and the JCJDE consultation in particular, such that certain practices (following Dunne 2009: 78) were rendered possible and others unthinkable. I argue that the process served to guarantee an outcome – the adoption of a Swedish style approach – through the attendant hegemony of neo-abolitionism as a discursive practice that necessarily closed the policy process to any other perspectives (Fitzgerald and McGarry

2015). Hence, I trace the content of the debates, noting the figuration of these discourses and points of contention beginning in October 2011 with the first Seanad motion. As we will see, this motion fell but served the institutionalisation process by casting neo-abolitionism as the policy standard against which all others would be measured, 'flushed out' alignments and forced the hand of the Minister for Justice. It allowed a reading into the record as canonical text (Neumann 2009: 67) on the sex industry in Ireland, the representation advanced by the ToRL (Kelleher *et al.* 2009) a source that received broad, uncritical reception and was repeatedly cited with reference to its findings and conclusions.

Neo-abolitionism and the upper house (the Seanad)

Senator Katherine Zappone's motion, 'The Human Trafficking and Prostitution Motion', tabled in the Seanad in October 2011, called on the government to criminalise sex purchasing as a means of tackling trafficking for the purposes of sexual exploitation and was supported by six other members of the house. The motion opened with reference to the Kelleher *et al.* (2009) report and its claim that 1,000 women were 'made available for paid sex on a daily basis all over Ireland and that up to 97 per cent of them are migrant women'. The motion cast prostitution and trafficking as a 'form of slavery', stated that the purchase of sex, mainly by men, was contrary to the values of a country committed to gender equality and cited Norway and Sweden as examples where criminal sanctions for the purchase of sex had deterred prostitution and trafficking (Seanad Éireann Debates 12 October 2011, Vol. 210, No. 13). Following a long debate, the motion was lost to a government counter motion proposing legal clarification first on strict liability and the principle of uneven criminalisation. However, the government representative in the House, Minister Kathleen Lynch (Labour Party), assured members that a way would be found around these challenges (ibid). A law reform process would begin within six month, she promised, without prejudice to any 'definitive' government decision.

The motion can be interpreted in two related ways, first in terms of the process it initiated and second, its discursive impact. The motion forced the government's hand, leading to a commitment to a law reform process within six months. Its discursive power rested upon foundational neo-abolitionist representations of sex work: that it was inseparable from sex trafficking which was, in turn, a function of (mainly) male purchasing of sex; that it was incompatible with gender equality and that criminalisation of sex purchasing worked. Several speakers urged the immediate introduction of an SPB on the basis that a consensus already existed in its favour both in the house and in wider society. Throughout, senators reiterated the ToRL data, for instance, the claim of 1,000 women per day in prostitution of whom 970 were migrants. For one, demand in the domestic sex industry created an 'insatiable appetite' for trafficked women and girls. Another argued that there were categories in society that 'must be protected by insisting that in certain circumstances, one simply cannot consent to something' (Seanad Éireann Debates 12 October 2011, Vol. 210, No. 13). Senators applauded the role of the ToRL in educating them on the topic, such as in highlighting the intrinsic link between prostitution and sex trafficking, and referred to ICI/Ruhama briefings in the parliament building, including one held the previous night, prior to the vote.[11] Minister Lynch concurred. Parliamentarians were 'informed extraordinarily well' by NGOs she said (ibid). Only one senator opposed the motion. She argued that criminalising the purchase of sex would be 'totally wrong', rejected the positive claims made about the Swedish law and denied that a full debate had been had in Ireland (Seanad Éireann Debates 12 October 2011, Vol. 210, No. 13).

In the event, the six month time frame set out by the Minister passed and the following April (2012), Senator Zappone was back in the house with a second motion proposing Swedish-style law. The government's delay, she argued, coincided with a time period in which 'on each day … more than 1,000 women and girls were made available for paid sex' (Seanad Éireann Debates 18 April 2012 Vol. 214, No. 12). Again, the motion was lost to the government amendments but it played an important role in discursively reiterating neo-abolitionist arguments and the debate echoed that surrounding the 2011 motion. Notable, however, was the presence of Justice Minister Shatter in the house and his clear flagging of opposition to neo-abolitionist foundational principles. While accepting that both prostitution and sex trafficking cased 'very serious harm' the Minister repeatedly distinguished one from the other and argued that there was room for reform in both areas. Citing the UNAIDS Advisory Group 2011 report on HIV and sex work, he said that this too should inform Ireland's deliberations. He argued against government foreclosure on policy options in advance of the pending law reform process, a view that was supported by an opposition-bench senator concerned with prejudicing the outcome (Seanad Éireann Debates 18 April 2012 Vol. 214 No. 12).

Although lost, both Zappone motions served critical discursive purposes. They set out, and then reiterated, a neo-abolitionist norm with a singular, overarching policy outcome: criminalisation of demand as the logical and solitary outcome of a law reform process. While the party whip applied and government-party members were obliged therefore to oppose both, their opposition was strategically justified with reference to the need for legal clarification and due process rather than substantial arguments. Notwithstanding Minister Shatter, both government parties had already supported the principle of an SPB, a positioning that legitimised the discursive narrowing of the law reform debate that would lead to, in effect, the criminalisation of demand as the only intervention to reduce both prostitution and sex trafficking.

Neo-abolitionism and the public consultation process

In June 2012, the government published its report entitled 'Discussion Document on Future Direction of Prostitution Legislation' to explore the 'future direction of legislation on prostitution in Ireland' (DJE 2012: 3). Simultaneously, the JCJDE was tasked with hosting the public consultation to bring forward recommendations to government.

Reflecting the Minister's stance, the report argued there was clear consensus on the 'evils' of child prostitution and of sex trafficking and there were 'different and genuinely held views' on criminalising demand. Prostitution and trafficking were separate phenomena and prostitution research that emphasised trafficking might not be helpful in addressing 'voluntary prostitution' (DJE 2012: 5). Studiously neutral, the report set out a stall in which neo-abolitionism was not assumed to *necessarily* have any greater power over any other regime. It evaluated four distinct options facing the state: total criminalisation, partial criminalisation, full decriminalisation or regulation and listed questions arising from the implications of each. A second report published by the Parliament's Library Research Service as part of the process highlighted knowledge difficulties. 'There is little information on whether prostitutes are safer and trafficking is reduced' under this (i.e. Swedish law) and other regimes examined (OLRS 2012).

The JCJDE enquiry process was structured around two stages. Firstly, written submissions were sought from the public and secondly, oral submissions were heard over six days, two of which, for former or current sex workers, were held in private. In addition, the committee members went on a fact-finding trip to Sweden (but nowhere else) in November 2012, prior to the oral hearings.

Given the constraints of this chapter, a comprehensive analysis of the extensive documentation produced for these stages is not possible. Moreover, while the committee was to later claim that the majority of all submissions supported the adoption of a Swedish-style regime[12] approximately 770 of the 800 written submissions received are not available.[13] The 24 written submissions that are available produced a substantial body of material. For example, the ICI submission alone ran to 80 pages and included legal briefs on the issues problematised in the Seanad in 2011. It was the authors of these written submissions who provided the pool of participants invited to participate orally and though their input was necessarily shortened for time considerations, content was subject to further questioning and commentary.

In their evaluation of oral submissions, Fitzgerald and McGarry (2015) argue that a universalised assumption about women in sex work dominated therein, premised on the view that consent was not possible or irrelevant in prostitution, which was in turn, inseparable from trafficking. The submissions formed a discursive strategy that constructed all women in prostitution as needing state protection, perennially helpless and lacking agency. The submissions, the majority of which were from ToRL members, served to establish the ToRL campaign as legitimately speaking for women in prostitution and for all women in Ireland, while delegitimising any other perspectives (ibid).[14]

Considering the organisations selected, the dominance of neo-abolitionist thinking was not surprising. Of the 15 organisations that spoke, 13 were campaign supporters[15], as were five of the nine individual speakers.[16]

Different and sometimes directly challenging views were aired by the remaining minority: the Gay Men's Health Project (GMHP), the Sex Workers Association of Ireland (SWAI)[17], a medical expert and a number of academics.[18]

However, the weight of opinion of witnesses favoured neo-abolitionism though refracted through sectional interests such as migration, health and women's rights. Many cited the ICI report and there were repeated reference to its configuration of 1,000 women and the 97 per cent migrants.[19] A concurrent and inter-related discursive loop was the invocation of prostitution's oppressive paradigm and its causality to trafficking, as illustrated in the below quote from one witness:

> Criminalising the purchase of sex would have a normative effect. It sends the message to the public that by treating human beings as commodities one is committing a crime. We believe that this will have a deterrent effect on prospective buyers. It could also serve to shrink the industry, making Ireland a less desirable destination for human trafficking.
>
> (Stapleton 2013)

During the sessions, parliamentarians largely concerned themselves with establishing further details from the presenters on the implications of the introduction of an SPB and on knowledge about the sex trade in Ireland, teasing out issues of technology, management, finances, health and consent within the sex trade. The question of alternative models to the Swedish approach, though raised in passing was largely absent, leading the GMHP to wonder if the focus on Sweden was because committee members had gone there and to wonder why the committee was not considering Canada or New Zealand, the latter a 'stronger model' for consideration in Ireland (GMHP 2013). Proceedings were framed not by deliberations arising from the four regime options set out by the Ministry but by one, the Swedish approach.

Before the committee's report was published, the ToRL campaign again claimed discursive ground and generated public pressure through media events with a private members bill, the *Criminal Law (Sexual Offences) (Amendment) Bill 2013*, tabled in the Dáil by opposition member Thomas Pringle (Independent). The bill, like the Zappone motions before, proposed Swedish-style legislation and Deputy Pringle thanked the ToRL for support in its drafting (Dáil Éireann Debates 3 May 2013). It was inevitably overturned but allowed a reiteration of neo-abolitionism's case and its representations of the problem of prostitution. The options presented were stark. 'You are either against exploitation or you are for it,' commented Deputy McGrath (Independent). It is a case of supporting either 'English pimps' or all the women's groups, commented Sinn Féin Deputy MacLochlainn (ibid.). A small number of left wing members dissented from the consensus evident as all political parties, now including Sinn Féin, supported the principle of criminalising the purchasing of sex as the principle instrument for prostitution law reform, with the government side, again basing its opposition on the need to await the committee's report.

Not long after this debate the JCJDE produced its report in which the committee made the case for the 'persuasive evidence' that the Swedish law had worked and could be transferred to Ireland to reduce both the harm in prostitution and sex trafficking. Members were influenced by the 'degree of support for the Swedish approach' from a cross section of Irish society and attached particular significance to the 'authoritative and independently verified evidence-based research' produced by the ICI (HoO 2013: 74–75). Although they welcomed the direct contributions made by current sex workers, greater weight was given to the views of former sex workers who had no interest in the outcome of the review process except minimising exploitation for sex workers. In addition, the committee recommended increased penalties for sex trafficking and for living off the earnings. It also created two new offences of recklessly permitting a premises to be used and of grooming a child or vulnerable person for sexual abuse or exploitation and the criminalisation of the act of accessing prostitution websites, as is under Irish law, accessing child pornography sites (ibid).

The Minister not for turning?

While the committee's report was applauded by ToRL and its members, the Minister's objections to key arguments subsequently became clarified. In the wake of the report's publication, Minister Shatter identified problems and sought clarifications in a letter to its chairperson, party colleague, Deputy Stanton producing a short but insightful correspondence between both men.

As a lawyer with a background in civil liberties, Minister Shatter's concerns were largely to do with constitutionality and the committee's 'legal over reach' in recommending an SPB given its 'fundamental departure' from the principle of equality underpinning the existing offence of solicitation in Irish law. The proposal of immunity for the seller of sex, did not take into account questions about age, consent and experience of both the seller and the buyer. Unequal criminalisation might not allow such considerations to be reflected. Despite differences in opinion heard during the consultation as to the 'voluntariness' of engagement in prostitution, the factual deficit regarding numbers engaged in prostitution in Ireland, and that there was a diversity of experiences in prostitution represented in submissions, the members were recommending, he said, a 'broadly applicable and discriminate offence'. Accordingly, he queried the committee's favouring of an anticipated social outcome, the reduction of prostitution, over civil liberties and constitutional rights including the right to equality before the law and a fair trial (Shatter 2013).

In response, and on behalf of the committee members, Deputy Stanton robustly repudiated each of the Minister's concerns and cited, in support, evidence heard at the enquiry. The reply, moreover, drew out a fundamental supposition of the committee. This was that what it termed 'social policy' trumped any individual rights that might be claimed to inhere in the act of selling sex, a supposition grounded in a rejection of the idea that prostitution was based on a relationship between consenting adults (Stanton 2013). Hence, the Minister's concerns about asymmetrical criminalisation were outweighed by the unequal power relationship in prostitution. Moreover, the legal precedent existed in Irish law to deny the validity of consent, in cases of statutory rape. Here the state already adjudged participants in under age sex unequally for the purposes of criminalisation, thus creating the precedent whereby social policy (protection of under age girls) trumped civil liberties. Moreover, an SPB was simply an enhancement of the extant legislative goal of reducing prostitution and added a 'new far more important normative value' concerning its exploitative nature. In relation to the Minister's concerns about a knowledge deficit, the committee cited the ICI report and other evidence presented and rejected the claim that there was a factual deficit in relation to prostitution in Ireland (Stanton 2013).

It is not known if Minister Shatter's aversion to the committee's recommendation on the adoption of Swedish-style legislation was invulnerable to pressure from Cabinet colleagues, especially from the Labour Party, or if this policy area was simply not a priority for the government, but there was no movement on the recommendation until Minister Shatter resigned, on a matter unrelated to this issue, in May 2014. His replacement, former children's minister Frances Fitzgerald, however, lost little time in effecting her long standing support for ToRL, eventually taking shape in the 2015 bill.

Discussion

This chapter examined a three-year prostitution law reform process, undertaken by the Irish state whose outcome was the bill proposing the adoption of Swedish-style legislation. I have argued that by the time the inter-parliamentary committee began its work, pivotal to that process, neo-abolitionism had already been internalised by the political elite. The process that followed hence became a means whereby the discursive power of neo-abolitionism was given full, largely uncontested rein to frame the outcome: the adoption of neo-abolitionism as state policy. By focusing on the trajectory of the idea through a series of parliamentary processes, the party alignment therein, as well as the content and hegemonic status of the discourse, we can identify the manner in which no other outcome was, in the end, conceivable.

The capacity of the ToRL to deliver the outcome it sought points to the political power of radical feminism in Irish politics, echoing the power of governance feminism in the US (Halley 2006) and undermining radical feminism's account of itself as silenced and delegitimised in Ireland (O'Connor 2008). As other chapters in this book attest, radical feminist activism on this issue is a global movement with capacities to unfold in harmony with local conditions, structures and processes. In Ireland, the presence of key femocrats, Katherine Zappone in the Senate and the Minister for Justice, Frances Fitzgerald (former director of the National Women's Council) was one such local, institutional factor. However, as I have argued here, neo-abolitionism's success in Ireland is pre-eminently explained by its capacity to dominate public and parliamentary discourse – in part explained further by the absence of any countervailing discourses such as strong sex worker organisations. The brilliantly run ToRL campaign, led by those who had cut their teeth successfully in relation to normalising the state to issues of violence against women, was the critical actor.

For ToRL the debate was never about review of prostitution law but about the adoption of one particular criminal justice measure – criminalisation of demand. Prior to being appointed to the task, arising from ToRL advocacy, the majority of committee members already supported this position (and the outlier, Sinn Féin in time also came on board). Witnesses to the committee's proceedings were, in the majority ToRL members and the committee cited the (unverifiable) majority of written submissions as providing final legitimisation for its view (HoO 2013). In the absence of any independent review of prostitution law in Ireland and/or demographic data on the sex trade, witnesses and committee members alike relied on the canonical text produced by the ToRL and its knowledge production.

At the heart of the argument here is a process whereby the framing of the problem by the ToRL, repeated throughout the media and in submissions to the committee, allowed legislators to condemn prostitution in the kind of unequivocal and simple moral terms found in US discourses on trafficking and prostitution (Zimmerman 2013: 53–54). Similarly, it became a *sine qua non* that there was only one way for Ireland to go. If there were indeed one thousand women subject to male violence each day, and if 97 per cent of them were migrants (for which read 'trafficking victims'), then the state's range of responses coalesced around only one possible outcome. The representation of daily violations of unknown (likely trafficked) victims, endlessly communicated, brought with it a 'built in guide for action' (Neumann 2009: 77): criminalisation of male demand. The binary presented by one Deputy – you are either against or for exploitation – reverberated deeply and the focus of parliamentary debates from 2011 onwards became, not so much whether and on what basis, but *how* the state could best implement an SPB. With the departure of Minister Shatter, Minister Fitzgerald carried from her previous role a bill that housed the SPB, symbolically conjoining the state's response to transactional sex with its protection of children, a symmetry anticipated perhaps by the committee's view that when it came to the selling of sex women were child-like, unable to consent and in need of protection from the state (HoO 2013).

Accordingly, the open discussion sought by the Minister for Justice for that process laid out in the report (DJE 2012), was actually foreclosed by the process itself. Neo-abolitionist hegemony allowed parliamentarians to bypass the range of possibilities as set out for them in that report. The ToRL provided a simple and compelling interpretation. At no stage was any other approach given comprehensive consideration. Parliamentarians travelled to Sweden only. Excepting the questions raised by Minister Shatter, neo-abolitionism was not subject to critical evaluation. The voices of those left wing Dáil members, dissenters from the Pringle Bill, were both a tiny minority and came late in process.

Thus, the campaign, as I argue here, marginalised all other discourses including those suggested by sex workers themselves through, for instance, the SWAI presentation at the oral hearings. Undoubtedly, the weak participation of sex workers in the process was partially a function of the organisational and financial deficiencies of the SWAI, but neo-abolitionism's essential exclusions were also at play. The chairperson of the JCJDE had no doubt that the contribution of sex workers was less valuable than that of former sex workers who, he said, had no apparent interest in the outcome of the process except in relation to exploitation in prostitution (Stanton 2013). This extraordinary comment implies that those who are, in fact, the focus of the law reform process, those selling sex, are not trusted voices and may not be concerned about harm in the sex trade – a theme repeated in the submissions (Fitzgerald and McGarry 2015). I have suggested that there was a discursive collapse of the complex reality of prostitution and its relationship to other phenomena (trafficking, migration, poverty, gender equality) into a single incontrovertible framework (Zimmerman 2013) of the anti-trafficking measures and the oppression paradigm of prostitution. The move to deny consent to all sex workers as a group, as a principle of law, and deny validity to their perspectives on their own subjectivity, set out by the committee in reply to the Minister, illustrates this collapse: complexity can not be accommodated.

If as Minister Shatter noted, there are multiple experiences rather than one singular experience in the sex trade and given the difficulties facing the Swedish state in validating its claims (noted in other chapters in this volume), then the (likely) enactment of the 2015 bill may raise challenges for the Irish state in testing its claims to reduce sex trafficking and prostitution. Like the Swedish state before it, Ireland does not have a base line study of the sex trade – the 'factual deficit' mentioned by Minister Shatter – against which it will be able to measure the impact of any change in the law. As hinted at by the committee the law may operate primarily symbolically giving 'a message to future generations concerning the exploitative nature of prostitution' (Stanton 2013). However, perhaps not ironically, the very absence of such data may serve neo-abolitionism well. Claims as to 'positive' outcomes may be neither verifiable nor confoundable in any meaningful way. A new abolitionist regime might thus both satisfy radical feminism's reach for power and influence and the state's need to be seen to be doing something, without having to do very much.

Notes

1 In a parallel situation, the Northern Ireland Minister for Justice, David Ford, unsuccessfully opposed the introduction of the SPB there in 2015.
2 The Irish parliament is bicameral: the Seanad (upper house) and the Dáil (lower house).
3 See www.oireachtas.ie/parliament/media/committees/justice/Witnesses-and-Submissions-on-Review-of-Legislation-on-prostitution.pdf for all submissions.

4 One Deputy argued for prostitution to be regulated and brought 'into the open' (see Dáil Éireann Debates, Vol. 432, 24 June 1993).

5 See Women's Aid blog 06.12.11. The figure is presumably derived from the several large membership organisations signed up, such as the Irish Congress of Trade Unions (ICTU) and the Irish Countrywomen's Association (ICA). In June 2013 a national newspaper cited 1.6 million ToRL supporters (Cork Examiner, 28 June 2013).

6 Notably, the EWL/CATW handbook on prostitution and sex trafficking was written by two Irish activists (O'Connor and Healy 2006). See also Women's Aid (2004) a precursor report.

7 For example, a campaign of male musicians, poets and others was launched in February 2011 and a billboard campaign in September 2012. In August 2014 campaign support by former US President, Jimmy Carter, received significant media coverage. See www.turnofftheredlight.ieabout/the-campaign-so-far.

8 A motion proposing the adoption of a SPB had previously been tabled (and lost) in the Senate in June by Independent Senator Ronan Mullen. However it came in advance of the knowledge-claims about the sex trade in Ireland detailed here.

9 Sinn Féin endorsed the ToRL in April 2013. See www.sinnféin.ie/contents/26446.

10 Fine Gael supported a Seanad motion that called for criminalisation of 'the purchase of sex so as to target demand in the sex exploitation industry' (Human Trafficking Motion, Seanad Éireann Debates, Vol.195, No. 16, 10 June 2009). Shadow cabinet member, Simon Coveney, supported criminalisation as far back as 2007 (Irish Times, July 6th 2007). The Labour Party proposed Swedish style legislation in 2006 and Labour Women joined the ToRL in 2010. Fianna Fáil confirmed its support in 2011.

11 Another senator spoke of a meeting organised by the ICI and Ruhama attended by the Police Service of Northern Ireland and a Swedish police Inspector.

12 The ToRL had organised a national submission campaign.

13 Access was refused by the Committee to protect author's identities. Personal communication from committee clerk, 29 July 2015. For available submissions see www.oireachtas.ie/parliament/media/committee/justice/Witnesses-and-Submissions-on-Review-of- Legislation-on-Prostitution.pdf

14 See www.oireachtas.ie/…/Witnesses-and-Submissions-on-Review-of-Legislation-on-prostitution.

15 These were, the Irish Medical Organisation, the National Women's Council of Ireland, Barnardos, the ICI, Ruhama, Action to Prevent Trafficking, One in Four, the Irish Immigrant Support Centre, the Irish Nurses and Midwives Organisation, Women's Aid, the Irish Feminist Network, Doras Luimní, and an Garda Síochana. The two non-supporters were the Sex Workers Alliance of Ireland and the Gay Men's Health Project.

16 They included a national television journalist, authors of the Kelleher *et al.* (2009) report, the Director of the Women's Health Project (ToRL member) and a member of An Garda Siochana (the police force).

17 The SWAI, the sole sex-worker organisation in the state was at this stage organisationally weak and relied on 'representatives' to speak.

18 Including the author.

19 The journalist told the committee that, from his investigations, between 500 and 700 women were available every day (JCJDE Debates, 6 February 2013).

References

Agustín, L. M. (2007) *Sex at the Margins: Migration, Labour Markets and the Rescue Industry.* London and New York: Zed Books.

Connolly, L. (2003) *The Irish Women's Movement*. Dublin: Lilliput Press.

Dunn, K. C. (2009) 'Historical Representations', in A. Klotz and D. Prakash (eds) *Qualitative Methods in International Relations*, Basingstoke: Palgrave McMillan/ECPR, pp.78–92.

Dáil Éireann Debates 28 January 2016 Vol. 904 No. 3

Dáil Éireann Debates 3 May 2013 Private Members Bill.

Dáil Éireann Debates 24 June 1993, Vol. 432.

Department of Justice and Equality (DJE) (2012) *Discussion Document on Future Direction of Prostitution Legislation*. Dublin: DJE.

Department of Justice Equality and Law Reform (DJELR) (1998). *The Law On Sexual Offences: A Discussion Paper.* Dublin: Government Publications.

Fitzgerald, F. (2014) 'Address at Immigrant Council of Ireland EU Anti-Trafficking Event', Dublin, 17 October, available at www.inis.gov.ie/JELR/Pages/SP14000291.

Fitzgerald, S. and McGarry, K. (2015) 'Problematizing Prostitution in Law and Polity in the Republic of Ireland: A Case for Reframing', *Social and Legal Studies* 1(21), doi: 10.1177/0964663915614886.

Flynn, J. (2016) 'The Church's Lingering Shadows on Sex Work in Ireland' *University Times*, TCD, Dublin, 22 April.

Galligan, Y. (1998) *Women and Politics in Contemporary Ireland.* London: Pinter.

Gannon, I. (1985) 'Linking Arms with Our Prostitute Sisters', in L. Steiner-Scott (ed.) *Personally Speaking: Women's Thoughts on Women's Issues.* Dublin: Attic Press. 105–115.

Government of Ireland (1993) *Second Commission on the Status of Women, Report to Government*. Dublin: The Stationery Office.

GMHP (2013) 'Review of Legislation on Prostitution Discussion (Resumed)', *JCJDE*, 1(41), 23 January.

Halley, J. (2006) *Split Decisions: How and Why to Take a Break from Feminism.* Princeton, NJ: Princeton University Press.

HoO – Houses of the Oireachtas (2013) Joint Committee on Justice Defence and Equality, *Report on hearings and submissions on the Review of Legislation on Prostitution*, 31/JDAE/010 (June).

Haughey, C. and Bacik, I. (2000) *Final Report: A Study of Prostitution in Dublin.* Unpublished report, Law School TCD/DJELR.

Kennedy, S. (2012) 'Prostitution: the New 'Abolitionism'?, *Irish Marxist Review*, 1(4): 16–21.

Kelleher, P. *et al.* (2009) *Globalisation, Sex Trafficking and Prostitution: The Experiences of Migrant Women in Ireland.* Dublin: ICI.

Law Reform Commission (1985) *Report on Vagrancy and Related Offences*, Dublin: Law Reform Commission.

Leahy, S. (2013) 'Scripting Bare Life: Legislating for the Trafficked Person in Ireland', Irish Centre for Human Rights Seminar, NUI Galway, 28 November.

Levine, J. (1982) *Sisters.* Dublin: Ward River Press.

Levine, J. and Madden, L. (1987) *Lyn: A Story of Prostitution.* Dublin: Attic Press.

Luddy, M. (2007) *Prostitution and Irish Society 1800–1940*. Cambridge: Cambridge University Press.

Lyon, W. (2013) 'The Trafficking Paradigm', *Irish Left Review*, 1(2): 75–84.

Neumann, I. (2009) 'Discourse Analysis' in A. Klotz and D. Prakash (eds) *Qualitative Methods in International Relations*, Basingstoke: Palgrave McMillan/ECPR, pp. 61–77.

O'Connor, M. (2008) 'Silencing Feminism: Making Sexual Exploitation Invisible and Legitimate', in U. Barry (ed.) *Where Are We Now?* Dublin: Tasc/New Ireland, pp. 130–162.

O'Connor, M. and Healy, G. (2006) *The Links between Prostitution and Sex Trafficking: A Briefing Handbook*. CATW/EWL.

Oireachtas Library and Research Service (2012) *Prostitution Regulation in Ireland: Which Way Now?* Houses of the Oireachtas Library and Research Service, *Spotlight* No. 6.

Purcell, B. (1985) 'Linking Arms with Our Prostitute Sisters: A Real End to Prostitution', in L. Steiner-Scott (ed.) *Personally Speaking: Women's Thoughts on Women's Issues*. Dublin: Attic Press, pp. 116–125.

Reilly, N. (2008) 'Global Norms and Local Action: Critical Approaches to Women's Human Rights in Ireland' in U. Barry (ed.) *Where Are We Now?* Dublin: Tasc/New Ireland, pp. 216–242.

Ryan, P. and Ward, E. (forthcoming 2017) 'Ireland: A Case Study' in H. Wagenaar and S. Okland Jahnsen (eds) *Prostitution Policies in Europe*. London: Routledge.

Scoular, J. (2004) 'The Subject of Prostitution', *Feminist Theory*, 5(3): 343–355.

Seanad Éireann Debates 18 April 2012 Vol. 214, No. 12.

Seanad Éireann Debates 12 October 2011, Vol. 210, No. 13.

Seanad Éireann Debates, 10 June 2009 Vol.195, No. 16.

Seanad Éireann Debates 29 June 1993 Vol. 137: 262.

Shatter, A. (2013) 'Letter to Chairman of JCJDE, 25 September', available at: www.oireachtas.ie/parliament/media/committees/justice/Addendum-to-Prostitution-Report.pdf.

Stanton, D. (2013) 'Letter to Shatter', 6 November, available at: www.oireachtas.ie/parliament/media/committees/justice/Addendum-to-Prostitution-Report.pdf.

Stapleton, P. (2013) 'Review of Legislation on Prostitution Discussion (resumed)' *JCJDE*, 1(41) 23 January.

ToRL (2012) 'Submission to the JCJDE', available at www.oireachtas.ie/parliament/media/committees/justice/Witness-and-Submissions-on-Review-of-Legislation-on-Prostitution.pdf.

Ward, E. (2010) 'From Prohibitionism to a Globalised Sex Trade', *Irish Political Studies*, 25(1): 47–65.

Ward, E. (2015) 'Methods and Methodologies in Researching the Sex Trade: Ireland and Croatia Considered', unpublished paper, *Gender Arc Research Workshop*, NUIG, 28 May.

Ward, E. (2013a) 'There is no Evidence that Prostitution Can be Abolished', *Irish Times*, 12 July.

Ward, E. (2013b) 'Migrants or Victims? Debating Prostitution Law Reform in Ireland', paper at *Irish Centre for Histories of Labour and Class inaugural conference*, NUIG, 21 November.

Ward, E. and Wylie, G. (2014) 'Reflexivities of Discomfort: Researching the Sex Trade and Sex Trafficking in Ireland', *European Journal of Women's Studies*, 21(3): 251–263.

Weitzer, R. (2010a) 'The Movement to Criminalise Sex Work in the United States', *Journal of Law and Society*, 37(1): 61–84.

Weitzer, R. (2010b) 'The Mythology of Prostitution: Advocacy Research and Public Policy', *Sexuality Research and Social Policy*, 7(1): 15–29.

Women's Aid (2004) *Position Paper: Prostitution and Trafficking*. Women's Aid: Dublin.

Zimmerman, Y. (2013) *Other Dreams of Freedom: Religion, Sex and Human Trafficking*. Oxford: Oxford University Press.

6 Almost abolitionism

The peculiarities of prostitution policy in England and Wales

Anna Carline and Jane Scoular

Introduction

This chapter will explore the current UK approach to abolitionism by examining how a popular Northern European prostitution agenda has been translated into the English context. We argue that while neo-abolitionism has, over the last decade, had a noticeable impact on prostitution policy and practice in the UK, this has its own peculiarities. Whilst mimicking the abolitionist tone of Sweden, governments in mainland Britain have thus far stopped short of criminalising all purchases of sexual services and decriminalising the activities of those who sell sex – who are deemed to be 'victims'. Rather, governments have opted to modify the existing liberal regime by creating bespoke measures which seek to combine increased punitive sanctions for some clients with efforts to promote the exiting of women by the imposition of enforced rehabilitation. This has led to what we term as almost abolitionism: which describes a fragmented process of problematisation, whereby prostitution is both a public nuisance and sexual offence. Consequently, while only some forms of sex purchasing are illegal, the activity as a whole is increasingly pathologised and sex workers, represented universally in policy discourse as women, oscillate between being constructed as both victim and offender.

Sidestepping the liberal/illiberal arguments that tend to dominate in this field, this chapter will provide a critical analysis of these developments. While it is important to keep in mind the critical work on abolitionism elsewhere (as discussed in this collection as a whole), the account is not based on generalisation from neighbouring states. Rather, and drawing upon England and Wales as a case study, we explore the local drivers and local impact of the distinctive interventions. More specifically, we critically analyse two key reforms introduced by the Policing and Crime Act 2009, which reflect how this abolitionism has taken hold in England and Wales: the strict liability offence of paying for the sexual services of a prostitute subject to exploitation (s14) and Engagement and Support Orders (hereafter ESOs) to facilitate exiting and 'rehabilitate' on-street sex workers (s17).[1] In relation to the latter we consider the findings of an empirical project which explored the effects of a 'compulsory rehabilitation' policy. In conclusion, we argue that this almost abolitionism – whilst reflecting the rhetoric of radical feminism and gender equality – results in a fundamentally responsibilising, punitive and coercive response to commercial sexual activity. This, in turn, eschews alternative feminist conceptualisations of prostitution as sex work and excludes any recognition of the complex causal factors of both prostitution and trafficking.

From nuisance to neo-abolitionism? The development of prostitution law and policy

A system of liberal governance, with a focus on prostitution as a public nuisance, has characterised the English approach to prostitution for almost a century. Emanating from the Wolfenden Committee, this public nuisance approach confines state intervention to the public aspects of prostitution, imposing a punitive regime upon the public acts of soliciting (Wolfenden 1957). From a liberal perspective, it was considered that being paid/paying for consensual sex was not *per se* harmful. Such an approach clearly reflects a liberal feminist standpoint that women have the right to determine how to use their bodies, and to do so without interference from third parties (Jagger 1991; Nussbaum 1999). Consequently, the liberal approach delineated 'a private sphere of non-intervention, creating an unregulated market in which private forms of commercial sex are, by omission, sanctioned and as such have very much proliferated' (Hubbard and Scoular 2009: 150; Matthews 1986). However, this also established and maintained a gender-asymmetry – with the woman who sells sex, rather than her male client, being the main focus of attention.

Accordingly, the law criminalises the more public side of prostitution and also the involvement of third parties. Offences include: loitering or soliciting in a street or a public place for the purpose of prostitution (s1 Street Offences Act 1959); soliciting another person in a street or a public place for the purposes of obtaining their sexual services as a prostitute (S52A Sexual Offences Act 2003); inciting or controlling prostitution for the purposes of gain (S52 and S53 Sexual Offences Act 2003); and managing or assisting in the management of a brothel (S33A Sexual Offences Act 1956); along with the use of anti-social behaviour orders to deal with street prostitution (Jones and Sagar 2001).

An impetus to reform the law of prostitution, however, developed again in the early part of the twenty-first century, which can be linked to multifarious factors, including: the increasingly global and diverse nature of sex work, the concerns pertaining to trafficking and exploitation, changing sexual and socio-economic norms and gender roles, in addition to the out-dated nature of the law. While aspects of the law were updated in 2003 (see the Sexual Offences Act 2003), a wholesale reform was considered necessary (Home Office 2000: 117). Consequently, this reform moment presented an opportunity for the implementation of more progressive regimes, for example the reconstruction of prostitution as work and a focus on labour laws. However, a neo-abolitionist perspective increasingly dominated the process (Home Office 2004; 2006; 2008).

Represented most evidently by the Swedish Sexual Purchase Act 1998, neo-abolitionism ostensibly flips the asymmetrical approach to prostitution, and draws upon a radical feminist rhetoric. Although in Sweden an array of legal provisions remain in place – for example offences relating to procuring/pimping and trafficking and regulations outlawing the use of accommodation to provide sexual services – the key distinguishing feature is the simultaneous criminalisation of purchasers and decriminalisation of sellers (see Florin 2012; Skilbrei and Holmström 2011, 2013). Male demand for sexual services is constructed as the 'root cause' of prostitution and trafficking (Ekberg 2004: 118), and therefore must be quashed. In contrast, women who engage in prostitution are victims who need support to exit, and hence should not be criminalised. Consequently, the 'burden' of criminal justice interventions shifts from sellers on to buyers.[2] As is well known, this is based on the presumption that 'sex work is the quintessential expression of patriarchal gender relations and male domination' (Weitzer 2013: 10). Thus, the eradication of prostitution is considered to be fundamental to the promotion of gender equality. Hence, through the schema of neo-abolitionism prostitution is fundamentally gendered, thus the real and complex diversity of commercial sex is ignored.

The subsequent influence of this neo-abolitionist agenda upon English law and policy is by no means serendipitous. Neo-abolitionist campaigners have attempted to universalise their understanding of commercial sex as an affront to human dignity and gender equality, and to ensure that the criminalisation of demand for sexual services and purchase of sexual services (i.e. the Swedish position) is adopted at national and international levels. To this end, the Swedish women's movement, activists and governmental ministers (see Ekberg 2004) have made some progress in this respect. A number of jurisdictions have already implemented or are considering adopting the Swedish approach.[3] Moreover, the campaign has also been further strengthened by a recent resolution of the European Parliament which asserts that prostitution is 'intrinsically linked to gender inequality in society and [has] an impact on the status of women and men in society and the perception of their mutual relations and sexuality' (European Parliament 2014: para E). While this body does not have law making power (any legislative change would need to come from the European Commission), it does carry significant symbolic and political weight. Press accounts, for example, note that the passing of the resolution 'formally establishes the EU's stance on prostitution and puts pressure on member states to re-evaluate their policies on sex work', pushing them towards the Nordic model (Oppenheim 2014). Indeed, the proposer of the motion, The British MEP Mary Honeyball, has since been encouraging states 'to be radical and ambitious enough to go Swedish' (Osborne 2014).

The evolution of neo-abolitionism in England and Wales

Whilst not as yet filtering through to legislation, in England and Wales numerous parliamentarians across the parties have explicitly expressed support for the Swedish model, as evidenced by the recommendation of the All-Party Parliamentary Group on Prostitution and the Global Sex Trade (APPG 2014). At the same time, the concerns embodied within the neo-abolitionism agenda are not new to the UK. Indeed, the subject of male licentiousness, concerns of sexual slavery and abolitionism have certainly been on the campaigning agenda since the Victorian era. National associations (such as the Ladies National Association under the leadership of Josephine Butler) campaigned against cruelty of the Contagious Diseases Acts regime of forced testing for sexually transmitted diseases. Nevertheless, it was only during the recent reform push that such issues were placed centre stage. Commencing with the publication of the Home Office report *Paying the Price,* a radical feminist perspective can be seen to dominate. Accordingly, prostitution was constructed and problematised as being inherently gendered, exploitative and victimising:

> Prostitution can have devastating consequences for the individuals involved and for the wider community. It involves the abuse of children and the serious exploitation of adults – many of whom are trafficked into and around the UK for this purpose.
>
> (Home Office 2004: 5)

Consequently, throughout the reform process the phrase 'commercial sexual exploitation' was invariably employed to signify sex work. For example, during the parliamentary debates, Labour MP Fiona McTaggart stated that there is a need to protect ' ... women from the exploitation inherent in every single occasion of purchasing and of prostitution' (House of Commons 2009a: col. 549). Hence, the need for a dual approach – which attempts to eradicate prostitution through reducing both demand and supply – was promoted:

> Prostitution may be driven by economic necessity but it can only exist because there is a demand for it. A coordinated strategy designed to reduce its prevalence must address demand as well as tackle the factors that lead individuals to become involved in its supply.
>
> (Home Office 2004: 12)

This approach, however, excludes 'the possibility of seeing the sale of sexual services as anything other than abusive and harmful' (Munro and Scoular 2013: 36). Herein we see the promotion of a radical feminist standpoint to the exclusion of other feminist perspectives, particularly those that conceptualise prostitution as labour (see further Carline 2011, 2012). Subsequently, various forms of regulation that could support individuals to work more safely and experience less exploitation (whether physical, economic and/or social, see Sanders 2005; Sanders and Campbell 2007; Sullivan 2010), were excluded as antithetical to the zero tolerance approach (Home Office 2006).

'Almost abolitionism': prostitution policy and neo-liberal responsibilisation

Nevertheless, while the rhetoric of neo-abolitionism is currently very strong internationally, policies do not simply jump across borders. Rather the process of policy transfer involves particular governmental processes, which operate in distinctive regulatory cultures. Moreover, it is important to appreciate the distinctiveness of the Swedish law. Few states will be able to achieve as complete a problematisation as Sweden, where a unique combination of ideas, alliances and actions *produced* the Swedish abolitionist model. National anxiety regarding an apparent 'influx' of 'trafficked' women from Eastern Europe and associated fears regarding Sweden's entry to the European Union (EU), a history of paternalism in social policy, a hegemonic and politically influential feminist movement and decades of social science work on the much neglected client: all help to make sense of the country's unique approach (see Kulick 2005; Scoular 2004; also Swanström this volume). Even in neighbouring Scandanavian countries, which have enacted similar laws (such as Norway and Iceland and Finland which enacted only a partial ban) and share similar political traditions, *empirical* researchers highlight significant differences, putting paid to any notion of a universal 'Nordic model' (Skilbrei and Holmström 2011). Such variation is even more pronounced in countries with different political cultures, greater diversity in feminist thinking and where sex work rights organisations are more established and better represented in the political discourse. Thus, there is an inevitable multiplicity in the manifestation of neo-abolitionist tendencies.

Accordingly, while in England and Wales the scene was set for the adoption of an asymmetrical neo-abolitionist approach – criminalising those who purchasing sex, whilst decriminalising the sale of sex – the resulting reforms produce their own unique form of abolitionism. During the reform process which culminated in the Policing and Crime Act 2009, we argue that the radical feminist perspective was co-opted by the state and transposed upon the pre-existing liberal/public nuisance framework, in a manner which only worked to extend the state's coercive reach. Hence, despite the official rhetoric that all women involved in prostitution are victims, the resulting reforms increasingly criminalise not only the buyers, but also the sellers of sex (Cusick and Berney 2005; Scoular and O'Neill 2007; Soothill and Sanders 2004). This 'almost abolitionism' is explored in further detail in the following two sections, as we examine the impact of two offences implemented in order to deter demand and facilitate exiting in England and Wales: ss14 and 17 Policing and Crime Act 2009. In so doing, we highlight the significant differences with the 'Nordic' approach. However, key to this analysis is the consideration of how, in England and Wales, the neo-abolitionist agenda has involved the proliferation of neoliberal responsibilisation.

As Scoular and O'Neill have argued (2007), the development of prostitution law and policy in the UK can be situated within the context of 'progressive governance', whereby power is dispersed and decentralised. They note that 'these new matrices of power are increasingly organised around specialist and expert forms of knowledge which seek to manage crime prevention and control through strategies of self-governance and responsibilization' (Scoular and O'Neill 2007: 767). Whilst the concept of, and a concern with, 'responsible citizens' is not a modern phenomenon, it has been argued that 'responsibility' has been 'colonised in public life and political rhetoric by neoliberal discourses of responsibilisation' (Trnka and Trundle 2014: 136).

As is well known, neoliberalism promotes 'a set of ideals and practices that involve a shrinking state mandate, deregulation and privatisation, a faith in markets to govern social life, and an increased emphasis on personal choice and freedom' (Trnka and Trundle 2014: 137). This connects with the notion of the responsible citizen, who is constructed to be autonomous and independent and empowered to 'fulfil their human potential' (Trnka and Trundle 2014: 138). However, ideal citizens are also responsible citizens. Citizens may have rights and freedoms, but they also have responsibilities, and a good citizen must exercise their autonomy responsibly (Clarke 2005: 451). As Clarke notes, '[c]itizens must manage their lifestyles so as to promote their own health and wellbeing. Members of communities must eschew anti-social behaviour so as to promote harmony, inclusivity and civility' (2005: 451). Within this neoliberal framework, citizens are subject to pervasive surveillance technologies, from both 'above and below: that is, by the state, the media, public groups, and individuals' (Trnka and Trundle 2014: 139), which entrenches responsibility within the subject. Accordingly:

> Responsibility becomes a form of reflexive prudence, and individuals and collectives must increasingly conduct moral evaluations of their actions in relation to their potential effects, calculating and designing their life course in ways that attempt to mitigate harm and risk, and maximise benefit to themselves and others.
>
> (Trnka and Trundle 2014: 136; see also Giddens 1999)

As we will explore further below, through these processes of neoliberal responsibilisation, the causes of and the solutions to prostitution are fundamentally – and problematically – individualised. Indeed, due to the mono-dimensional construction of clients and sex workers, both the (male) purchasers and the (female) sellers of sex are subject to techniques of responsibilisation. The male purchaser's demand for sexual services is constructed as causative of not only prostitution, but also trafficking. He therefore needs to be educated as to the realities of the sex industry, and disciplined should he fail to cease purchasing sex. On the other hand, a woman is only perceived to sell sex because of her dire economic and life circumstances; accordingly, she has to be empowered (or coerced) to reform and improve her life. Consequently, she is expected to exit sex work and required to engage in state approved employment. Throughout this process, however, the state fails to acknowledge the impact of structural injustices and its own role in their continuation.

Shifting the burden? Deterring demand, reducing supply and the Police and Crime Act 2009

Whilst the female sex worker has tended to dominate the policy focus, since the 1980s male street clients have been increasingly seen as dangerous in the English context. Media anxiety surrounding the multiple murders of women by the 'Yorkshire Ripper' (Ward Jouve 1986) in particular, created considerable fear and anger, which Walkowitz (1992) argues fuelled an anti-violence campaign, and paved the way for increased legal surveillance and criminal penalties to be attached to certain purchasers. Thus, the Sexual Offences Act 1985 created the offence of kerb crawling, which though never used to any great extent, created a new category of offender, who was positioned somewhere between a sex offender and public nuisance. This new offender became a target for new interventions, such as the experiments with kerb-crawler rehabilitation/diversion schemes for clients (Bindel 1998), and further criminal sanction. Hence, certain groups of clients have been subjected to increased policing and criminalisation (Brooks-Gordon 2010; Brooks-Gordon and Gelsthorpe 2003; Sanders 2005; Sanders 2009a; Sanders and Campbell 2008). However, in *Tackling the Demand*, the Home Office set out that more was needed in order to eradicate prostitution: 'To truly tackle the problem of commercial sexual exploitation more needs to be done to target those who contribute to the demand, those that pay for sex' (Home Office, 2008: 9). Similarly, during the parliamentary debates, the then Home Secretary stated: ' … it has been clear to me for some time that tackling the demand side of the equation is one of the best ways we have of fighting back against the misery of prostitution and human exploitation' (House of Commons 2009a: col. 524).

To this end, the Policing and Crime Act 2009 brought in two provisions. With respect to on-street prostitution, s19 further extended the reach of the criminal law, by replacing the offence of 'kerb crawling' with a generalised soliciting offence. Significantly, there is no longer a need for the conduct amounting to soliciting to be persistent, which arguably undermines the nuisance-based rationale of the law. Accordingly, the offence is transformed into what is known as a status-based crime, whereby the offence is not premised upon any positive act or behaviour of the offender, but occurs due to the existence of a certain state of affairs. Moreover, and pivotal to the policy agenda of deterring demand, s14 criminalised paying for the sexual services of a prostitute who has been exploited by a third party.

Ostensibly introduced to deal with the issue of trafficking, and turning the focus of the criminal law to off-street prostitution, s14 is similar to the Finnish regime, which has adopted a partial ban, outlawing the purchase of sexual services from trafficked victims (see further Skilbrei and Holmström 2011, 2013). Hence, the liberal approach to prostitution is *prima facie* retained by this new offence – as ostensibly it only criminalises purchasing sexual services from exploited individuals, with exploitation being defined to encompass deception, threats, both physical and otherwise, and also coercion. Hence, while this is clearly not limited to women who have been trafficked, the section is seemingly restricted to non-consensual forms of prostitution, thus drawing upon liberal notions of consent and autonomy. However, peculiarities exist and the liberal sentiment of s14 is undermined by the radical feminist construction of prostitution which was drawn upon throughout the reform process, as mentioned above (see further Carline 2011, 2012). Concomitantly, the circumstances which potentially fall within the scope of the offence are significantly expansive in scope. A Home Office circular, published at the time when the offence came in to force, for example, states that threats to stop the supply of drugs or alcohol, and threats to end the relationship, or withdraw love/affection, would fall within the section's remit (Home Office 2010a).

Moreover, under s14 the client's knowledge regarding the exploitation is irrelevant, hence the crime is one of strict liability, which is a controversial move. The imposition of a strict liability is contrary to basic criminal law principles which require fault – and therefore a level of knowledge – whether this be assessed objectively or subjectively (Archard 2008; Ashworth and Zedner 2008; Hart 2008). However, and once again drawing upon a radical feminist rhetoric, those in favour of the offence stipulated that the crime must be one of strict liability, in order to effectively deter clients. To this end, it was argued that the offence would cause the sex buyer to contemplate how their behaviour funds the sex industry and perpetuates the exploitation of women (House of Commons 2009b: col. 25) and to act with 'vigilance and circumspection' (House of Commons 2009d: col. 289). Significantly, however, no evidence was provided to support the contention that the offence would operate as an effective deterrence. Indeed, research does not suggest that it will (Von Hirsch *et al.* 1999). Further difficulties arise as the offence is premised upon the assumption that men who buy sex are ignorant of the realities of the sex industry, as well as lacking knowledge of the law. For example, during the Policing and Crime Act parliamentary debates, Vernon Coaker MP surmised that many men simply think: '"I'll purchase the sex." They do not think "Is this somebody who is exploited?"' (House of Commons 2009c: col 110). This conceptualisation is not, however, supported by empirical research into clients (Sanders 2009a; Sanders 2005). Moreover, the offence produces a significant incongruity, whereby the maximum punishment for a person who pays for the sexual services of someone who is deceived or coerced into prostitution is a mere fine of £1000.

Hence, the extent to which this offence responds effectively to the harm of trafficking is debatable. Nevertheless, s14 was deemed to provide an effective solution. MP Alan Campbell, for example, stated:

> People who are serving on this Committee will look back on the measure in the future, when strict liability is working, when we would have reduced the demand for prostitution, helped women out of prostitution

> and helped to tackle some of the worst examples of exploitation and trafficking, and be proud of the work that they have done on the Bill.
>
> (House of Commons 2009d: col. 304)

These claims of effectiveness were unsubstantiated throughout the reform process and significantly doubted by numerous bodies, including the Metropolitan Police (see House of Commons 2009d: col. 294). Further, recent research suggests that the offence has had a limited impact (Kingston and Thomas 2014). According to the findings of a Freedom of Information request regarding the use of s14, the offence 'had not been used by the majority (81%) of police forces across England and Wales' (Kingston and Thomas 2014: 262. See also House of Commons 2014). This lack of implementation, Kingston and Thomas suggest, may well reflect reluctance amongst the forces to utilise the criminal law to deal with trafficking. The failure of police to respond adequately to violence against women – particularly when the women are involved in prostitution – is, unfortunately, not uncommon (Dellinger Page 2010; Kingston 2013; Kingston and Thomas 2014: 262–264). Research also demonstrates a significant lack of awareness with regards to trafficking, with examples of the police charging trafficked victims with immigration related offences (Kingston and Thomas 2014: 264, discussing Centre of Social Justice 2013). However, the limited use of the offence may also emanate from a lack of cases involving the requisite exploitation, with research and previous police operations suggesting that the level of trafficking is by no means as prolific as official arguments suggest (Kingston and Thomas 2014: 264; Mai 2009). Furthermore, Kingston and Thomas' findings also suggest that the law is being misapplied. Information provided by Avon and Somerset police forces – which recorded 81 arrests under s14 in 2012 – indicated that the offence had been used for those who '[s]olicit another for the purpose of obtaining their sexual services as a prostitute in a street/public place' (2014: 265). Such conduct is, however, covered by the s19. These findings substantiate fears that s14 may be used to deal with the more public aspects of prostitution (Scoular and Carline 2014).

Through the implementation of s14, this 'shifting the burden' of criminalisation on to clients in England and Wales is clearly intended to be instrumental. It is believed that the approach will not only be effective in reducing prostitution, but is essential to that end. This, however, overestimates the ability of the criminal law to produce both significant behavioural change and fundamentally reduce what is a diverse and complex industry. Furthermore, Florin (2012) has argued that in Sweden the criminalisation of clients was more of a symbolic move, intended to complement the measures brought in to facilitate exiting prostitution. Hence, in the Nordic countries, the reduction in prostitution is to be achieved by supporting women to exit prostitution, which, in turn is to be achieved through social work measures. While this produces conflicts, particularly between the promotion of desistance, on the one hand, and harm-reduction and social work ethos on the other (Skilbrei and Holmström, 2013), it is significant that exiting is facilitated by social work as opposed to criminal justice mechanisms.

From 'common prostitutes' to vulnerable victims? Almost abolitionism and sex sellers

The term 'common prostitute' was first introduced into law by s3 of the Vagrancy Act 1824, which criminalised any 'riotous' or 'indecent behaviour' by a common prostitute in public. This set the tone for the focus upon the visible aspects of sex work and a construction of on-street soliciting as a public nuisance. The term remained on the statute books until 2009, when it was eventually abolished by s16 of the Policing and Crime Act. During the reform process, it was recognised that the term 'dehumanise[d] people who deserve our sympathy as much as our condemnation – if not more' (Jack Straw, then Home Secretary, House of Commons 2007: col. 69–70). Hence, and mimicking the tone of neo-abolitionism and radical feminism, the prostitute-as-victim script is replete in official documentation. Whilst in *Paying the Price* on-street prostitution is a key focus, the issue of trafficking increasingly dominated the reform agenda. However, the victim status of both is emphasised: female prostitutes are either drug addicted street prostitutes or women who have been trafficked or otherwise forced into prostitution (see Home Office 2004, 2006, 2008).

Significantly, however, despite the focus upon the vulnerable victim status of the 'prostituted woman', English abolitionism sits in stark contrast to Nordic models in its refusal to decriminalise those who sell sex. Throughout the reform process, calls to abolish the soliciting offences were dismissed and herein the public nuisance discourse once again came to the fore. For example, Alan Campbell argues that 'women cannot act with impunity: they cause a nuisance and create concern in local communities' (House of Commons 2009d: col. 316). In such situations he felt that 'the community has the right to expect that, if they have been given every opportunity to leave prostitution, they will be gently pushed in that direction' (House of Commons 2009d: col. 316). Hence, the on-street sex worker is both a vulnerable victim and a public nuisance and, despite the government's rhetoric that the desire is to enable women to exit prostitution, there is a complete failure to acknowledge that criminal records 'institutionalise women in prostitution' (Niki Adams, English Collective of Prostitutes, House of Commons 2009b: col. 26). Indeed, the reach of the criminal justice net has been extended. While the phrase 'common prostitute' was rightly abolished, in its place we have a statutory definition of persistence: two or more occasions over a period of three months. This is a significant extension on the previous requirement of two or more occasions in one month.

Consequently, the government in England and Wales has thus far persisted with a criminal justice approach. This involves increased enforcement (including the use of Anti-Social Behaviour Orders (ASBOs)) for street sex work in particular, raids on indoor establishments under the guise of tackling trafficking and exploitation and the tightening of restrictions on licences for sexual entertainment venues (Hubbard 2015). These mechanisms operate alongside interventions that promote prevention and support for women to exit prostitution. A prime example of this twin-track approach is the Engagement and Support Orders (ESOs) introduced in England and Wales by the Policing and Crime Act 2009.

Enforcing exit through coercion? Evaluating Engagement and Support Orders

ESOs provide an alternative penalty for those convicted of soliciting in a street or public place for the purposes of prostitution. As opposed to receiving a fine, an offender can now be required to attend three meetings with an 'appropriate person', during which they must 'address the causes of the conduct constituting the offence' and 'find ways to cease engaging in such conduct in the future'. However, as with kerb crawling, the legal basis of this new order is unclear. The offending conduct that triggers the order is soliciting in a public place. Thus, in theory, 'ceasing to engage in such conduct' could be achieved by working indoors or in ways that do not constitute a nuisance. It appears, however, from policy guidance and from practise (see Carline and Scoular 2015), that it is prostitution *per se* that is considered to be the 'offending conduct' – although this is not by virtue of law. Furthermore, an ESO may be passed without the consent of the offender, and a failure to attend a meeting without a reasonable excuse will result in a breach. Whether or not a breach has occurred is to be determined by the 'appropriate person', who must report the matter to the court, whereby the magistrate may revoke the order and re-sentence. This re-sentence could involve the imposition of another order, or a fine. A summons to attend court may follow a breach, and failure to attend may result in a warrant for her arrest. If arrested, the offender can be detained for up to 72 hours before the court appearance (Policing and Crime Act 2009, Schedule 1).

To analyse the impact of these new orders, we now turn to the key findings of an empirical project, which aimed to explore the anticipated and unanticipated effects of a policy of 'forced welfarism' (Scoular and O'Neill 2007; Sanders 2009b).[4] Significantly, and drawing upon the data obtained via a Freedom of Information request, ESOs have not been implemented evenly across England and Wales. Study participants considered that this was an inevitable consequence of nationally variable and contingent policing priorities. Nevertheless, when orders had been implemented participants – including recipients – were invariably not against them. However, it needs to be stressed that this favourable attitude flowed from the negative impact of fining those involved in sex work. Hence, the orders were considered to be 'the best of a bad' situation, given the on-going criminalisation of those who solicit in a public place for the purposes of selling sex.

In the majority of areas, ESO supervision was undertaken by agencies who were already engaging, whether voluntarily or otherwise, with those involved in sex work. Hence, for many recipients, an order simply involved on-going engagement with a known project worker, which consequently enabled (in most areas) the three meetings to be completed without significant difficulty. There was also a general reluctance to declare the offender had breached the terms of the ESO, with projects concerned to protect their relationships with their client group. Given the involvement of pre-existing agencies, supervisors were from a diverse range of projects including NHS funded services, probation, drug intervention projects, various charities and sexual health organisations. Accordingly, a range of differing perspectives on the problematic nature of prostitution could be seen. Nevertheless, there was similarity in practice, with most supervisors adopting a primarily needs-focused and person-centric approach.

Hence, whilst facilitating exiting was the official rationale behind the implementation of the orders, which reinforces neo-liberal responsibilisation and individualises the causes of prostitution, supervisors were able to employ different forms of practice, which went beyond that presupposed by official policy (Home Office 2010b). The orders were utilised by many support workers to provide an opportunity for a more holistic and non-judgmental engagement. Thus, the wider social, economic and health issues faced by recipients tended to be the main focus of the meetings. This included accompanying them to medical appointments, help with benefits and housing, assistance with purchasing appliances such as a washing machine and a microwave and support to obtain food parcels, as well as harm-reduction techniques. Accordingly, supervisors resisted the coercive nature of the criminal justice system, as it was considered to be counterproductive.

Research on female offenders identifies such personal and practical support as essential to reducing offending, and thus such practices could be seen as facilitating desistance (Corston 2007; Corston 2011; Hedderman *et al.* 2011). However, the extent to which ESOs amounted to an effective mechanism to facilitate desistance was doubted by supervisors, due to the inadequacy of orders to deal with the numerous and complex difficulties faced by many involved in sex work (Pitcher 2006). As a result, repeat orders were accepted as inevitable by project workers, as was the reality that many recipients would continue to work whilst on an ESO. Moreover, whilst some agencies recognised exiting to be a longer-term goal, many doubted whether complete desistance could, for some, ever been achieved. It is also well known that exiting prostitution is an exceptionally difficult and lengthy process and often involves periods of re-engaging in sex work (see for example Hester and Westmarland 2004; Cusick *et al.* 2011).

In contrast, a tension arose for the police, as they struggled to negotiate the contradiction emanating from the sex worker's dual victim/offender status. Whilst officers were cognisant of the complex vulnerabilities of ESO recipients, they also felt the political and community pressure to reduce – if not eradicate – on-street prostitution, in a timely manner. This in turn led some to suggest more coercive disposals, including the use of ASBOs and the threat of imprisonment, for those who failed adequately to transform their lives. Such perspectives reflect the potential carceral consequences of utilising criminal justice mechanisms to enforce exiting. This involves a 'shift in governance' (Scoular and O'Neill 2007: 773) which:

> … locates individual women as being responsible for the social problem they encounter, thereby justifying a punitive response when, despite the best efforts of the support agencies around them, they continue with their involvement in prostitution.
>
> (Phoenix and Oerton 2005: 100)

Hence, the ESOs result in various difficulties, tensions and conflicts which have to be managed by the relevant agencies. Problematically, much needed support for vulnerable individuals is dependent upon the involvement of criminal justice agencies, with some recipients commenting that support was often only available to those who had been convicted. Indeed, whilst it was acknowledged that the order at times facilitated initial contact with some hard to reach individuals, a significant tension arose from the zero tolerance approach to sex work, as it inevitably leads to geographical displacement (Pitcher *et al.* 2006). Thus, project workers were increasingly dependent upon criminalising women in order to facilitate outreach. Accordingly, projects are placed in a complex situation, whereby they are required to negotiate the criminal justice system, and monitor and potentially discipline sex workers. Concomitantly, it can also be argued that the government's policies involve a regulation of support projects, whereby they are expected to endorse the government rhetoric that prostitution is an unlivable life choice, and that the only solution is desistance. This, however, may lead to the provision of unwanted and/or irrelevant services (Cusick *et al.* 2011: 153), which diminish the support provided to this group.

Consequently, it is argued that the orders institute a moralistic, individualistic and tokenistic response, which demonstrates a willful refusal to acknowledge the well-known complexities of prostitution. Prostitution is recognised by many to be ' … a gendered survival strategy often used by poor women trying to create a better future for themselves and their dependents' (Phoenix 2008: 38). Hence, in addition to decriminalisation, it is recognised that the most effective way in which to enable exiting is to provide sufficient resources to address each woman's 'particular economic needs' (Niki Adams, English Collective of Prostitutes (ECP), House of Commons 2009b: col. 27).

Conclusion

This chapter has traced the evolution of prostitution law and policy in England and Wales, and explored its impact upon various subjects and spaces of sex work. While neo-abolitionism, and the correlating radical feminist discourse, has influenced law reform and policy developments, the public nuisance perspective nevertheless remains influential. The interaction of these two frameworks is felt acutely by street-based workers who are under intense pressure to exit, as demonstrated by the implementation of ESOs. Under the guise of promoting gender equality, sellers are increasingly cast as victims. However, this construction takes place in the context of an existing criminal justice framework and in a declining welfare system in which citizenship and assistance is increasingly conditional. At the same time, the vulnerability and victim status of the female sex worker is used to justify the need to tackle demand through the increased criminalisation of those who purchase sex. Indeed, the neo-abolitionist schema involves subjecting male sex buyers to the same pathologising and responsibilising tendencies previously applied to female sex workers. Subsequently, as opposed to focusing on the crimes committed, the law has collapsed harm, disease and anti-social behaviour with the activity of purchasing sex, which becomes a problematic identity *per se*. It is, thus, impossible to be both a good responsible citizen, and a purchaser of sexual services (Kulick 2005: 215, 217).

Throughout this process a fundamental and problematic slippage occurs, as buying and selling sex are not criminal offences, yet subjects are invariably penalised. This, we argue, signifies how the grafting of the radical feminist rhetoric of neo-abolitionism on to the pre-existing liberal framework of the law facilitates processes of neoliberal responsibilisation. Hence, both purchasers and sellers are increasingly disciplined for engaging in what is fundamentally legal activity. Concomitantly, 'ignorant men', and their demand for sexual services, are constructed as causative of prostitution and trafficking, while women who fail to adequately transform their lives are punished. However, the 'almost abolitionism' reflects a neo-abolitionism approach in policy-speak only, as it results in a system which is more akin to conservative moralistic criminalisation regimes. Throughout this process alternative feminist perspectives, which recognise prostitution as a form of labour, are rejected and the state eschews the complex causal factors of both prostitution and trafficking. These include the multifarious structural, material and economic inequalities, the impact of globalisation and restrictive immigration practices (see for example Andrijasevic 2010; Doezema 2010; Murray 1998; Sanders and Campbell 2008: 174). In contrast, we argue that the next generation of reform in the UK should be informed by a sex work discourse, which acknowledges and responds to the complexities of prostitution and trafficking.

Notes

1 Acts of Parliament contain numbered sections, which provide the detail of the law. Throughout this chapter, sections are referred to as 'sX'. Hence, the offence regarding the purchasing of sexual offences is contained in section 14 of the Policing and Crime Act 2009.

2 The title of a recent All-Party Parliamentary Group on Prostitution and the Global Sex Trade report is: *Shifting the Burden: Inquiry to Assess the Operation of the Current Legal Settlement on Prostitution in England and Wales* (APPG 2014).

3 The policy has subsequently been mirrored, to some extent, by parliaments in Norway and Iceland (leading some to refer to it as Nordic), and in part, or in tone, by South Korea, France, Finland, Israel, the United Kingdom, Northern Ireland and the Republic of Ireland.

4 The research project employed a three-part research methodology, triangulating data from academic commentary, policy documents and reports and semi-structured interviews. To commence, and in order to reveal the extent to which ESOs had been implemented, and the rates of breaching, we submitted a Freedom of Information Request. Thereafter, we conducted interviews with 31 participants, comprising of supervisors/project workers (13), police offices (11) and ESO recipients (8), across eight cities. Participants were asked questions pertaining to the impact and efficacy of ESOs, along with perspectives on best practice and suggestions for reform. Ethical approval was obtained from the University of Strathclyde. For a more detailed discussion of the methodology see Scoular and Carline (2014).

References

All-Party Parliamentary Group on Prostitution and the Global Sex Trade (APPG) (2014) *Shifting the Burden: Inquiry to Assess the Operation of the Current Legal Settlement on Prostitution in England and Wales.* Available at: http://appgprostitution.files.wordpress.com/2014/04/shifting-the-burden.pdf. Accessed 15 April 2014.

Andrijasevic, R. (2010) *Migration, Agency, and Citizenship in Sex Trafficking.* New York: Palgrave Macmillan.

Archard, D. (2008) 'Criminalising the Use of Trafficked Prostitutes: Some Philosophical Issues', in V. Munro and M. Della Giusta (eds) *Demanding Sex: Critical Reflections of the Regulation of Prostitution.* Aldershot: Ashgate, pp. 149–162.

Ashworth, A. and Zedner, L. (2008) 'Defending the Criminal Law: Reflections on the Changing Character of Crime, Procedure, and Sanctions', *Criminal Law and Philosophy*, 2: 21–51.

Bindel, J. (1998) 'Out of the Gutter: The First School to Reform Kerb Crawlers Opened Last Week in Leeds', *The Independent*, 12 November: 9.

Brooks-Gordon, B. (2010) 'Bellwether Citizens: The Regulation of Male Clients of Sex Workers', *Journal of Law and Society*, 37(1): 145–170.

Brooks-Gordon, B. and Gelsthorpe, L. (2003) 'Prostitutes' Clients, Ken Livingstone and a New Trojan Horse', *The Howard Journal of Criminal Justice*, 42(5): 437–451.

Carline, A. (2012) 'Of Frames, Cons and Affects: Constructing and Responding to Prostitution and Trafficking for Sexual Exploitation', *Feminist Legal Studies*, 20(3): 207–225.

Carline, A. (2011) 'Criminal Justice, Extreme Pornography and Prostitution: Protecting Women or Promoting Morality?' *Sexualities*, 14(3): 312–333.

Carline, A. and Scoular, J. (2015) 'Saving Fallen Women Now? Critical Perspectives on Engagement and Support Orders and their Policy of Forced Welfarism', *Social Policy and Society*, 14(1): 103–112.

Centre of Social Justice (CSJ) (2013) *It Happens Here: Equipping the UK to Fight Modern Slavery.* London: Centre for Social Justice.

Clarke, J. (2005) 'New Labour's Citizens: Activated, Empowered, Responsibilized, Abandoned?' *Critical Social Policy*, 25(4): 447–463.

Corston, J. (2011) *Women in the Penal System: Second Report on Women with Particular Vulnerabilities in the Criminal Justice System*. London: Howard League for Penal Reform.
Corston, J. (2007) *The Corston Report: A Review of Women with Particular Vulnerabilities in the Criminal Justice System*. London: Home Office.
Cusick, L. and Lee Berney, L. (2005) 'Prioritizing Punitive Responses Over Public Health: Commentary on the Home Office Consultation Document Paying the Price', *Critical Social Policy*, 25(4): 596–606.
Cusick, L., Brooks-Gordon, B., Campbell, R. and Edgar, R. (2011) '"Exiting" Drug Use and Sex Work: Career Paths, Interventions and Government Strategy Targets', *Drugs: Education, Prevention and Policy*, 18(2): 145–156.
Dellinger Page, A. (2010) 'True Colors: Police Officers and Rape Myth Acceptance', *Feminist Criminology*, 5(4): 315–334.
Doezema, J. (2010) *Sex Slaves and Discourse Masters: The Construction of Trafficking*. London: Zed.
Ekberg, G. (2004) 'The Swedish Law that Prohibits the Purchase of Sexual Services: Best Practices for Prevention of Prostitution and Trafficking in Human Beings', *Violence Against Women*, 10(10): 1187–1218.
European Parliament (2014) *European Parliament Resolution of 26 February 2014 on Sexual Exploitation and Prostitution and its Impact on Gender Equality*. Available at: www.europarl.europa.eu/sides/getDoc.do?pubRef=-//EP//TEXT+TA+P7-TA-2014-0162+0+DOC+XML+V0//EN.
Florin, O. (2012) 'A Particular Kind of Violence: Swedish Social Policy Puzzles of a Multipurpose Criminal Law', *Sexuality Research and Social Policy*, 9: 269–278.
Giddens, A. (1999) 'Risk and Responsibility', *Modern Law Review*, 62(1): 1–10.
Hart, H. L. A. (2008) *Punishment and Responsibility: Essays in the Philosophy of Law* (2nd edn). Oxford: Oxford University Press.
Hedderman, C., Gunby, C. and Shelton, N. (2011) 'What Women Want: The Importance of Qualitative Approaches in Evaluating Work with Women Offenders', *Criminology and Criminal Justice*, 11(1): 3–19.
Hester, M. and Westmarland, N. (2004) *Tackling Street Prostitution: Towards a Holistic Approach*. London: Home Office.
Home Office (2010a) *Home Office Circular 006/2010: Policing and Crime Act 2009 – New Prostitution Provisions*. London: Home Office.
Home Office (2010b) *Guidance on section 17 Policing and Crime Act 2009: Engagement and Support Orders*. London: Home Office.
Home Office (2008) *Tackling the Demand for Prostitution: A Review*. London: Home Office.
Home Office (2006) *A Coordinated Prostitution Strategy and a Summary of Responses to Paying the Price*. London: Home Office.
Home Office (2004) *Paying the Price: A Consultation Paper on Prostitution*. London: Home Office.
Home Office (2000) *Setting the Boundaries: Reforming the Law on Sexual Offences*. London: Home Office.
House of Commons (2014) *Sexual Offences: Prosecutions*. House of Commons, Daily Hansard Written Answers, 11 March. Available at: www.publications.parliament.uk/pa/cm201314/cmhansrd/cm140311/index/140311-x.htm. Accessed 15 April 2014.
House of Commons (2009a) HC Debates Vol. 486 (137). *Policing and Crime Bill 2008–2009*, 19 January.

House of Commons (2009b) Public Bill Committee 1st Sitting, *Policing and Crime Bill 2008–2009*, 27 January.

House of Commons (2009c) Public Bill Committee 4th Sitting, *Policing and Crime Bill 2008–2009*, 29 January.

House of Commons (2009d) Public Bill Committee 9th Sitting, *Policing and Crime Bill 2008–2009*, 10 February.

House of Commons (2007) HC Debates Vol. 464. *Criminal Justice and Immigration Bill 2007–2008*, 8 October.

Hubbard, P. (2015) 'Law, Sex and the City', *International Journal of Law in the Built Environment*, 7(1): 5–20.

Hubbard, P. and Scoular, J. (2009) 'Making the Vulnerable More Vulnerable? The Contradictions of Street Prostitution Policy', in D. Canter, M. Ioannou and D. Youngs (eds) *Safer Sex in the City*. Farnham: Ashgate, pp. 135–153.

Jagger, A. (1991) 'Prostitution', in A. Soble (ed.) *The Philosophy of Sex: Contemporary Readings*. Lanham, MD: Rowman and Littlefield, pp. 260–274.

Jones, H. and Sagar, T. (2001) 'Crime and Disorder Act 1998: Prostitution and the Anti-social Behaviour Order', *Criminal Law Review*, Nov.: 873–885.

Kingston, S. (2013) *Prostitution in the Community: Attitudes, Action and Resistance*. London: Routledge.

Kingston, S. and Thomas, T. (2014) 'The Police, Sex Work, and Section 14 of the Policing and Crime Act 2009', *The Howard Journal of Criminal Justice*, 53(3): 255–269.

Kulick, D. (2005) 'Four Hundred Thousand Swedish Perverts', *GLQ: A Journal of Lesbian and Gay Studies*, 11(2): 205–235.

Mai, N. (2009) *Migrant Workers in the UK Sex Industry: Full Research Report ESRC End of Award Report, RES-062-23-0137*. Swindon: ESRC.

Matthews, R. (1986) 'Beyond Wolfenden? Prostitution, Politics and the Law', in R. Matthews and J. Young (eds) *Confronting Crime*. London: Sage Publication, pp. 188–210.

Munro, V. and Scoular, J. (2013) 'Harm, Vulnerability and Citizenship: Constitutional Concerns in the Criminalisation of Contemporary Sex Work in the UK', in R. A. Duff, L. Farmer, S. E. Marshall, M. Massimo Renzo and V. Tadros (eds) *The Constitution of Criminal Law*. Oxford: Oxford University Press, pp. 30–52.

Murray, A. (1998) 'Debt-Bondage and Trafficking: Don't Believe the Hype', in K. Kempadoo and J. Doezema (eds) *Global Sex Workers: Rights, Resistance, and Redefinition*. New York: Routledge, pp. 51–64.

Nussbaum, M. (1999) *Sex and Social Justice*. Oxford: Oxford University Press.

Oppenheim, M. (2014) '*MEPs Vote to Criminalise Buying Sex*', *The Guardian*. Available at: www.theguardian.com/global-development/2014/feb/26/meps-vote-criminalise-buying-sex-european-parliament.

Osborne, H. (2014) 'Nordic Model of Prostitution Approved by European Parliament', *International Business Times*. Available at: www.ibtimes.co.uk/nordic-model-prostitution-approved-by-european-parliament-1438009.

Phoenix, J. (2008) 'Economic Exploitation, Male Violence and Prostitution Policy in the UK', in V. Munro and M. Della Guista (eds) *Demanding Sex: Critical Reflections on the Regulation of Prostitution*. Aldershot: Ashgate, pp.35–50.

Phoenix, J. and Oerton, S. (2005) *Illicit and Illegal: Sex, Regulation and Social Control*. Cullompton: Willan Publishing.

Pitcher, J. (2006) 'Support Services for Women Working in the Sex Industry', in R. Campbell and M. O'Neill (eds) *Sex Work Now*. Cullompton: Willan Publishing, pp. 235–262.

Pitcher, J., Campbell, R., Hubbard, P., O'Neill, M. and Scoular, J. (2006) *Living and Working in Areas of Street Sex Work*. Joseph Rowntree Foundation, Bristol: The Policy Press.

Sanders, T. (2009a) 'Kerbcrawler Rehabilitation Programmes: Curing the "Deviant" Male and Reinforcing the "Respectable" Moral Order', *Critical Social Policy*, 29(1): 77–99.

Sanders, T. (2009b) 'Controlling the "Anti Sexual" City', *Criminology and Criminal Justice*, 9(4): 507–525.

Sanders, T. (2005) *Sex Work: A Risky Business*. Cullompton: Willan Publishing.

Sanders, T. and Campbell, R. (2008) 'Why Hate Men who Pay for Sex? Exploring the Shift to "Tackling Demand" in the UK', in V. Munro and M. Della Giusta (eds) *Demanding Sex: Critical Reflections of the Regulation of Prostitution*. Aldershot: Ashgate, pp. 163–179.

Sanders, T. and Campbell, R. (2007) 'Designing out Vulnerability, Building in Respect: Violence, Safety and Sex Work Policy', *The British Journal of Sociology*, 58(1): 1–19.

Scoular, J. (2004) 'Criminalising 'Punters', Evaluating the Swedish Position on Prostitution', *Journal of Social Welfare and Family Law*, 26(2): 195–210.

Scoular, J. and Carline, A. (2014) 'A Critical Account of a "Creeping Neo-abolitionism": Regulating Prostitution in England and Wales', *Criminology and Criminal Justice*, 14(5): 608–626.

Scoular, J. and O'Neill, M. (2007) 'Regulating Prostitution: Social Inclusion, Responsibilisation and the Politics of Prostitution', *British Journal of Criminology*, 47(5): 764–778.

Skilbrei, M.-L. and Holmström, C. (2013) *Prostitution Policy in the Nordic Region. Ambiguous Sympathies*. Farnham: Ashgate.

Skilbrei, M.-L. and Holmström, C. (2011) 'Is there a Nordic Prostitution Regime?' *Crime and Justice*, 40(1): 479–517.

Soothill, K. and Sanders, T. (2004) 'Calling the Tune? Some Observations on Paying the Price: A Consultation on Prostitution', *Journal of Forensic Psychiatry*, 15(4): 642–659.

Sullivan, B. (2010) 'When (Some) Prostitution is Legal. The Impact of Law Reform on Sex Work in Australia', *Journal of Law and Society*, 37(1): 85–10.

Trnka, S. and Trundle, S. (2014) 'Competing Responsibilities: Moving Beyond Neoliberal Responsibilization', *Anthropological Forum*, 24(2): 136–153.

Von Hirsch, A., Bottoms, E., Burney, E. and Wikstrom, P. (1999) *Criminal Deterrence and Sentencing Severity: An Analysis of Recent Research*. Oxford: Hart Publishing.

Walkowitz, J. (1992) *City of Dreadful Delight: Narratives of Sexual Danger in Late-Victorian London*. London: Virago.

Ward Jouve, N. (1986) *The Streetcleaner: The Yorkshire Ripper Case on Trial*. London: Marion Boyars Publishing Ltd.

Weitzer, R. (2013) *Legalizing Prostitution: From Illicit Vice to Lawful Business*. New York: New York University Press.

Wolfenden Report (1957) *Report of the Committee on Homosexual Offences and Prostitution*. London: HMSO.

7 Against the trend

Resistance to neo-abolitionism in Australian anti-trafficking policy debates

Erin O'Brien

Introduction

Battles over policy responses to sex work have raged in Australia for many decades, often centred on a fundamental dispute between some feminists and other activists who argue that sex work is a form of violence against women, and others who seek recognition of sex work as a legitimate form of employment. Traditionally the policy purview of regional governments of Australia (states and territories), debate on sex work legislation has more recently emerged within federal policy-making forums focused on the eradication of human trafficking. Within these forums, neo-abolitionist activists have strongly criticised legalised sex work, and pushed the Australian Federal Government to endorse the 'Nordic Model' as a tool of anti-trafficking. The 'Nordic Model' is the criminalisation of the purchase of sex, alongside the decriminalisation of the selling of sex, first implemented in Sweden, and subsequently (in varying forms) in Finland, Norway and Iceland (Skilbrei and Holmström 2011). This chapter provides a critical account of neo-abolitionist activism within human trafficking policy-making in Australia over the last 15 years. It argues that neo-abolitionist activism in Australia is reactive to the status of sex work in Australia, where the trend is towards liberalisation of sex work laws. In this policy environment, the appeal from neo-abolitionist activists is one focused on demonstrating the failures of the current approach, and asserting a causal connection between legalised sex work and increased sex trafficking in order to push for the adoption of the Nordic Model.

This chapter first discusses the policy environment in which neo-abolitionist activists lobby. It highlights the intricacies of debating sex work policy in a federal system of government where power to make laws pertaining to sex work is delegated to regional governments. This chapter then charts neo-abolitionist activism across two key parliamentary inquiries that have influenced Australia's legislative responses to human trafficking, identifying the key assumptions embedded within this activism. Third, this chapter considers some of the reasons behind the failure of neo-abolitionist activism, despite the existence of some key intersections between neo-abolitionist ideology and the Australian government's current neo-liberal approaches to border security.

Sex work and human trafficking policy-making: state matters in federal forums

Australia is one of only a handful of nation-states that have legalised a range of sex work practices beyond those of sole operators. Responsibility for criminal law pertaining to sex work is retained by the state and territory governments of Australia,[1] and thus legislation differs from state to state. In the 1990s and early 2000s several states of Australia moved to liberalise sex work laws with Queensland, Victoria, and the Australian Capital Territory adopting a licensing system for brothels and escort agencies, while New South Wales adopted a decriminalisation approach[2]. While brothel work and solicitation remain illegal in several states of Australia, there has been considerable pressure recently to liberalise these laws, with the South Australian and Western Australian parliaments expected to consider bills to legalise or decriminalise sex work in the next few years (Al Jazeera 14 June 2015; ABC News 11 September 2014). This liberalisation has occurred primarily due to consensus support for harm minimisation (Weitzer 2009: 100), rather than overwhelming societal acceptance of sex work as a legitimate form of labour.

Advocates of the Nordic Model have been active in policy debate at the state level (CATWA 2015) but have not restricted their activism to political debate on sex work. While constitutional responsibility for sex work law rests with each regional government, neo-abolitionists have capitalised on the federal deliberations about human trafficking in seeking another avenue through which to lobby for the adoption of the Nordic Model. Anti-trafficking policy debates have thus become an important site of neo-abolitionist activism in Australia.

Australia's federalised political system has not only offered neo-abolitionist activists the opportunity to lobby several levels of government, it has also shaped the nature of neo-abolitionist activism in the nation's political debates. As activists have sought to critique sex work policy through anti-trafficking debates at the federal level, the first hurdle they confront arises from the question of whether or not the federal government is even empowered to implement the Nordic Model. This political question seems largely unresolved. In the past, the Australian parliament has cited the restriction on federal powers in dismissing the proposed Nordic Model (Parliament of Australia APJC Report 2004: 60). However, other nation-states faced with a similar restriction on federal powers have nevertheless managed to influence state policy on sex work. For instance, the United States of America imposed anti-trafficking legislation at the federal level that made grants available to state-based police services for increased raids on brothels (US Congress 2005). In the USA example, however, federal moves simply supported the enforcement of existing state policies criminalising sex work. Should the Australian Federal Government adopt the Nordic Model, it would produce a significant policy contradiction between the federal and state levels. This federal factor has not, however, diminished neo-abolitionism within Australian trafficking debates. Rather, it has simply required a strategic approach that both criticises the current state-based systems of legalised sex work and tries to persuade federal legislators of the efficacy of the Nordic Model in helping Australia to meet its international obligations to combat human trafficking.

Neo-abolitionist activism at the Australian parliamentary inquiries

Advocates of the neo-abolitionist perspective in Australia typically hail from two distinct camps. On the one hand, some religious or family groups decry sex work as immoral. On the other hand, some organisations identifying as feminist advocate the belief that sex work is the ultimate expression of men's power over women. While these feminist groups might reject the conservative values underpinning the neo-abolitionism of religious organisations, both advance the argument that in order to abolish sex trafficking, sex work must be abolished.

Neo-abolitionists have sought to influence Australian federal policy on sex work through two key federal parliamentary inquiries into human trafficking. Throughout these inquiries, neo-abolitionist calls for sex work to be abolished in order to combat sex trafficking rested upon two key assumptions: first, that sex work is indistinguishable from trafficking; and second, that legalisation of sex work creates the conditions for demand for sexual services to flourish, fuelling increased sex trafficking. Premised on these assumptions, neo-abolitionists in Australia have called for the introduction of the Swedish, or Nordic, Model that criminalises the purchaser of sexual services, while decriminalising the seller. In the following sections, the emergence of these two key assumptions during the Australian human trafficking inquiries is charted, examining first the Joint Parliamentary and Senate Committee Inquiries on Sexual Servitude held between 2003 and 2005, and then the 2012–2013 Inquiry on Human Trafficking and Forced Labour.

Inquiry into the Trafficking of Women for Sexual Servitude 2003–2005

The first major inquiry into human trafficking in Australia was the Australian Parliamentary Joint Committee (APJC) on the Australian Crime Commission Inquiry into the Trafficking of Women for Sexual Servitude commencing in 2003. This was supplemented by a Senate Legal and Constitutional Legislation Committee (LCLC) Inquiry in 2005 to review proposed new legislation developed following the 2003 inquiry. These initial inquiries focused on defining human trafficking and establishing legislation to meet Australia's obligations in ratifying the *United Nations Protocol to Prevent, Suppress and Punish Trafficking in Persons, Especially Women and Children.* The 2003 inquiry exclusively examined trafficking for sexual exploitation, offering some insight into the focus of policy and discourse at the time, where concern centred predominantly on women trafficked for sex. The centrality of the sex industry to concerns about human trafficking offered a tremendous opportunity for neo-abolitionists to push for the adoption of the Swedish Model (as it was then called) as a response to human trafficking for sexual exploitation.

During this 2003 phase of consultation and policy development by the Federal Government, some organisations sought to position sex work and sex trafficking as indistinguishable from each other. Where, in other industries, labour is typically characterised as 'forced', or 'free', neo-abolitionists argued that sex work is never 'free' labour, because the sex industry should never be considered as a legitimate labour industry. The argument that sex work is not legitimate labour was presented in a few different ways through the inquiries. The Australian Catholic Migrant and Refugee Office[3] relied on a conservative moral agenda, arguing that sexuality should not be reduced to a commodity. In their submission to the 2005 Senate Inquiry they quoted a letter from Pope John Paul II:

> The disturbing tendency to treat prostitution as a business or industry not only contributes to the trade in human beings, but is itself evidence of a growing tendency to detach freedom from the moral law and to reduce the rich mystery of human sexuality to a mere commodity.
>
> (Australian Catholic Migrant and Refugee Office, LCLC Submission 2005: 3)

Feminist neo-abolitionists also argued that there was an inherent difference between sexual labour and other forms of labour, resting on the assumption that it is impossible to consent to sex work. Considered inherently harmful, dehumanising, and oppressive to women (Barry 1995: 11), prostitution is characterised by neo-abolitionists as always coercive and always forced because one cannot freely consent to harm. This assumption was clearly evident during the initial Australian inquiries into human trafficking. First articulated by the Coalition Against Trafficking in Women Australia (CATWA)[4], neo-abolitionists declared the distinction between trafficking and sex work to be a 'false distinction' (CATWA Submission 2003: 5). They argued that:

> Trafficking is represented as requiring explicit force and lack of consent. Prostitution in which no force is obvious is considered to be 'free' and frequently represented as ordinary 'work' or even as the exercise of women's 'choice'. The creation of such a distinction suggests that there could be a form of prostitution that is not damaging to the women and young people involved.
>
> (CATWA Submission 2003: 6)

In addition to these arguments positioning sex work as inherently different to other forms of work, and therefore indistinguishable from sex trafficking, neo-abolitionists also argued that trafficking was fuelled by an existing sex industry in Australia. In particular, it was the legalised nature of the industry that was argued to contribute significantly to the exploitation of women through sex trafficking. Elizabeth Evatt, on behalf of the Australian Section of the International Commission of Jurists[5], tentatively suggested that legalisation may play a role in human trafficking. In her submission to the inquiry she stated that:

> While the decriminalisation of prostitution is not a direct cause of trafficking, it does appear that the relaxation of legal prohibitions may enable exploitation of trafficked women to occur, without undue interference by legal authorities.
>
> (Evatt APJC Submission 2003: 4)

Other groups were more explicit in their condemnation of legalised sex work as the cause of sex trafficking in Australia. The Catholic Women's League of Australia[6] argued that:

> Efforts to legalise prostitution must be understood as inhibitors to the prosecution of those running illegal brothels, and trafficking women. Providing a shield to pimps, traffickers and buyers to escape or lessen penalties, such legislation functions to perpetuate this vicious cycle.
>
> (Catholic Women's League of Australia, APJC Submission 2003: 2)

That legalised sex work would increase trafficking was not always the primary focus for organisations providing testimony to the initial parliamentary inquiries. In 2003 Project Respect[7] agreed that addressing demand was an 'absolutely fundamental issue' (Parliament of Australia, APJC Hearing 18 November 2003: 47). However, while most neo-abolitionist groups maintained that sex work was indistinguishable from sex trafficking, Project Respect discussed the complexities behind trafficking demand dynamics. Sheila Jeffreys, a prominent feminist neo-abolitionist and academic, gave testimony on behalf of CATWA to parliament arguing, 'Male buyers do not make a special demand for trafficked women to use; they simply demand to buy prostituted women' (Parliament of Australia, APJC Hearing, 19 November 2003: 56). By contrast, Kathleen Maltzahn of Project Respect questioned:

> why there is a demand for women who cannot refuse certain sexual acts, numbers of sexual acts, certain customers and sex without a condom. We have to start asking questions about what people are buying when they buy trafficked women.
>
> (Parliament of Australia, APJC Hearing, 18 November 2003: 47)

While both Project Respect and CATWA criticised existing systems of legalisation as playing some role in fuelling human trafficking, the evidence presented by Maltzahn suggests that there is a distinction to be drawn between demand for trafficked sexual services and demand for sexual services *per se*.

This is not a distinction that neo-abolitionists typically draw, arguing instead that all demand for sex work fuels the demand for trafficking. Several organisations proposed a solution to this problem – the criminalisation of demand.

The Swedish Model was first proposed during the 2003 parliamentary inquiry by CATWA and the Catholic Women's League of Australia. CATWA constructed the Swedish Model as the logical step to take, premised on the assumption that the demand for trafficking could not be separated from the demand for sexual services. In her testimony to the parliamentary hearing, Sheila Jeffreys laid out four recommendations that neo-abolitionists hoped legislators would follow:

> First, that Australia should ratify the 2000 protocol on trafficking; second, Australia should commit itself to fulfilling its commitments under article 9, which are towards ending the demand; third, Australian states and territories should be encouraged to look again at their policies of legalisation, which lead to huge increases in the legal and illegal sex industries and create the demand for trafficking; and fourth, the Swedish Model should be examined as a way forward for Australia.
>
> (Parliament of Australia, APJC Hearing, 18 November 2003: 57)

Despite calls by CATWA and the CWLA for the consideration of the Swedish Model, surprisingly little of the discussion during the 2003–2005 inquiries focused on regulatory systems of sex work and their relationship to sex trafficking. In a brief discussion at the public hearings about legal approaches to sex work, one committee member, Senator Duncan Kerr, responded negatively to advocacy for the Nordic Model from CATWA representative Sheila Jeffreys, declaring that:

> Our only response cannot be 'wind back the legalisation of prostitution'; we have to have a response that accepts that, at least in some Australian jurisdictions, there is going to be a regulated sector and an unregulated sector.
>
> (Parliament of Australia, APJC Hearing, 18 November 2003: 60)

This reluctance to consider the proposal was also evident in the final report from the 2003–2004 Committee Inquiry. While the committee acknowledged the proposal for Australia to take action to curb men's demand for sexual services, it ultimately dismissed it, declaring discussions about the legality of sex work to be:

> a somewhat broader (and older) debate, that the Committee does not intend to enter into and which is, in any case, beyond its terms of reference.
>
> (Parliament of Australia, APJC Report 2004: 60)

The second major inquiry into human trafficking was announced in 2012, nearly a decade after the first, with the intention of reviewing existing laws and examining possible initiatives to adopt in the fight against human trafficking. Having examined neo-abolitionist activism at the federal level between 2003 and 2005, I now turn to an examination of this most recent federal parliamentary inquiry.

Inquiry into Slavery, Slavery-like Conditions and People Trafficking 2012–2013

The Australian Joint Standing Committee (AJSC) on Foreign Affairs, Defence and Trade 'Inquiry into Slavery, Slavery-like Conditions and People Trafficking' moved away from an overt focus on merely trafficking for sexual exploitation and explored trafficking for all forms of labour. This inquiry expressly called for submissions with a focus on 'Australia's efforts to address people trafficking … ways to encourage international action' and 'international best practice to address all forms of slavery' (Parliament of Australia, AJSC Report 2013f: xi), with no specific mention of sex work or even sexual servitude within the terms of reference. Fuelled by increasing political attention towards border security in the context of a moral panic about irregular migration (Martin 2015), this inquiry demonstrated a shift towards locating human trafficking as a problem primarily associated with migration, implicitly de-prioritising the sex industry as the locus of the problem. Despite the broader focus of the second inquiry, an increased number of organisations lobbied for a neo-abolitionist approach to sex trafficking, calling for the adoption of the Nordic Model.

Nearly ten years after first giving evidence to the 2003 inquiry, CATWA submitted again to the 2012 inquiry the declaration that 'a false distinction has been created between those who supposedly travel to prostitution in Australia of their own free will, and those who are forced to do so' (CATWA Submission 19, 2012: 4). The framing of sex work as a form of violence against women, and therefore always illegitimate, was also put forward by religious organisations at the 2012 inquiry. Christian Faith and Freedom, an interdenominational NGO, declared in a submission to the 2012 inquiry that:

> The link between human trafficking and prostitution needs to be recognised, that prostitution is a manifestation of gender inequality, and a form of violence against women, with a need to move toward practical action to reduce the demand for prostituted women by criminalising the purchase of sex in Australia.
>
> (Christian Faith and Freedom, Submission 32, 2012: 32)

It is notable that, while from a religious organisation, the submission clearly adopts language typically associated with some feminist critiques of sex work. Traditionally, religious groups could be expected to condemn sex work as a threat to family values and sexual morality – a characterisation evident in the submission from the Catholic Migrant and Refugee Office during the 2003 inquiry. However, this submission from Christian Faith and Freedom clearly frames the issue as one of gender equality and violence. This adoption of feminist language is reflective of a convergence between Christian and radical feminist opposition to sex work that has been so successful in other countries in advancing a neo-abolitionist agenda (O'Brien, Hayes and Carpenter 2013: 46–48; Chuang 2010: 1665).

The characterisation of sex work as violence against women and a commodification of human sexuality underpins much of the neo-abolitionist activism in the Australian inquiries. This was not however an overt focus of most of the abolitionist organisations making submission to the hearings. Several groups echoed the comments of Christian Faith and Freedom and the Catholic Migrant and Refugee Office in declaring an undeniable link between sex work and sex trafficking. However, most submissions focused on a criticism of Australia's liberal laws in relation to sex work, rather than a detailed critique of the legitimacy of sex work *per se*.

Advocacy during the 2012 inquiry also mirrored neo-abolitionist arguments from the 2003 inquiry arguing that legalised sex work was responsible for fuelling human trafficking. The Australian Christian Lobby's[8] submission to the 2012 inquiry argued that:

> There is an undeniable connection between people trafficking and legalised prostitution. In addressing the broader issues of slavery, slavery like conditions, and people trafficking, consideration must be given to prostitution and sex trafficking.
>
> (Australian Christian Lobby, Submission 42, 2012: 3)

This 'connection' between legalised sex work and sex trafficking was characterised by neo-abolitionist activists as strongly causal. They argued that legalised sex work fuelled the trafficking of women to work in the sex industry. One organisation contributing to the 2012 inquiry referred to Australia as a 'welcoming environment' for traffickers (Collective Shout, Submission 5, 2012: 3). This argument was implicit in much of the neo-abolitionist advocacy at the 2003 inquiry, however during the 2012 inquiry it appeared in more detail. Neo-abolitionist activists argued that legalised sex work, and the 'welcoming environment' it created, was problematic firstly because it made Australia an attractive destination for trafficking due to a flourishing legal sex industry, and secondly because it led to increases in human trafficking.

The legalised sex industry was positioned not only as an inhibitor to prosecution, but also as an enticement to traffickers. Lyle Shelton from the Australian Christian Lobby told the hearing that 'Australia's culture of legal prostitution – that is, treating it like any other form of work – makes it easier for traffickers to lure women into sexual slavery in legal and illegal brothels here' (Parliament of Australia, 20 November 2012b: 36). Family Voice

Australia[9] declared that, 'The fact that prostitution is legal in parts of Australia is used by traffickers to help recruit women for sexual servitude' (Family Voice Australia, Submission 2, 2012: 2). Collective Shout[10] also attacked the liberalisation of sex work laws as a cause of human trafficking. It argued that:

> Australia is seen as an 'attractive' destination for pimps and traffickers because most of the country's sex industry operates free of government monitoring and intervention ... This kind of welcoming environment for sex industry businesses makes Australia an attractive target for sex industry investors, and therefore makes Asian women vulnerable to cross-border trafficking into Australia.
>
> (Collective Shout, Submission 5, 2012: 3)

Collective Shout makes its attack on the legalised sex industry very clear in recommending that the Australian government 'reframe its understanding of trafficking as a crime largely commissioned by the sex industry, and intrinsically intertwined with the business of prostitution' (Collective Shout, Submission 5, 2012: 3).

These neo-abolitionist arguments centre largely on the impact of the relaxation of regulations surrounding sex work. However, the target of greatest ire among neo-abolitionists during the inquiries was the role of legalisation of sex work in condoning and promoting the demand for sexual services. The Australian Christian Lobby summarised this argument most clearly in declaring that, 'legalised prostitution drives demand up, and in doing so increases the demand for trafficked women and women working in sexual slavery' (Australian Christian Lobby, Submission 42, 2012: 3). CATWA argued that without a market for sex work, there would be no trafficking in women for sex work. Meagan Tyler, representing CATWA at the parliamentary inquiry public hearing characterised trafficking as caused by a social acceptance of sex work. She declared that:

> The link that is now being shown by not only social analysts but also economists is one of demand: legalising prostitution expands the market for prostitution and also fosters the promotion of demand for prostituted women.
>
> (Parliament of Australia, AJSC Committee Hearing, 8 May 2013d: 41)

Family Voice Australia, Collective Shout, the Australian Christian Lobby and Christian Faith and Freedom joined CATWA in positioning the demand for sexual services, fuelled by a legalised industry, as the cause of sex trafficking. All of these groups advocated for the adoption of the Nordic Model in glowing terms telling of its great success in Europe. The Australian Christian Lobby claimed that the Model has 'been successful in decreasing the demand in Sweden for the purchase of sex by men, and it is unlikely that all of that demand has spilled over borders' (Australian Christian Lobby Submission 42, 2012: 3). Christian Faith and Freedom compared Sweden's law to the

German Prostitution Act legalising sex work, stating that, 'Sweden appears to be the only country in Europe where prostitution and sex trafficking has not increased' while 'The German Prostitution Act had failed to improve conditions for women in the prostitution industry' (Christian Faith and Freedom Submission 32, 2012: 30–31). While several organisations pointed to the alleged success of the Nordic Model in reducing sex trafficking, CATWA was the only organisation to elaborate on how the Nordic Model could work, arguing that:

> it addresses those in a more privileged position actually to change their circumstances and their behaviour. So it targets the buyers: the fact that they are then penalised in some way for engaging in buying people in prostitution; and then it does not target those most marginal who are mistreated.
> (Parliament of Australia, AJSC Committee Hearing, 8 May 2013d: 42)

During this inquiry, advocates of the Nordic Model attempted to link it closely with the inquiry's terms of reference. This may have been, by some, an attempt to overcome the declaration by the 2003–2004 Parliamentary Committee that discussion of legal approaches to sex work was beyond the scope of the initial inquiry. Several groups highlighted the Nordic Model as a 'best practice' approach, directly responding to the third item in the terms of reference for the committee 'To inquire into and report on … international best practice to address all forms of slavery, slavery-like conditions and people trafficking' (Parliament of Australia, AJSC Final Report 2013f: xi). Collective Shout described the Nordic Model as 'currently the world's best practice approach' (Collective Shout Submission 5, 2012: 5). Lyle Shelton of the Australian Christian Lobby explicitly linked the Nordic Model to the inquiry's terms of reference. During his witness statement he said, 'I just think that, to achieve the third dot point of your terms of reference, this very much has to be part of the solution' (Parliament of Australia, AJSC Committee Hearing, 20 November 2012b: 41). CATWA representative Meagan Tyler also told the 2012–2013 Parliamentary Inquiry that adopting the Nordic Model would meet Australia's international obligations under the Palermo Protocol. She said:

> It [the Nordic Model] addresses article 9 of the Palermo Protocol, which calls on states to discourage either through legislation or educative measures, social or cultural measures as well, to prohibit and discourage the demand that fosters exploitation that leads to trafficking.
> (Parliament of Australia, AJSC Committee Hearing, 8 May 2013d: 42)

In comparison to the initial parliamentary inquiries of 2003–2005, the discussion at the 2012–2013 Parliamentary Inquiry about the asserted link between legalised sex work and sex trafficking and the Nordic Model, was rather more extensive. This is likely a result of the increased number of neo-abolitionist organisations providing witness testimony at public hearings. However, despite the greater number of voices calling for consideration of the

Nordic Model, they appeared to gain very little traction with the committee members in persuading them of its efficacy. Advocates of the Nordic Model were extensively grilled about the evidence base behind it and their assertion that legalised sex work leads to increased sex trafficking. Committee member Phillip Ruddock MP said to Lyle Shelton of the Australian Christian Lobby:

> All I am asking for is the original research that proves the proposition. When somebody tells me that there is evidence that I can take as being credible, that if you legalise prostitution it makes sex slavery grow, I want to see the evidence.
>
> (Parliament of Australia, AJSC Committee Hearing, 20 November 2012b: 36)

It should be noted that the call to provide supporting evidence was not unique to neo-abolitionist advocates. Committee members expressed frustration throughout the hearings at the lack of reliable data from primary sources available for scrutiny. Seemingly unpersuaded by the evidence provided by neo-abolitionists in support of the Nordic Model, however, the Committee members also sought the views of other public hearing witnesses.

Objections to the Nordic Model were raised by other witnesses. Their criticisms centred on a lack of evidence, challenges to claims of the model's efficacy, and concerns about negative impacts on workers' and migrants' rights. The Law Council of Australia[11], World Vision Australia[12], Anti-Slavery Australia[13], and Scarlet Alliance[14] all indicated that they did not support the adoption of the Nordic Model. Fiona McLeod responded to questions from committee members about the Nordic Model indicating that the Law Council of Australia would have an objection to its adoption from a 'human rights perspective', and believed the evidence purported to show the Nordic Model's effectiveness was 'controversial' (Parliament of Australia, AJSC Committee Hearing, 20 November 2012b: 21). Laura Beacroft from the Australian Institute of Criminology also questioned the reliability of data that supposedly demonstrates a link between legalised sex work and trafficking (Parliament of Australia, AJSC Committee Hearing, 21 November 2012c: 19) and Jennifer Burn from Anti-Slavery Australia referred to research from the UN Special Rapporteur on trafficking which found 'no conclusive evidence that linked a legalised sex industry with trafficking of sex workers' (Parliament of Australia, AJSC Committee Hearing, 22 April 2013b: 31). Burn added, in response to questions about the Nordic Model, 'At this stage, there is not the evidence that says that such a scheme is effective' (Parliament of Australia, AJSC Committee Hearing 22 April 2013b: 31).

Jennifer Burn from Anti-Slavery Australia questioned whether or not the model had led to a wholesale reduction in sex work, or if perhaps there was merely a reduction in the visibility of sex work due to the legislation's focus on street-based sex work (Parliament of Australia, AJSC Committee Hearing, 22 April 2013b: 32). Melissa Stewart, giving testimony on behalf of World Vision, raised similar objections to those raised by the Law Council of Australia, stating:

> We are always concerned that any criminal justice approach takes a strong look at the impact and whether it has unintended consequence of pushing an industry farther underground in order to make people more vulnerable and victims less identifiable by law enforcement agencies.
>
> (Parliament of Australia, AJSC Committee Hearing, 20 November 2012b: 56)

Jules Kim, representing prominent Australian sex worker organisation the Scarlet Alliance, echoed this concern, declaring that 'criminalisation of our work, our clients and our workplaces makes us vulnerable to exploitation, reduces our choice and does not protect migrant sex workers' (Parliament of Australia, AJSC Committee Hearing, 23 April 2013c: 13).

Project Respect, an organisation that has criticised the legal sex industry in the past, put forward an alternative policy suggestion. They advocated for the introduction of 'an offence for the reckless purchase of sex services from trafficked individuals, to discourage the 'pull' end of the trafficking cycle' (Project Respect, Submission 38, 2012: 7). This proposal differs from the Nordic Model approach of criminalising the purchase of all sex services, and instead specifies that the purchase of trafficked sex services should be criminalised. In so doing, the buyer does not escape responsibility for their role in contributing to human trafficking, but a distinction is maintained between 'forced' and 'free' sexual services. Neo-abolitionist organisation CATWA vehemently rejected this proposal, declaring it to be 'manifestly ineffective' (CATWA Submission 19, 2012: 8).

Ultimately, legislators did not endorse either this suggestion, or the Nordic Model. Advocates for the Nordic Model came up against the same roadblock as that experienced by CATWA during the 2003 Parliamentary Inquiry. Resistance to the model from government members was articulated in terms of concerns about federal and state legislative powers, rather than questions concerning the effectiveness or consequences of the model. The fact that sex work was a state, not a federal issue, was raised several times during the inquiry. Senator Moore responded to neo-abolitionist advocacy by Christian Faith and Freedom, declaring that, ' … as you well know, prostitution law is a state issue' (Parliament of Australia, AJSC Committee Hearing, 20 November 2012b: 8). While Iain Anderson from the Attorney General's Department clearly indicated the Federal Government's reluctance to engage on a state matter. He said, in response to questioning concerning NGOs' access to brothels in Victoria, 'Just to note that regulation of the sex industry is a matter for the states and territories. I am loath to stray into an area that is primarily for them' (Parliament of Australia, AJSC Committee Hearing, 14 May 2013e: 4).

The limitation on federal powers was openly acknowledged by several neo-abolitionists. CATWA spoke of their work in trying to lobby state governments of Australia to adopt the Nordic Model (Parliament of Australia, AJSC Committee Hearing, 8 May 2013d: 44), while ACL representative Lyle Shelton told the inquiry that,

> We know this is a Commonwealth inquiry, but trafficking of women for sex cannot be considered without acknowledging the role that state governments play – again, perhaps unwittingly – in fostering demand.
>
> (Parliament of Australia, AJSC Committee Hearing, 20 November 2012b: 35)

Despite the acknowledgement by activists and statements by some committee members that regulation of the sex industry (and thus a decision on criminalisation of aspects of the industry) was a state matter, there was some acceptance of the Federal Government's ability to intervene on state matters, to a certain extent. Rebekah Kilpatrick, also from the Attorney General's Department, said, not in relation to the proposal of the Nordic Model, but in response to a request for NGO access to brothels, that:

> In terms of whether we could pursue it with the states, as part of the revised national action plan … we are also exploring ways to better engage with high-risk industries that are outside areas of typical Commonwealth concern, such as the sex industry.
>
> (Parliament of Australia, AJSC Committee Hearing, 14 May 2013e: 4)

This proposal from the Attorney General's Office is reflected in the National Action Plan on Human Trafficking adopted in December 2014. However, the extent to which the Federal Government has attempted to influence sex work policy at the state level is limited, with the plan declaring an intent to strengthen 'the connectedness of the Australian Government response with States and Territories' through unspecified increased cooperation (National Action Plan 2014: 21). This falls well short of any attempt by the Federal Government to impose a particular policy agenda on state governments in relation to sex work.

One committee member seemingly offered an alternative window of opportunity for advocates of the Nordic Model to pursue a neo-abolitionist agenda at the federal level. Phillip Ruddock asked witnesses, more than once during the hearings, if Australia's international obligations under treaties and conventions might provide some legal route through which the Federal Government could influence state legislation in relation to sex work. In questioning representatives from Christian Faith and Freedom, he asked:

> It seems to me that you are arguing that we should assert that there is a Commonwealth power to legislate to make unlawful the use of prostitutes in Australia and abroad, based upon the Swedish Model. Where do you believe we have that power? Is it derived from some international treaties? Which treaties? If we are to recommend what you seem to be suggesting, that the use of prostitutes be made unlawful here and abroad [sic].
>
> (Parliament of Australia, AJSC Committee Hearing, 20 November 2012b: 7)

Ruddock reiterated this query to representatives from the Law Council of Australia, and the Australian Christian Lobby (Parliament of Australia, AJSC Committee Hearing 20 November 2012b: 21 and 41). None of the witnesses questioned were able to provide a definitive response to Ruddock's request for an avenue through which the federal government could influence state policy. However, during Ruddock's exchange with Lyle Shelton of the ACL, the Parliamentary Committee Chair Melissa Parke MP interjected:

> CHAIR: There is a UN Convention against Transnational Organized Crime with a Protocol on Trafficking in Persons, especially Women and Children.
> RUDDOCK: There you are, you see!
> SHELTON: We will leave that to the wisdom of the committee, but I am sure that the committee would be able to find a way.
>
> (Parliament of Australia, AJSC Committee Hearing, 20 November 2012b: 41)

In the final report from the committee, however, the members offered no indication of an intention to stretch Commonwealth powers to intervene in state matters, or to even recommend adoption of the Nordic Model by state governments of Australia. The final report emerging from the 2012 Parliamentary Inquiry acknowledged the submissions and witnesses calling for the adoption of the Nordic Model, as well as those who criticised it, in the section considering 'community perceptions on international best practice' (Parliament of Australia, AJSC Report 2013f: 95–97). However, the committee made no direct comment or recommendation in relation to the Nordic Model whatsoever. This dismissal by omission is likely borne out of more than simply a limitation of federal powers in relation to sex work law. In other sections of the report, the committee indicated an inclination to view trafficking into the sex industry alongside trafficking for other forms of labour (Parliament of Australia, AJSC Report 2013f). The section of the report concerning definitions of trafficking makes no specific mention of trafficking for sex work, reflecting the overall approach of the second parliamentary inquiry in moving on from the first inquiry's almost exclusive focus on trafficking for sexual exploitation.

Obstacles to neo-abolitionism in Australia

Australian policy-makers are showing clear signs of moving beyond an overt focus on the sex industry and disputes concerning the legitimacy of sex work. These two factors, alongside the limited remit of the Federal Government to make laws pertaining to sex work (discussed in detail earlier), are key reasons why neo-abolitionist activism has thus far failed to resonate with human trafficking policy-makers. This section explores these two key factors, then considers the conflicts and intersections between neo-abolitionism and the Australian government's neo-liberal approach to migration.

Neo-abolitionist advocacy at the 2003–2005 and 2012–2013 inquiries demonstrates a clear strategic approach to not only challenge the legitimacy of sex work as a form of labour, but also to critique Australia's existing sex work laws, characterising them as directly causative of human trafficking. In countries where sex work is illegal, the Nordic Model offers a multi-faceted approach of decriminalising sex workers, while criminalising buyers. On face value, it demonstrates an understanding of the legal vulnerability of sex workers and the need to afford them some protections, while at the same time maintaining a condemnation of sex work. This contrasts with the Australian context where the need to provide legal protection to sex workers has already been recognised and legislated for, to an extent, through legalisation and decriminalisation models. The task of neo-abolitionist advocates in Australia is thus distinct to the task of neo-abolitionists in North America and most states of Western Europe where legislators are yet to make the symbolic shift from criminalised prostitution to legalised sex work.

Despite this strategic approach, neo-abolitionists were pushing against the trend not only in relation to sex work laws, but also discourse on trafficking more generally. There is a clear trend in Australian policy-making towards viewing sex trafficking alongside, rather than distinct from, trafficking for other forms of labour. The exclusive focus of the 2003 inquiry on trafficking for sexual servitude likely offered the best window of opportunity for policy responses that are unique to sex trafficking, such as the Nordic Model, to have salience with decision-makers. The expansion of the terms of reference of the 2012 inquiry, which sought responses to addressing trafficking for labour more generally, perhaps resulted in a narrowing of the policy window for neo-abolitionism.

The failure of neo-abolitionists to persuade decision-makers to adopt an anti-sex work agenda could perhaps also be explained by contrasting ideologies. Some have argued that the legalisation of sex work in Australia reflects a neo-liberal approach where individual choice, especially consumer choice is paramount (Carson and Edwards 2011: 79). This contrasts sharply with the 'protectionist' approach adopted by Sweden in enacting a model that criminalises clients in an effort to protect women harmed by the sex industry (Carson and Edwards 2011: 86). However, a neo-liberal political ideology manifests differently when it comes to migration policy. Free markets are encouraged, but free movement of people is not. In the intersection between debates on trafficking and debates on migration, the choices of people to migrate for work are questioned and demonised, rather than exalted. In this intersection, neo-abolitionist activism is not entirely inconsistent with current federal government approaches to human trafficking.

In the construction of victims, neo-abolitionism describes a victim that is completely passive, lacking in agency. Even those women who claim to have consented to sex work are stripped of their capacity to consent within the neo-abolitionist ideology. This understanding of victims intersects with government responses to human trafficking and border security. During the 2012

Parliamentary Inquiry much of the discussion at the hearings centred on the requirement for victims of trafficking to assist with prosecutions of traffickers in order to secure a protection visa (Parliament of Australia, APSC Hearings 19 October 2012a: 18–19, 19 March 2013a: 1–2; 22 April 2013b: 1–2). This assumption is premised on a characterisation of victims of trafficking that is subscribed to by neo-abolitionists whereby victims are always harmed by their experiences. The corresponding assumption is that they should therefore always be inclined to seek retribution against their exploiter. This simplistic construction of victims overlooks a wider range of experiences of people who may view the person who brought them to Australia as a 'facilitator', not a trafficker.

The victim lacking in all choice and agency reflects the binary thinking that dominates government responses to irregular migration, distorting the true nature of much irregular migration as existing on a complex continuum (Kelly 2002: 14). The neo-abolitionist emphasis on the impossibility of choice for all women involved in sex work perpetuates the government's delineation between victims lacking in choice and criminals exercising choice. When it comes to border security, the dominant Australian political rhetoric condemns and criminalises asylum seekers for making a choice to get on a boat (Grewcock 2009; Rowe and O'Brien 2014), while showing compassion to those assumed to have had all choice stripped away. The central element of choice in this construction categorises irregular migrants as victim or criminal. In the characterisation of all migrant women in sex work as automatically victimised, neo-abolitionism erases the category of migrant women making choices to travel for work, and justifies border control policies that prevent women from travelling as a protective measure. Neo-abolitionist ideology thus has the unintended consequence of supporting a problematic governmental agenda of creating strict categories of migrant in order to exclude, rather than include.

Conclusion

For more than a decade neo-abolitionists have lobbied the Australian Federal Government to consider the Nordic Model as an anti-trafficking tool. This activism has been consistent with neo-abolitionist activism around the world in putting forward central assumptions that view sex trafficking as a unique problem distinct from trafficking for other forms of labour, and asserts a causal relationship between legalised sex work and sex trafficking. In Australia, the trend towards legalising or decriminalising sex work by several regional governments has put neo-abolitionist activists in the unique position of calling for a winding back of laws that have already made the symbolic shift from criminalisation to legalisation. This, alongside the limited remit of the Federal Government to intervene on sex work policy, has hindered neo-abolitionists in their attempts to persuade decision-makers to adopt the Nordic Model. Despite an ideological intersection between the radical feminist approach to sex trafficking, and neo-liberal approaches to border security, neo-abolitionists may struggle to remain relevant in the federal debate. The conversation on human trafficking in Australia is moving on from an overt focus on the sex industry to a consideration of trafficking within a broader frame of forced labour in a range of industries.

Notes

1 Australia has a federal system of government, with six state governments and two territory governments forming as the Commonwealth of Australia. There are some constitutional differences between the states and territories in relation to the autonomy they have over political decision-making, however all states and territories have the remit to determine policy on sex work within their borders.
2 Queensland, Victoria, and the Australian Capital Territory have legalised sex work to include licensed or registered brothels and private workers. In New South Wales sex work is decriminalised, allowing for street based sex work in designated areas, brothels, escort agencies and private workers. In the Northern Territory escort agencies are licensed, and private workers may operate without a license. In South Australia and Western Australia brothels and solicitation remain illegal, and in Tasmania brothels are also criminalised, however self-employed workers may operate legally (Quadara 2008, 1–17).
3 A non-government organisation established by the Australian Catholic Bishops' Conference www.acmro.catholic.org.au.
4 The Australian branch of the feminist international anti-trafficking non-government organisation the Coalition Against Trafficking in Women www.catwa.org.au.
5 A non-government organisation devoted to utilising the legal system to promote human rights www.icj-aust.org.au.
6 The Catholic Women's League of Australia is a peak body representing non-government organisations of Catholic women in Australia. A peak organisation or peak body is an Australian term for an advocacy group or trade association, an association of industries or groups with allied interests.
7 An Australian non-government feminist organisation providing services for women experiencing violence and exploitation in the sex industry www.projectrespect.org.au.
8 One of the most prominent political action groups lobbying for the inclusion of Christian values in policy-making in Australia www.acl.org.au.
9 A Christian non-government political lobbying organisation www.fava.org.au.
10 An Australian non-government campaigning group opposed to the sexualisation and objectification of women www.collectiveshout.org.
11 The peak body representing legal practitioners in Australia www.lawcouncil.asn.au.
12 The Australian branch of the international non-government organisation World Vision www.worldvision.com.au.
13 A research and policy group within the Faculty of Law at the University of Technology Sydney www.antislavery.org.au.
14 The peak body representing sex workers and sex workers organisations in Australia www.scarletalliance.org.au.

References

ABC News (2014) 'WA Prostitution Laws Still on the Agenda, Despite Opposition from Liberal MPs', *ABC News*, 11 September. Available at: www.abc.net.au/news/2014-09-11/wa-government-still-plans-to-introduce-prostitution-laws/5736518. Accessed 14 July 2015.

Al Jazeera (2015) 'Australia: the Fight to Decriminalize Prostitution', *Al Jazeera*, 14 June. Available at: www.aljazeera.com/indepth/features/2015/06/australia-fight-decriminalise-prostitution-150614062103562.html. Accessed 14 July 2015.

Australian Catholic and Migrant Refugee Office (2005) *Submission to the Senate Legal and Constitutional Legislation Committee Inquiry on the Criminal Code Amendment (Trafficking in Persons Offences) Bill 2004.*

Australian Christian Lobby (2012) *Submission 42, Parliamentary Standing Committee Inquiry into Slavery, Slavery-like conditions and People Trafficking.*

Barry, K. (1995) *The Prostitution of Sexuality.* New York: New York University Press.

Carson, L. and Edwards, K. (2011) 'Prostitution and Sex Trafficking: What are the Problems Represented to Be? A Discursive Analysis of Law and Policy in Sweden and Victoria, Australia', *Australian Feminist Law Journal*, 34: 63–87.

Catholic Women's League Australia (2003) *Submission 20, Parliamentary Joint Committee on the Australian Crime Commission Inquiry into the Trafficking of Women for Sexual Servitude.*

CATWA (2015) 'Submissions', *Coalition Against Trafficking in Women Australia.* www.catwa.org.au/?q=submissions. Accessed 21 July 2015.

CATWA (2012) *Submission 19, Parliamentary Standing Committee Inquiry into Slavery, Slavery-like conditions and People Trafficking.*

CATWA (2005) *Submission to the Senate Legal and Constitutional Legislation Committee Inquiry on the Criminal Code Amendment (Trafficking in Persons Offences) Bill 2004.*

CATWA (2003) *Submission 39, Parliamentary Joint Committee on the Australian Crime Commission Inquiry into the Trafficking of Women for Sexual Servitude.*

Christian Faith and Freedom (2012) *Submission 32, Parliamentary Standing Committee Inquiry into Slavery, Slavery-like conditions and People Trafficking.*

Chuang, J. (2010) 'Rescuing Trafficking from Ideological Capture: Prostitution Reform and Anti-Trafficking Law and Policy', *University of Pennsylvania Law Review*, 158(6): 1655–1728.

Collective Shout (2012) *Submission 5, Parliamentary Standing Committee Inquiry into Slavery, Slavery-like conditions and People Trafficking.*

Evatt, E. (2003) Australian Section of the International Commission of Jurists. *Submission 8, Parliamentary Joint Committee on the Australian Crime Commission Inquiry into the Trafficking of Women for Sexual Servitude.*

Family Voice Australia (2012) *Submission 2, Parliamentary Standing Committee Inquiry into Slavery, Slavery-like conditions and People Trafficking.*

Grewcock, M. (2009) *Border Crimes: Australia's War on Illicit Migrants.* Sydney: Institute of Criminology Press.

Kelly, L. (2002) 'Journeys of Jeopardy: A Review of Research on Trafficking in Women and Children in Europe', *IOM Migration Research Series.* No. 11.

Martin, G. (2015). 'Stop the boats! Moral panic in Australia over Asylum Seekers', *Continuum: Journal of Media and Cultural Studies*, 29(3): 304–322.

National Action Plan (2014) National Action Plan to Combat Human Trafficking and Slavery2015–2019, Commonwealth of Australia. Available at: www.ag.gov.au/CrimeAndCorruption/HumanTrafficking/Documents/Trafficking-NationalActionPlanToCombatHumanTraffickingAndSlavery2015-19.pdf.

O'Brien, E., Hayes, S., and Carpenter, B. (2013) *The Politics of Sex Trafficking: A Moral Geography.* Basingstoke: Palgrave Macmillan.

Parliament of Australia (2005) House of Representatives, *Official Hansard*, 21 and 24 June.

Parliament of Australia (2004) Parliamentary Joint Committee on the Australian Crime Commission. *Inquiry into the Trafficking of Women for Sexual Servitude: Final Report*. The Parliament of Australia, June.

Parliament of Australia (2003) Australian Parliamentary Joint Committee on the Australian Crime Commission. *Inquiry into the Trafficking of Women for Sexual Servitude: Public Hearing Transcript*. The Parliament of Australia, 18–19 November.

Parliament of Australia (2013a) Parliamentary Standing Committee *Inquiry into Slavery, Slavery-like conditions, and People Trafficking: Public Hearing Transcript*. The Parliament of Australia, 19 March.

Parliament of Australia (2013b) Parliamentary Standing Committee *Inquiry into Slavery, Slavery-like conditions, and People Trafficking: Public Hearing Transcript*. The Parliament of Australia, 22 April.

Parliament of Australia (2013c) Parliamentary Standing Committee *Inquiry into Slavery, Slavery-like conditions, and People Trafficking: Public Hearing Transcript*. The Parliament of Australia, 23 April.

Parliament of Australia (2013d) Parliamentary Standing Committee *Inquiry into Slavery, Slavery-like conditions, and People Trafficking: Public Hearing Transcript*. The Parliament of Australia, 8 May.

Parliament of Australia (2013e) Parliamentary Standing Committee *Inquiry into Slavery, Slavery-like conditions, and People Trafficking: Public Hearing Transcript*. The Parliament of Australia, 14 May.

Parliament of Australia (2013f) *Trading Lives: Modern Day Human Trafficking: Inquiry of the Human Rights Sub-Committee*. June 2013. Australian Parliamentary Joint Standing Committee (APSC) on Foreign Affairs, Defence and Trade: Canberra.

Parliament of Australia (2012a) Parliamentary Standing Committee *Inquiry into Slavery, Slavery-like conditions, and People Trafficking: Public Hearing Transcript*. The Parliament of Australia, 19 October.

Parliament of Australia (2012b) Parliamentary Standing Committee *Inquiry into Slavery, Slavery-like conditions, and People Trafficking: Public Hearing Transcript*. The Parliament of Australia, 20 November.

Parliament of Australia (2012c) Parliamentary Standing Committee *Inquiry into Slavery, Slavery-like conditions, and People Trafficking: Public Hearing Transcript*. The Parliament of Australia, 21 November.

Project Respect (2012) *Submission 38, Parliamentary Standing Committee Inquiry into Slavery, Slavery-like conditions and People Trafficking*.

Project Respect (2003) *Submission 25, Parliamentary Joint Committee on the Australian Crime Commission Inquiry into the Trafficking of Women for Sexual Servitude*.

Quadara, A. (2008) "Sex Workers and Sexual Assault in Australia: Prevalence, Risk and Safety', *ACSSA Issues 8*. Melbourne: Australian Institute of Family Studies.

Rowe, E. and O'Brien, E. (2014) '"Genuine" Refugees or Illegitimate "Boat People": Political Constructions of Asylum Seekers and Refugees in the Malaysia Deal Debate', *Australian Journal of Social Issues*, 49(2): 171–193.

Skilbrei, M.-L. and Holmström, C. (2011) 'Is There a Nordic Prostitution Regime?', *Crime and Justice*, 40(1): 479–517.

US Congress (2005) *Trafficking Victims Protection Reauthorization Act of 2005*.

Weitzer, R. (2009) 'Legalizing Prostitution: Morality Politics in Western Australia', *British Journal of Criminology*, 49(1): 88–105.

8 In search of a fair and free society

The regulation of sex work in New Zealand

Gillian Abel

Introduction

> Commitment to human rights for all citizens is of great importance in New Zealand. The country has fought hard for human rights and now it works to keep them.
>
> (Barnett, Healy *et al.* 2010: 71)

Sex workers in New Zealand (NZ) fought a long battle for human rights and in 2003 they achieved this when the Prostitution Reform Act (PRA) was passed. Getting decriminalisation of sex work on the agenda has been problematic in the global context, given the growing dominance of a neo-abolitionist discourse which equates prostitution with trafficking. To the rest of the world, it seemed somewhat surprising that this discourse was muted in NZ. New Zealanders have traditionally been 'wired' by a cultural preoccupation with fairness and the need for everyone to be able to have a 'fair go' (Bromell 2014). In an interesting comparison of the history of NZ and the United States of America, Fischer (2012) wrote, amongst other things, of the issue of women's rights. Whilst women's rights campaigners in the USA concentrated on liberty and freedom in their search for equality, in NZ social and political justice and notions of fairness were the key messages that resonated. This difference was not only pertinent to women's rights, but to all societal issues. He suggested that this difference came about because of the different ways in which these countries were occupied. Whilst the USA was settled in the seventeenth century by people who considered themselves to be victims of tyranny and persecution, NZ was occupied in the nineteenth century by people who felt themselves to be victims of social injustice and inequity (Bromell 2014). Consequently, while people in the USA fought for the principle of liberty and freedom from oppression, those in NZ were more focused on the principle of fairness and equity. Could it be that the cultural context of fairness in NZ silenced the neo-abolitionist voice?

It is in the context of social and political justice that Tim Barnett, a Labour Party Member of Parliament (MP) introduced the Prostitution Reform Bill to the NZ Parliament in September 2000. The architect of this Bill was the New

Zealand Prostitutes' Collective (NZPC), a sex workers' rights organisation founded in 1987. The Bill proposed the scrapping of all laws which regulated sex work activities, paving the way for a decriminalised sex industry in NZ. The stated aim of the Bill was to decriminalise prostitution and in so doing:

- safeguard the human rights of sex workers and protect them from exploitation;
- promote the welfare and occupational health and safety of sex workers;
- create an environment which is conducive to public health;
- protect children from exploitation in relation to prostitution.

Sex work is a contentious issue and neither of the main political parties (Labour and National) in NZ would have been prepared to introduce decriminalisation as a party initiative. Instead, it entered parliament as a Private Member's Bill and it was left up to individual MPs to vote according to their consciences. This meant that lobbying was almost solely confined to this population. There were no public debates on this issue, no rallies and no public referendum. The public were able to have their say through submissions to the Justice and Electoral Committee of the NZ Parliament, but ultimately the decision to decriminalise sex work was left to MPs. In June 2003, following the final reading of the Bill, 60 MPs voted for decriminalisation with 59 against and one MP abstaining.[1]

The principle of fairness set the scene for the introduction of the Bill to parliament but as will be argued in this chapter, it was not enough to sustain its passage through the three readings. Freedom had to also take the stage. But this was not freedom in the sense of 'freedom from oppression' rather it was freedom of choice and freedom to be able to have a 'fair go'. There remain questions as to how the dominant abolitionist voice of 'freedom from oppression' was seemingly absent when it enjoys so much power in other Western countries. What makes NZ different? An analysis of the debate that took place in parliament on the Bill seems a useful place to start to address this question.

To analyse any public policy one needs to first make the 'problem' explicit before scrutinising it. Bacchi (2009) maintains that 'problems' are created within the policy-making process and that therefore 'problems' can be seen as shaped by policies not addressed by them. She poses six questions which need to be addressed when analysing any 'problem':

- What is the 'problem' represented to be?
- What are the assumptions underlying the representation of the 'problem'?
- How has the 'problem' come to be represented in this way?
- Can this 'problem' be thought about any differently?
- What effects do the representation of the 'problem' produce?
- How or where has the representation of the 'problem' been produced, disseminated and defended?

Carson and Edwards (2011) utilised Bacchi's framework to analyse sex work policy in Sweden and Victoria, Australia, with a particular focus on the 'demand side' of sex work and its relationship to sex trafficking. They suggested that this provided a systematic way of unpacking the main issues at play. This paper takes up this suggestion, but does not seek to make comparisons with any other mode of regulation of sex work. What it does provide is some insight into the arguments that framed sex work in NZ as an occupation of choice and not a symbol of oppression. In the remainder of this chapter, I will use Bacchi's six questions to analyse the debates on the Bill between October 2000 and June 2003.

Before embarking on the analysis, it is necessary to situate myself in the debate about the regulation of sex work as the lens I bring to the analysis cannot be value-free. My position on sex work is grounded in my commitment to public health principles of social justice. Much of the public health emphasis in the past has been on minimising harm, and this drive has been behind the calls for decriminalisation of sex work. But more and more, public health is acknowledging the human rights issues associated with criminalising people who, of their own volition, work in the sex industry. Human rights are essential to addressing underlying determinants of health (World Health Organization 2007) and this is the focus of public health. Any response to sex work should begin with the perspectives of those who work in this industry and all should take a collective responsibility in intervening through harm minimisation practices and policies (O'Neill 2001; Beyrer, Crago *et al.* 2014). Decriminalisation of sex work is an example of effective public health policy which was developed collaboratively in New Zealand (Abel, Fitzgerald *et al.* 2010). The public health philosophy of harm minimisation and human rights were at the heart of this regulatory change. I use the terms 'sex work' and 'prostitution' interchangeably in this chapter depending on the theoretical context of the argument.

What's the problem represented to be?

The Bill was drafted by NZPC, with the help of lawyers, academics and others, to 'meet the needs of sex workers' (Barnett, Healy *et al.* 2010: 62) and protect their wellbeing (Harrington 2012). It accepted sex work as an occupational choice and that the laws criminalising sex work activities denied sex workers' human rights and placed them at risk of harm. In analysing the intentions of the Bill (stated in the introduction), it is evident that the assumptions were that the old law did not give sex workers the right to refuse to provide any commercial service as they were susceptible to coercion by others, such as brothel operators or clients; did not provide sex workers with employment protections which were afforded to workers in other occupations; did not encourage safer sex practices; and did not protect children (under the age of 18) from enticement into the sex industry. The implication was that these risks would be minimised by new legislation that provided rights to sex workers and saw them engaged in recognised, legal work. Clients were depicted as a problem only insofar as they could coerce or exploit sex workers working in the context of the then current legislative environment.

What assumptions underlie the representation of the problem?

The assumptions underlying the position that criminalisation of sex work activities created risks and denied human rights was driven from a combination of a sex worker rights and public health perspective. Sex work research carried out in NZ has mostly been participatory, 'by and for' sex workers, and Harrington (2012) has suggested that this has produced knowledge which has given sex workers a voice in policy. She argues that politicians, policy-makers and academics have not problematised male commercial sex conduct and have failed to critique the commercialisation of sex and to a large extent this is correct. As far back as the early 1990s, NZPC had developed links with public health academics and several research projects were undertaken using a community-based participatory approach. Whilst most research looked at the health and safety of sex workers in a criminalised environment (Chetwynd 1992, Chetwynd 1996, Plumridge and Abel 2000, Plumridge 2001, Plumridge and Abel 2001), some small pieces of research were conducted with clients and findings did position them as being relatively benign (Chetwynd and Plumridge 1993, Chetwynd and Plumridge 1994, Plumridge, Chetwynd *et al.* 1996, Plumridge, Chetwynd *et al.* 1997a,Plumridge, Chetwynd *et al.* 1997b). This was echoed by most participants in the research carried out in NZ who, while able to cite at least some unpleasant experiences with clients, did on the whole say that they liked their clients and enjoyed contact with them (Plumridge and Abel 2000, Abel 2010). The research provided evidence that criminalisation created a barrier to a safe sex industry and Barnett drew on this in constructing his speeches over the three parliamentary readings. They were thus very much focused on public health issues of social justice and harm minimisation.

When Barnett introduced the Bill in its first reading in October 2000, the focus was almost entirely on social justice as he emphasised the 'genuine' and 'real' injustices in the law:

> I do not stand alone and my cause is driven by a passion born of injustice. This bill replaces moralistic law with fair law … .The injustices in the present law are plain and predictable, and they are real. The last 5 years have seen 410 people convicted, countless hours of police time engaged on essentially moral and unproductive crusades, and genuine criminality hidden from view by the secrecy and mystery generated by current prostitution law. Reforming this law can be seen as cleansing the stables of a century of accumulated mess, removing the layers of Victorian hypocrisy, scraping off the abuse of sex workers sanctioned by our current prostitution laws, washing away the public health dangers generated by criminalisation of the oldest profession, and replacing the stench

of stigma affecting sex workers because of the position the law puts them in. Members may disagree with me about how best to clean the stables, where to start, and how best to remove the stains. Would anybody in this House really try to claim that the stable was not filthy in the first place? If any member thinks that prostitution law needs a clean-up, then support for this bill is our only option … . The issues raised by this bill may be difficult, but they should not be seen by anyone in this House as threatening. They are lifeblood concerns for some people in our community. It is absolutely right and proper for this Parliament to address them.

(Prostitution Reform Bill, First Reading, 11 October 2000)

Barnett urged MPs to purge the old laws that criminalised sex work activities and made for an unsafe sex industry, to make way for more modern, liberal and 'fair law'. He challenged MPs to disagree that the law was the 'problem' and none rose to refute this. The moralistic, outdated laws, he claimed, made the industry an unsafe and unjust one and a public health danger. He and the supporters of the Bill referred to this 'bad law' as being Victorian. The linking of the law to Victorian times was also reinforced by the analogy Barnett provided in his first speech, likening the cleaning up of the law to the cleaning of stables. Metaphors are frequently used, particularly in media reporting, to signify that sex work is dirty, wrong and evil (Stenvoll 2002, O'Neill and Campbell 2006). It was interesting in this case, that Barnett had turned this on its head. Although he was reinforcing the 'dirty' nature of sex work, he laid the blame for this on the law and not the work itself. The tone of the speech evoked images of the public health sanitary movement in Victorian England – ridding the towns of sewage, rotting garbage and miasmas in an effort to combat diseases. This provided a good springboard for his later public health arguments of harm minimisation.

Ten MPs addressed parliament following Barnett's opening address: six spoke for the Bill (five of whom were women) and four against (all men). Those supporting decriminalisation followed Barnett's lead in highlighting the injustices and inequities caused by the existing legislation, as is evident in the following examples:

the objections I have heard do not hold weight against the basic injustice that is written into our laws.

(Liz Gordon, Alliance Party, Prostitution Reform Bill, First Reading, 11 October 2000)

Our current laws are unworkable and just plain discriminatory. They stigmatise and punish mostly the female workforce. … They (sex workers) can suffer arbitrary and unfair work rules.

(Anne Tolley, National Party – Women's Affairs spokesperson, Prostitution Reform Bill, First Reading, 8 November 2000)

> I look forward to the day when women and men in this country will no longer be persecuted because of out-dated and inequitable laws.
>
> (Sue Bradford, Green Party, Prostitution Reform Bill, First Reading, 8 November 2000)

Although social justice percolated under the surface in the second and third readings of the Bill, what came to the foreground was a discourse which had more emphasis on law which protected and minimised risks; a discourse that freed sex workers from the harms they incurred through the old law. It was not that the pro-decriminalisation MPs had changed their minds on 'fair law' but that they perceived that harm minimisation was more marketable than human rights. Indeed, Barnett reflected that some MPs who had a personal antipathy towards sex work were persuaded to vote for decriminalisation by the harm minimisation argument (Barnett, Healy *et al.* 2010).

How did the 'problem' come to be represented in this way?

The turn to a harm minimisation argument came about after the first reading when the Bill was sent to the Justice and Electoral Committee. The committee considered 222 submissions from individuals and organisations, debated amongst themselves and then made amendments directly addressing 'potential harm and risks unique to prostitution' (Tim Barnett, Labour Party, Prostitution Reform Bill, Third Reading, 25 June 2003). They presented the current law as untenable in that it inflated risks and identified what risks could be dealt with by law and what risks needed special prostitution-focused law. Social justice was very much a secondary issue.

The main arguments of those MPs against decriminalisation were that prostitution was morally corrupt, unhealthy and harmful and if it was decriminalised it would encourage more people into the industry, there would be more crime, more drugs, more gangs, more trafficking and more underage workers. These arguments were rebuffed well by the harm minimisation rhetoric in the second and third readings where the focus was on individual freedom and choice. Barnett reminded MPs of the arguments made against other law changes in the past, such as homosexual law reform and the implementation of a needle exchange system, which had, 'not led to disaster. Indeed, those measures and others have led to more complete less risky lives and have enhanced their individual freedom. The Prostitution Reform Bill does just that'. (Barnett, Prostitution Reform Bill, Second Reading, 19 February 2003). The pragmatic public health argument that 'prostitution is here to stay' and therefore there is a need to 'work out the best way of controlling these harms' was Barnett's strong drive-home message in his final reading of the Bill:

> It (the Bill) is a decriminalisation measure, similar to our whole family of public health-related laws. It does not seek to label prostitution as

> normal, but it does accept its inevitability. … . Having accepted that prostitution is here to stay, like it or not, the next thing is to identify what problems it generates … . The next stage is to work out the best ways of controlling those harms. That is harm minimisation.
>
> (Prostitution reform Bill, Third Reading, 25 June 2003)

There were fewer speakers who rose to speak for the Bill (four) than those who spoke against (13) in the final debate. Sue Bradford (Green Party) spoke for the Bill in all three readings and her discourse like Barnett's had evolved. She cited respected organisations like the World Health Organization and the United Nations Children's Fund who supported decriminalisation, 'because they know that restrictive laws merely encourage violence, trafficking, rape, and the spread of HIV/AIDS – not the opposite. The way to combat these things is through the harm minimisation approach promoted in the bill before us today' (Prostitution Reform Bill, Third Reading, 25 June 2003).

She returned briefly to a focus on human rights and social justice by appealing to other women in parliament to vote for the right of women to choose to work in the sex industry and to end the state of affairs that disempowered women in sex work. She then merged this with a harm discourse by arguing for promotion of the rights and wellbeing of vulnerable and exploited groups, claiming that 'a harm to one is a harm to all. Until that harm is removed, none of us can be truly free' (Prostitution Reform Bill, Third Reading, 25 June 2003).

Can the problem be thought about differently?

The focus on harm minimisation left gendered power unexplored in the debate. Radical feminists have highlighted inequalities in prostitution. The buying of sex is seen as violence against women and represents male privilege and power (Scoular 2004). Women are mere sexual objects to be bought and sold in a practice of sexual slavery (Jeffreys 1997). This has fuelled the argument that all women involved in prostitution are trafficked and there is little regard given to women's agency and alternative stories of the women involved (Scoular 2004). Other feminists do not see sex work as inherently oppressive and acknowledge women's agency, albeit that in some cases agency is constrained (O'Neill 2001). It is the latter liberal feminist perspective that features more strongly in New Zealand.

Fifty-six of the public submissions to the Justice and Electoral Committee drew on feminist arguments, with 40 submissions arguing for decriminalisation and only 16 against (Laurie 2010). Most of these submissions, both for and against decriminalisation, drew on article 6 of the Convention for the Elimination of Discrimination Against Women (CEDAW):

'States/Parties shall take appropriate measures including legislation to suppress all forms of traffic in women and exploitation of prostitution of women' (UN Women 1979).

Those feminist groups or individuals who drew on article 6 to argue against decriminalisation stated that decriminalisation would increase the trafficking and exploitation of women, whilst those who argued for decriminalisation drew on this article to claim that trafficking in women would be reduced by removing the illegality of their work. Sandra Coney, one of the most prominent radical New Zealand feminists, wrote personally to each MP arguing that decriminalisation would 'make New Zealand a key link in the global trade in women and create the potential for New Zealand to become a prostitution tourism destination' (Laurie 2010). She proclaimed prostitution to be a symbol of gender inequality and proposed the 'Nordic Model' as an exemplar of the way to regulate and ultimately abolish prostitution.

Coney was supported by a Labour Party MP, Dianne Yates, who was one of only nine Labour Party members to vote against the Bill. She proposed an amendment to the Bill (Supplementary Order Paper 56) to make it unlawful to be a client of a prostitute. She heralded the 'Nordic model' as 'providing greater equality between men and women'. She had little support in parliament and her amendment was voted down by 19 votes to 96. Only four female MPs supported this amendment. Other female MPs distanced themselves from the stance taken by Yates and Coney, taking a liberal position that women have the right to self-determination, especially with regard to their bodies and sexuality. For example, in the words of Sue Bradford:

> I fundamentally question the right of the State in this day and age to interfere with the rights of people 18 years and over to have consensual sex with each other. There is no way that sex workers – mainly women – should continue to be open to harassment and prosecution for a victimless crime. Nor should we turn to the Swedish model, which prosecutes men who pay for sex. The Swedish experience shows that all that does is drive prostitution underground. … I come from another strand of feminist thinking that believes that it is our job to do everything we can to make life better for women, even those who are in this most vulnerable of occupations. Unless we truly believe that prostitution is going to disappear altogether and soon, I believe that the best we can do as feminists is to maximise the conditions that will help to end the worst excesses of violence, coercion and exploitation, rather than allow prostitution to continue as a subset of the criminal world. … I would rather do everything I can, right now, to help protect and empower those who, for whatever reason, have chosen to make prostitution their occupation.
>
> (Sue Bradford, Labour Party, Prostitution reform Bill, Second Reading, 19 February 2003)

The mainstream liberal feminist organisation, the National Council of Women in NZ (NCWNZ), an umbrella organisation of 43 women's groups and societies, was a key player in the achievement of decriminalisation of sex work in NZ (Laurie 2010). Although they felt strongly that prostitution represented a power imbalance between men and women, they deemed it essential that sex workers be protected irrespective of whether they choose to work in sex work or not. They indicated in their submission that sexual slavery was no different from other kinds of occupational slavery and rejected the 'Nordic Model' because of the danger it would place sex workers in if they were forced underground. They emphasised that decriminalisation was vital to 'the rights of sex workers and children to be protected against exploitation and violence' (Laurie 2010: 94). This was echoed by the female MPs who voted for decriminalisation:

> It is about giving some people the same rights as other New Zealand people. … I do not condone prostitution. I think people are entitled to a better life than one that can be provided by selling sex. I would be heartbroken if one of my children decided to enter the sex industry – prostitution plays no part in my dreams for them – but if they did, I would want to know that they had the same rights as any other New Zealander.
>
> (Katherine Rich, National Party, Prostitution Reform Bill, Second Reading, 19 February 2003).

Many MPs did speak about the double standard of the sex worker being criminalised and not the client. However, for them the solution was not to criminalise the client. It was a matter of being treated equally as, ' … common decency demands that we give sex workers the same status in law as the client – buyers and sellers must be treated equally. The status quo is simply abhorrent' (Anne Tolley, National Party, Prostitution Reform Bill, First Reading, 8 November 2000).

Self-determination was emphasised and because individual choice was prioritised, protections needed to be put in place to minimise risks. Lynne Pillay said, 'I support this bill as a woman, because it is about the right to choose and to be safe and secure in that choice' (Lynne Pillay, Labour Party, Prostitution Reform Bill, Second Reading, 19 February 2003):

> I have talked to a number of prostitutes and people from the Prostitutes' Collective who do not see what they do as degrading to them. If it is an activity that they are indulging in through free choice, then there is nothing degrading about it … whether it is degrading is the decision of the person who is engaging in the activity.
>
> (Helen Duncan, Labour Party, Prostitution Reform Bill, Second Reading, 19 February 2003)

In a neoliberal environment like NZ, in which government seeks to deregulate and achieve government from a distance, emphasis is put on self-regulation and self-surveillance (Bacchi 2009). There were arguments that government should not be in the business of regulating morals – individuals should be regulating themselves. 'Society has no part to play in making moral judgments about prostitution. It must become a self-regulating activity. ... In my view there needs to be no blame attached to this industry. These issues should be ruled by people's individual morality, not by the laws of the land' (Liz Gordon, Alliance Party, Prostitution Reform Bill, First Reading, 11 October 2000). Or, 'ACT is a party that believes in the freedom of people to conduct their own business' (Penny Webster, ACT Party, Prostitution Reform Bill, First Reading, 8 November 2000).

What effects are produced by this representation of the problem?

Bacchi and Eveline (2003: 111) have argued that 'policies produce particular kinds of subjects'. The PRA has produced the sex worker in New Zealand – a worker engaged in an occupation with similar rights to individuals engaged in any other form of occupation. In the eyes of the law, sex workers are agentic beings, freely choosing to be a sex worker. It is acknowledged that there are risks to working in this occupation that relate to health and safety, exploitation and coercion and policy provides protections to minimise these risks. What this policy does not produce is the trafficked woman; a victim in need of protection.

How/where is this representation of the 'problem' produced and defended?

Decriminalisation of sex work makes sense in the context of a neoliberal philosophical position of minimal state intervention, self-regulation and economic individualisation. It also makes sense in a country that prides itself on gender equality, to have sex workers given the same rights and status as their clients. More than 12 years following decriminalisation, and with a now centre-right National government in its third term of office, the state continues to defend the position of sex work as an occupational choice.

There have been few concerns since the passing of the Prostitution Reform Act. The review of the Act, published five years after enactment, concluded that it had been effective in achieving its purposes and that most sex workers were better off than they were when their activities were criminalised (Prostitution Law Review Committee 2008). There have been some concerns raised by two district councils regarding street-based work in their cities, but there is little political will to make changes to a mode of regulation that is working well for most.

There are a minority of groups in NZ who still put up some resistance but this is weak and unsupported. For instance, in 2013 the 'Nordic Model' was raised again when Elizabeth Subritzky submitted a petition on behalf of the group 'Freedom from Sexual Exploitation' to the Justice and Electoral Committee of the House of Representatives (Petition 2011/60). This is a small religious-based group in New Zealand committed to seeing change in the areas of prostitution and the trafficking of women and children for sex. The petitioners proposed that the Prostitution Reform Act (2003) be changed to allow prosecution of all clients of sex workers and claimed that prostitution should not be seen as separate from trafficking (Justice and Electoral Committee 2013). The petition also called for an eradication of the street-based sector. The claim was that decriminalisation was to blame for enticing women (victims) into selling sex. The Ministry of Justice supported the Prostitution Law Review Committee's recommendation that New Zealand not pursue an approach that criminalises the client as this would expose sex workers to more risk and make them more vulnerable. Moreover:

> The purpose of the PRA was to enable sex workers to have the same protections afforded to other workers. The PRA regulated the business of prostitution while not endorsing or morally sanctioning it or its use. The Act recognised that sex workers are not necessarily victims but require the same protections as other workers regardless of gender or sexual orientation.
>
> (Ministry of Justice 2013: 5)

Sex workers are working within a policy framework where they have rights; however they are still negotiating their lives within a cultural context where there is social ambivalence and strong moral discourses towards the sex industry and its workers (Abel, Fitzgerald *et al.* 2010). Sullivan (2010) suggests that even in a decriminalised context, sex workers may struggle to gain an identity as a 'worker' outside of these dominant discourses. There will undoubtedly be periodic efforts to tweak and change the Prostitution Reform Act as these moral discourses wax and wane.

Conclusion

What was interesting in the push for decriminalisation was an alliance of sorts between four philosophical positions. Firstly, the political context within which the debate occurred was one in which neoliberal principles of economic individualism and self-regulation prevailed. Harrington (2012: 338) has argued that the decriminalisation of sex work in NZ 'exemplifies advanced liberal technologies of agency' with the ideal being freedom and 'assuming free individuals will take care of their own wellbeing'. Neoliberal states like NZ favour a 'rhetoric of choice' both ideologically and as a 'legitimatory device' and in doing so it has been argued that gender becomes invisible (Scambler 2007: 1092).

The sex workers' rights voice was the second important position in the debate on sex work in NZ as it was this voice that informed the drafting of the Bill. The sex worker voice calls for sex work to be seen as a work issue; that it is service work that should be respected and protected like work in any other service occupation (Alexander 1997; Jenness 1993; Simmons 1999). There is an understanding that most sex workers choose to work in the sex industry and the rights and ability of these individuals to exercise this agency should be supported (Simmons 1999). The demand side of sex work is not an issue that produces much discussion, as sex work is not seen as violence against women. Harrington's (2012: 343) analysis of the discourse on sex work in Sweden and New Zealand suggests that the expert knowledge network informing the debate on policy in New Zealand privileged the sex worker voice, problematised their lack of freedom, and was not engaged in any critical analysis of 'commercial sex markets and their contribution to constructing social hierarchy'. There was no strong belief that sex buyers and exploitation of women were the source of the problem throughout the debates on sex work legislation in New Zealand. The debate did begin with an emphasis on inequalities, but these were not so much issues of gender inequality, but inequalities in citizenship rights which were framed as unfair.

The third argument for decriminalisation was a liberal feminist one which stressed the right of women to choose to work in sex work. Sex work as an occupational choice which required protection of rights, was relevant for most women, both within and outside of parliament. Twenty-five per cent of submissions on the Bill drew on feminist arguments and only a quarter of these argued against decriminalisation on the grounds that prostitution was violence against women. There was a strong representation of women in parliament – 33 of the 120 MPs were women and 22 of these MPs (two-thirds) voted for decriminalisation. At the time that the Bill was going through parliament, New Zealand had a female Prime Minister (who voted for the Bill), as well as a female Governor General, Speaker of the House and Chief Justice. Whilst prostitution as violence against women was not totally absent from the debate, it was weak and side-lined as not attending to the empowerment and protection of those who choose to work in sex work.

The fourth and ultimately most persuasive argument was the public health one of harm minimisation. There is a history of successful public health policy reforms in New Zealand informed by harm minimisation principles. Most notable are the Homosexual Reform Act and the implementation of needle exchanges in the 1980s to help minimise the spread of HIV/AIDS. The public health stance towards sex work has generally been a pragmatic one. Prohibitionist laws have never achieved their aim of eradicating sex work and have only served to drive the industry underground, where sex workers are vulnerable to a number of harms (Davis and Shaffer 1994; Jordan 2005; World Health Organization 2005). The public health emphasis has therefore been on minimising harm through acknowledging this and decriminalising all activities associated with sex work. This was an argument that won over many of the MPs who were undecided on which way to vote.

Ultimately, the neoliberal argument of freedom of choice, the sex workers' rights and feminist positions of the right of women to choose, and the harm minimisation argument of protecting women who choose to work in the sex industry were all framed as issues of fairness. The argument for decriminalisation of sex work started and ended on fairness. The Human Rights Act (1993) states that the 'intention is to help ensure that all people in New Zealand are treated fairly and equally'. Former Vice-chancellor of the

University of Auckland in New Zealand, Raewyn Dalziel, reinforced New Zealand's tradition of fairness in stating that justice and rights have always been a focus in this country. In talking about women's suffrage in New Zealand she stated that the message 'New Zealand conveyed to the outside world was not only about New Zealand women and New Zealand's political life, but about social and political justice' (cited in Fischer 2012: 262). Fairness effectively silenced the neo-abolitionist voice in NZ and in doing so women (as well as men and transgender people) have obtained their freedom to choose to be sex workers.

Note

1 The Labour Party was in power at the time the Bill went through parliament and thus they had the most seats in parliament. Forty-one of their 51 sitting MPs as well as nine from the Green Party voted for decriminalisation. The other ten votes came from the centre-right ACT (4) and National (6) Parties. Those voting against decriminalisation were mostly centre or centre-right. The only left-wing votes against the Bill came from nine Labour Party members and both the Progressive Party MPs. The abstention was from a Labour Party member.

References

Abel, G. (2010) 'Decriminalisation: A Harm Minimisation and Human Rights Approach to Regulating Sex Work', *Public Health and General Practice*, Christchurch: University of Otago.

Alexander, P. (1997) 'Feminism, Sex Workers, and Human Rights', in J. Nagle (ed.) *Whores and Other Feminists*. New York: Routledge, pp. 83–97.

Bacchi, C. (2009) *Analysing Policy: What's the Problem Represented To Be?* Frenchs Forest, NSW: Pearson.

Bacchi, C. and Eveline, J. (2003) 'Mainstreaming and Neoliberalism: A Contested Relationship', *Policy and Society* 22(2): 98–118.

Barnett, T., Healy, C., Reed, A. and Bennachie, C. (2010) 'Lobbying for Decriminalisation', in G. Abel, L. Fitzgerald, C. Healy and A. Taylor (eds) *Taking the Crime out of Sex Work: New Zealand Sex Workers' Fight for Decriminalisation*. Bristol: Policy Press, pp. 57–73.

Beyrer, C., Crago, A., Bekker, L., Butler, J., Shannon, K., Kerrigan, D., Decker, M., Baral, S., Poteat, T., Wirtz, A., Weir, B., Barré-Sinoussi, F., Kazatchkine, M., Sidibé, M., Dehne, K., Boily, M. and Strathdee, S. (2014) 'An Action Agenda for HIV and Sex Workers', *The Lancet*, 385: 287–301.

Brents, B. and Sanders, T. (2010) 'Mainstreaming the Sex Industry: Economic Inclusion and Social Ambivalence', *Journal of Law and Society* 37(1): 40–60.

Bromell, D. (2014) '"A Fair Go" in Public Policy', *Policy Quarterly*, 10(2): 12–21.

Carson, L. and Edwards, K. (2011) 'Prostitution and Sex Trafficking: What are the Problems Represented to Be: A Discursive Analysis of Law and Policy in Sweden and Victoria, Australia', *Australian Feminist Law Journal*, 34: 63–87.

Chetwynd, J. (1996) 'The Prostitutes' Collective: A Uniquely New Zealand Institution' in P. Davis (ed.) *Intimate Details and Vital Statistics: AIDS, Sexuality and the Social Order in New Zealand*. Auckland: Auckland University Press, pp. 136–148.

Chetwynd, J. (1992) 'HIV/AIDS and Sex Workers', *New Zealand Medical Journal*, 105: 227.

Chetwynd, J. and Plumridge, E. (1994) 'Knowledge, Attitudes and Activities of Male Clients of Female Sex Workers: Risk Factors for HIV', *New Zealand Medical Journal*, 107: 351–353.

Chetwynd, J. and Plumridge, E. (1993) *Clients of Female Sex Workers: A Pilot Study*. Christchurch: Christchurch School of Medicine.

Davis, S. and Shaffer, M. (1994) *Prostitution in Canada: The Invisible Menace or the Menace of Invisibility?* Available at: www.walnet.org/csis/papers/sdavis.html.

Eldred-Grigg, S. (1984) *Pleasures of the Flesh: Sex and Drugs in Colonial New Zealand 1840–1915*. Wellington: AH and AW Reed.

Fischer, D. (2012) *Fairness and Freedom: A History of Two Open Societies New Zealand and the United States*. Oxford: Oxford University Press.

Harrington, C. (2012) 'Prostitution Policy Models and Feminist Knowledge Politics in New Zealand and Sweden', *Sexuality Research & Social Policy*, 9: 337–349.

Human Rights Act (1993) *Human Rights Legislation in New Zealand*. Available at: www.legislation.govt.nz/act/public/1993/0082/latest/whole.html.

Jeffreys, S. (1997) *The Idea of Prostitution*. Melbourne: Spinifex Press.

Jenness, V. (1993) *Making it Work: The Prostitutes' Rights Movement in Perspective*. New York: Aldine de Gruyter.

Jordan, J. (2005) *The Sex Industry in New Zealand: A Literature Review*. Available at: www.justice.govt.nz/pubs/reports/2005/sex-industry-in-nz-literature-review/index.html.

Laurie, A. (2010) 'Several Sides to this Story: Feminist Views of Prostitution Reform', in G. Abel, L. Fitzgerald, C. Healy and A. Taylor (eds) *Taking the Crime out of Sex Work: New Zealand Sex Workers' Fight for Decriminalisation*. Bristol: Policy Press, pp. 85–101.

Ministry of Justice (2013) Petition 2011/60 of Elizabeth Subritzky on Behalf of Freedom from Sexual Exploitation and 2,910 others. Submission of the Ministry of Justice: Wellington, NZ.

O'Neill, M. (2010) 'Cultural Criminology and Sex Work: Resisting Regulation through Radical Democracy and Participatory Action Research (PAR)', *Journal of Law and Society*, 37(1): 210–232.

O'Neill, M. (2001) *Prostitution and Feminism: Towards a Politics of Feeling*. Cambridge: Polity Press.

O'Neill, M. and R. Campbell (2006) 'Street Sex Work and Local Communities: Creating Discursive Spaces for Genuine Consultation and Inclusion' in R. Campbell and M. O'Neill (eds) *Sex Work Now*. Cullompton: Willan, pp. 33–61.

Plumridge, E. and Abel, G. (2000a) *Safer Sex in the Christchurch Sex Industry. Study 2: Survey of Christchurch Sex Workers*. Christchurch, Christchurch School of Medicine and Health Sciences: University of Otago.

Plumridge, E. and Abel, G. (2000b) 'Services and Information Utilised by Female Sex Workers for Sexual and Physical Safety', *New Zealand Medical Journal*, 113(1117): 370–372.

Plumridge, E., *et al.* (1997a) 'Control and Condoms in Commercial Sex: Client Perspectives', *Sociology of Health and Illness*, 19(2): 228–243.

Plumridge, E., *et al.* (1997b) 'Discourses of Emotionality in Commercial Sex: the Missing Client Voice', *Feminism and Psychology*, 7(2): 165–181.

Plumridge, E., *et al.* (1996) 'Patrons of the Sex Industry: Perceptions of Risk', *AIDS Care*, 8(4): 405–416.

Plumridge, L. (2001) 'Rhetoric, Reality and Risk Outcomes in Sex Work', *Health, Risk and Society*, 3(2): 199–217.

Plumridge, L. and Abel, G. (2001) 'A "Segmented" Sex Industry in New Zealand: Sexual and Personal Safety of Female Sex Workers', *Australian and New Zealand Journal of Public Health*, 25(1): 78–83.

Prostitution Law Review Committee (2008) *Report of the Prostitution Law Review Committee on the Operation of the Prostitution Reform Act 2003*. Wellington: Ministry of Justice.

Prostitution Reform Bill, First Reading, First Session, Forty-sixth Parliament 11 October and 8 November 2000. See www.parliament.nz/en/pb/hansard-debates/rhr/document/47HansD_20030219_00001132/prostitution-reform-bill-second-reading.

Prostitution Reform Bill, Second Reading, 19 February 2003. Available at: www.parliament.nz/en/pb/hansard-debates/rhr/document/47HansD_20030219_00001132/prostitution-reform-bill-second-reading.

Prostitution Reform Bill, Third Reading, 25 June 2003. Available at: www.parliament.nz/en/pb/hansard-debates/rhr/document/47HansD_20030625_00001319/prostitution-reform-bill-procedure-third-reading.

Scambler, G. (2007) 'Sex Work Stigma: Opportunist Migrants in London', *Sociology* 41(6): 1079–1096.

Scoular, J. (2004) 'The "Subject" of Prostitution: Interpreting the Discursive, Symbolic and Material Position of Sex/Work in Feminist Theory', *Feminist Theory*, 5(3): 343–355.

Simmons, M. (1999). 'Theorizing prostitution: The question of agency', in B. Dank and R. Refinetti (eds) *Sex Work and Sex Workers: Sexuality and Culture*. London: Transaction Publishers, pp. 125–148.

Stenvoll, D. (2002) 'From Russia with Love? Newspaper Coverage of Cross-Border Prostitution in Northern Norway, 1990–2000', *The Journal of Women's Studies*, 9(2): 143–162.

Sullivan, B. (2010) 'When (Some) Prostitution is Legal: The impact of law reform on sex work in Australia', *Journal of Law and Society*, 37: 85–104.

UN Women (1979) *Convention on the Elimination of all forms of Discrimination Against Women*. Available at: www.un.org/womenwatch/daw/cedaw/text/econvention.htm.

World Health Organization (2007). *Violence against Women and HIV/AIDS: Critical Intersections*. Available at: www.who.int/gender/documents/sexworkers.pdf.

Conclusion

Carceral feminism, the state and the sex worker in a globalised era. Whose power?

Eilís Ward and Gillian Wylie

Introduction

Neo-abolitionist ideas and policies have become ubiquitous. In many parts of the world, it is a simple given that criminalising the purchasing of sex will reduce sex work and thus automatically cause a reduction in the demand that, the argument goes, fuels trafficking for the purposes of sexual exploitation. Hence, in one fell swoop, along with the abolition of prostitution, sex trafficking will also come to a halt. As the chapters of this book illustrate, these ideas nowadays animate international political frameworks and shape many state policies towards sex work. Even in country contexts seemingly immune to the lure of the idea, neo-abolitionist activists plug away determinedly in the public sphere, impacting on local politics and civil societies. But, as this book also illustrates, there are many problems and challenges in this line of argument and these problems are rendered in turn more complex by interactions between neo-abolitionist ideals and international regimes, local political cultures and contending values. By way of conclusion, we offer some synthesising reflections on the analysis of neo-abolitionism's trajectory, found across the chapters of this book, as well as some thoughts on the political and social implications of this radical feminist project.

Neo-abolitionist claims and drivers

The claim that 'Sweden works' is an important rallying and legitimating cry for neo-abolitionist activism – and one that we refer to at the beginning of this book. Yet, throughout the chapters the idea that there is a strong evidence base for the Swedish Model or sex purchase bans is repeatedly shown to be flimsy, not least in Yvonne Swanström's chapter which raises the lack of proper evaluation of the Sex Purchase Ban. Throughout the book the empirical basis for advocating criminalising male demand is questioned. For example, the chapter on Ireland shows that the often-cited statistics used to make the neo-abolitionist case are dubious. Overall, the conflation of the issue of sex trafficking with prostitution is a central conceit of neo-abolitionism because the predominant image of the violated, innocent trafficking victim bolsters calls to criminalise demand and trumps any 'liberal' concerns with harm reduction, choice or agency or claims as to the complexity and diversity within the sex trade and the workability of the proposal. But here too the evidence base on the nature and extent of sex trafficking is highly problematic and politicised (Feingold 2010; Vance 2011). What we are suggesting here is that the spreading influence of neo-abolitionism cannot be accounted for in terms of established 'facts' or proven policy efficacy, rather its undoubted rise and rise has political and ideological roots. This book attempted to tease out those roots and the interplay between a very powerful idea (the radical feminist account of the sex trade) with political processes and institutions across the states selected here.

At the outset of this book we identified a number of drivers of neo-abolitionism, derived from an overview of the contributed chapters. We suggested that these drivers: the Swedish exemplar; radical feminist transnational activism; violence against women movements; old fashioned morality politics; the 'trafficking imaginary'; evangelical Christianity; global and local political cultures; and the strength of sex work activism, all intersect to produce varying degrees of traction for neo-abolitionism across differing contexts. We hope that, now at the close of the book, the specific way these combined drivers exert influence within each context has become clearer to readers and helps make analytical sense of why neo-abolitionism flourishes or fails in each place.

That neo-abolitionist activism has global reach is clear from the impact of transnational feminist activism at the UN and the EU and the strategic alliances activists made with nation-states pushing the agenda internationally (particularly the US and Sweden). After Palermo and its follow-up in regional organisations like the EU, nation-states came under pressure to adopt new anti-trafficking frameworks which are often closely associated with neo-abolitionist measures to curb demand for commercial sex. Yet new international norms do not translate seamlessly to nation-states (Acharya 2004). Here the other drivers are also crucial in terms of the alliances, strategic or more long term, between radical feminists, religious groups and political parties, the presence or absence of counter voices and the nature of political structures, prevailing policies and political mores. From Sweden to New Zealand, the US to Australia and destinations in between, the book has suggested that we need to study each place 'from the ground up', and with an eye to its international situatedness, to analyse why neo-abolitionism takes root or not through a contextualised reading of these intermingling factors.

Of course, it is necessary to introduce the usual caveat here that 'more research is needed'. Our reach in terms of case studies and each chapter's content was necessarily constrained by space and it is indeed possible that other drivers are played out in the contexts under study. The role of the media, for instance, is mentioned throughout the chapters, but outside the brief of the book's focus and perhaps requires specific attention. Moreover, our brief was for advanced liberal democratic states and within that only a selected handful. Exploration is needed of the experiences of other European states such as Greece, Italy and Hungary, and of states in Latin America, Asia and Africa. More research, indeed, is needed – but the drivers identified here, we suggest, provide a useful framework to help further such comparative research.

Prostitution, feminism and the state

While the emphasis in this book is on nuanced readings of the impact of neo-abolitionism on particular places and spaces, there is an overarching concern, embedded in the book's title to explore what all these cases tell us about the relations between 'prostitution, feminism and the state' in contemporary, advanced, liberal democracies. As is clear in each discussion, neo-abolitionism reads prostitution as an embodiment of gender inequality and a form of violence against women. It also links contemporary prostitution to the imaginary of sex trafficking which rests on a crude binary. This binary denies the possibility of consent or agency to those who sell sex and presents the trafficker or the buyer of sex as always male, powerful and criminal. This reading legitimates state responses to the sex trade which are punitive and prosecutorial, with the ire of the state (and feminists) ostensibly targeted at men but, more often than not, creating ever-more complex positions for those who sell sex. As such neo-abolitionists are archetypal examples of carceral feminists (Bernstein 2010), allying with states to criminalise those whom they see to be the perpetrators of inequality. Yet in making these alliances with states they end up coalescing in politics which are a) designed to promote neo-liberal approaches to social problems and b) bolster the exclusion of migrant workers.

The UK chapter by Scoular and Carline provides one example of the first of these tendencies. Although not a wholeheartedly neo-abolitionist regime, the regulation of prostitution in England and Wales is moving in this direction with increasingly punitive measures being taken against male buyers. These policies are paralleled by neo-liberal measures of responsibilisation directed at women who sell sex, with the expectation that they will engage in self-reform. However, as we noted at the outset, the complexity of each case mean that other forms of feminism can equally find themselves in cahoots with state welfare policies under conditions of widespread neo-liberalism, as the long tradition of state feminism in Sweden illustrates.

Almost every chapter is shadowed by an acknowledgement of the ways that feminist neo-abolitionism plays into the second of these tendencies. Especially following the intertwining of thinking about prostitution with assumptions about transnational sex trafficking, neo-abolitionist policies can end up implicated in the justification of a carceral approach to border politics. This is crystal clear, for example, in O'Brien's chapter on Australia that demonstrates how discourses of the criminality and illegality of migration, exemplified by trafficking, bring neo-abolitionist aspirations in line with the legitimation of exclusionary migration policies. Swanström suggests that the use of the sex purchase ban to play the politics of migration and trafficking was not the aim of its feminist advocates, concerned as they were for their ideals of gender equality. Yet Halley (2006) suggests that the determination of 'governance feminists' to 'walk the halls of power' and advocate for carceral approaches has problematic consequences which they should have foreseen. Again though, it is important to acknowledge that other influences within feminism can also find themselves in cahoots (intentionally or not) with the politics of migration control. Heumann *et al.*'s chapter on the Netherlands reveals that the political impetus for the legalisation of prostitution came from an intent to separate legal local workers from irregular foreign ones rather than a purist commitment to sex workers' rights. Ironically, the 'mirror-image' Swedish approach may also produce a hierarchy of victims of the sex trade, dividing 'native' victims from 'foreign' sex workers (Skilbrei and Holmström 2013).

The book therefore shows how radical feminism, energised into neo-abolitionist activism, has drawn feminism and many women's organisations and movements into a worrisome connection with statist and neo-liberal agendas. Moreover the negative consequences of neo-abolitionism for women who sell sex and migrant women in the contradictory world of neo-liberal globalisation seem clear.

Conclusion

The stories told in this collection are thus about the movements and alliances of many large ideas and powerful institutions. They are about the movement of a radical feminist idea into mainstream state criminal justice apparatuses. They are about the profound shifts that have occurred in the sex trade brought about by technological innovation and the challenges therein to both policing and our views of fairness, rights, morality, inclusion and exclusion. They are about state securitisation in the face of migration and global inequalities. They are about the fraught relationship between evidence and policy making in a policy arena that is troubled by knowledge-production. They are also stories about how some states, Sweden and the USA, utilise certain ideas for their own statecraft purposes in international relations. Yet, threaded throughout this entire book and the concerns of the authors is not the imaginary but the reality of the sex worker and in particular the migrant sex worker. Our focus on the political, ideational and the institutional in the book, necessarily lifted the lens away from this reality and bracketed the more sociological and personal narratives necessary to explore this realm. However, we would like to conclude by drawing together again all of these realms, from the interrogation of state power, governance feminism and ideas about neo-liberalism to the every day reality of sex workers. Given feminism's liberal and inclusionary agenda, its rejection of the politics of domination and its valorisation of subjectivity, it is most troubling that radical feminism's 'primary logic' (Sandbeck 2012) within neo-abolitionism is a law and order agenda of criminal justice mechanisms, carcerality, state securitisation and the onward march of neo-liberal politics. Radical feminism has allowed state power to essentialise, objectify and victimise the bodies of those migrant sex workers and all sex workers.

References

Acharya, A. (2004) 'How Ideas Spread: Whose Norms Matter? Norm Localization and Institutional Change in Asian Regionalism', *International Organization*, 58(2): 239–275.

Bernstein, E. (2010) 'Militarized Humanitarianism Meets Carceral Feminism: The Politics of Sex, Rights and Freedom in Contemporary Anti-trafficking campaigns', *Signs*, 36(1): 45–71.

Feingold, D. (2010) 'Trafficking in Numbers: the Social Construction of Human Trafficking Data' in P. Andreas and K. Greenhill (eds) *Sex, Drugs, and Body Counts: The Politics of Numbers in Global Crime and Conflict*. New York: Cornell University Press, pp. 46–74.

Halley, J. (2006) *Split Decisions: How and Why to Take a Break from Feminism*. Princeton, NJ and Oxford: Princeton University Press.

Sandbeck, S. (2012) 'Towards an Understanding of Carceral Feminism as Neo-liberal Biopower' unpublished paper delivered at the annual conference of the Canadian Political Science Association, University of Alberta, Canada.

Skilbrei, M. L. and Holmström, C. (2013) *Prostitution Policy in the Nordic Region: Ambiguous Sympathies*. Farnham and Burlington, VA: Ashgate.

Vance, C. (2011) 'States of Contradiction: Twelve Ways to Do Nothing About Trafficking while Pretending to', *Social Research*, 78(3): 933–948.

Index